FootprintItalia

# Venice & Ve

D0356047

Shona Main

# Introducing
# the region

# About the region

# Venice

# Padua & around

# Treviso &
# the north

# Contents

# About the author

**Shona Main** grew up in Shetlands and at 17 moved to Dundee to train as a magazine journalist with D.C. Thomson & Co. Ltd, working on *Blue Jeans* and *Jackie* where she was the Pop Editor, a career high. After studying law, she then had a misguided and rather lacklustre foray into politics before returning to writing at the turn of the century. She writes mainly about Italy, Scotland and politics. Her partner, Nick Bruno is also a writer and they split their time between Scotland and Italy, eating and drinking too much.

# Acknowledgements

The biggest thanks goes to Nick, who is so very useful and amusing. Thanks also to the Main family whose love and disinterest in the frippery of my career keeps my feet on the ground and to the Eames and Brunos for warm welcomes. Thanks to Petrie, whose hospitality, horse balls and high quality rants keep us cheery. To Gerardo (the great gourmand), Francesca, Dario, Federica, Robert, Giuliana and Beatrice for all the food, wine, stories and laughs. Thanks to Michele and Andrea Barison for always helping. To Miriam for her enthusiasm about the Veneto. To Federica for her effervescence and to her husband, Antonio Manno for writing the best art book about Venice. Thanks to Stefania Gatta at ENIT and the good folks in Venice and the Veneto who helped along the way, particularly Cristina Gibellato and Gisella Portelli in Padova, Matteo Tassan in Venice and Luca Rizzardi and Monica Viviani in Verona, Luca Giannini in Mestre and Pier Luigi Bertotti in Treviso. To my dear chums in Dundee – especially Poppy, Jams, Sir Robin, Lady Pauline, Laurie, the Grimmondos, Foxy, Fiona, Alan and Pao and DGDave - who were constantly bombed out and whinged at for the three months I spent writing this book. To Jo, for coming to Venice. To Bill Duncan for telling me about San Sebastian. To Ian at Dundee Train

Station for cheery goodbyes. To Norma and Lesley at Boots make-up counter for words of encouragement. To the inventor of the tubi grip for stopping my arms from falling off and to Borders Milk Chocolate Gingers for keeping me going. Finally, a monumental thank you to my braw editors, Alan Murphy and Sophie Blacksell, and to Kassia and Angus at Footprint for having the patience of saints.

# About the book

The guide is divided into four sections: Introducing the region; About the region; Around the city/region and Practicalities.

**Introducing the region** comprises: **At a glance**, which explains how the region fits together by giving the reader a snapshot of what to look out for and what makes this region distinct from other parts of the country; **Best of Venice & Veneto** (top 20 highlights); **A year in Venice & Veneto**, which is a month-by-month guide to pros and cons of visiting at certain times of year; and **Venice & Veneto on screen & page**, which is a list of suggested books and films. **About the region** comprises: **History**; **Art & architecture**; **Venice & Veneto today**, which presents different aspects of life in the region today; **Festivals & events**; **Sleeping** (an overview of accommodation options); **Eating & drinking** (an overview of the region's cuisine, as well as advice on eating out); **Entertainment** (an overview of the region's cultural credentials, explaining what entertainment is on offer); **Shopping** (what are the region's specialities and recommendations for the best buys); and **Activities & tours**. **Around the city/region** is then broken down into five areas, each with its own chapter. Here you'll find all the main sights and at the end of each chapter is a listings section with all the best sleeping, eating & drinking, entertainment, shopping and activities & tours options plus a brief overview of public transport.

**Sleeping price codes**
€€€€  over €300 per night for a double room in high season.
€€€  €200-300
€€  €100-200
€  under €100

**Eating & drinking price codes**
€€€€  over €40 per person for a 2-course meal with a drink, including service and cover charge
€€€  €30-40
€€  €20-30
€  under €20

# Map symbols

| | | | |
|---|---|---|---|
|  | | | |

Informazioni
Information

Luogo d'interesse
Place of Interest

Museo/Galleria
Museum/Gallery

Teatro
Theatre

Negozi
Shopping

Ufficio postale
Post Office

Chiesa Storica
Historic Church

Giardini
Gardens

Vaporetto
Waterbus

Vaporetto Imbarco
Waterbus boarding

Traghetto

Monumento
Monument

Stazione Ferroviaria
Railway Station

Escursioni a piedi
Hiking

Metropolitana
Metro Station

Mercato
Market

Funicolare
Funicular Railway

Aeroporto
Airport

Universita
University

Percorsi raccomandati
Recommended walk

# Picture credits

**Superstock** Pages 1, 250, 251: PRISMA; pages 2, 3, 9, 17, 26, 27, 31, 33, 34, 48, 50, 53, 54, 55, 63, 64, 68, 70, 72, 79, 97, 101, 146, 151, 188, 189, 205, 212, 213, 215, 216, 222, 229, 232, 258, 260, 261, 263, 264, 267, 268, 273: Age fotostock; pages 16, 17, 43, 94, 101, 111, 122, 125: superstock inc; pages 16, 44, 45, 123, 124, 137, 194: De Agostini; page 30: Image Asset Management Ltd; page 40: Bridgeman Art Library London; page 46, 128: Ben Mangor; pages 54, 97, 132: Axiom Photographic Limited; page 154, 275: Hemis.fr.

**Shutterstock** Pages 2, 6, 7, 49: Franck camhi; pages 2, 9, 166, 167, 169, 173, 239, 241, 243: Vladimir Daragan; page 10: Jiri Miklo, Perove Stanislav; page 11: Andrejs Pidjass; page 12: Sailorr; page 12, 19, 157: Luciano Mortula; pages 15, 36, 92: David Davis; pages 17, 24: Stephanie Schoenebein; page 18: Oleg Babich; page 20: rfx; page 35: Route66; page 38: Vuk Vukmirovic; page 39: David Mckee; page 47: Stefanie Schoenebein; pages 59, 94: Newphotoservice; pages 84, 85, 88: Eugene Mogilnikov; page 90: Villedieu Christophe; page 91: Pavel K; page 93: CSLD; pages 106, 110, 112: Claudio Zaccherini; page 116: William Casey; page 117: Silvio Verrecchia; pages 119, 162: WH CHOW; pages 120, 255: Soundsnaps; page 126: Khirman Vladimir; page 127: PixAchi; page 134: Sematadesign; page 136: Alistair Scott; page 137: imageshunter; page 143: David Peta; page 145: Senorcampesino; page 156: Alexander Raths; page 161: Jozef Sedmak; page 185: Jo Chambers; page 191: The cloister; page 193: Maria Veras; page 201: Roberto Romanini; page 205: Claudio Giovanni Colombo;

page 214: Davide Marzotto; page 224: Thomas M Perkins; page 237: Huang Yuetao; pages 238, 248, 252: Skowron; page 245: Tan Kim Pin; page 246: Alfredo Ragazzon; page 247: Nando Machado.

**Nick Bruno** Pages 2, 3, 9, 15, 28, 29, 32, 37, 48, 51, 52, 67, 76, 77, 78, 79, 99, 100, 103, 105, 108, 135, 139, 140, 141, 142, 147, 149, 150, 159, 161, 163, 164, 168, 169, 171, 172, 175, 178, 180, 183, 184, 186, 187, 190, 195, 196, 199, 210, 219, 225, 227, 228, 234, 235, 236, 240, 244, 249, 253, 257, 259, 263, 265, 266, 269, 270, 271, 274, 275.

**Julius Honnor** Pages 13, 14, 257.

**Shona Main** Pages 15, 39, 53, 67, 69, 98, 107, 113, 115, 140, 144, 152, 153, 160, 197, 198, 230, 232, 245, 262.

**tips images** Page 21: Marcella Pedone; pages 51, 56, 57, 71, 109, 158, 254: Mark Edward Smith; page 60: Francesco Tomasinelli; page 75: Giovanni Lunardi; page 138, 226: Stefano Scata; pages 218, 220: Marc Chapeaux.

**Random House** Page 25.

**Bertinetti-Edizioni Whitestar** page 25.

**Ca'Maria Adele** Page 62, 143.

**De Agostini Picture Library** Page 73.

**Matteo Danesin** Pages 174, 176, 177.

**Colli Euganei** Page 181.

**Albergo Verdi** Page 182.

**Villa Margherita** Page 184.

**Cortina Tourism** Page 202.

**Monterosa Ski Archive** Page 203.

**Bisol and Dachota Renneau at communiqu** Page 207.

**Albergo al Sole** Page 211.

**Girolibero cycling** Page 233.

**Alan Copson/jonarnoldimages.com** Front cover.
**Veer** Back cover.
**Shutterstock** (Sailorr) Back cover.

# Contents

Venice is a testament to the
power of human imagination.

Introducing the region

# Introduction

**V**enice is an unbelievable city that floats in a world of its own. A city of romance and riches that is defined by its past. And what a past. During the Italian Renaissance this former maritime superpower was where east met west and where power and affluence fuelled unsurpassed creativity and the untrammelled pursuit of pleasure. This legacy, recalled in the city's prolific art and architecture, is there for all to see and admire. Today, only great ingenuity stops its transcendent testimonies to the power of the imagination from crumbling into the sea. However, as their history proves, the Venetians can teach us all a thing or two about surviving, in style.

Beyond the marshlands of the lagoon lies the prosperous region of Veneto. Venice turned to its territories on terra firma when its maritime dominance began to wane and reaped the benefits of this fertile and industrious area. Veneto is strewn with Renaissance villas, fortified towns and undulating vineyards and topped by the snow-capped peaks of the Dolomites. It has other truly great cities too: Padua, with its awe-inspiring frescoes and illustrious university; the architectural splendour of Vicenza, a showcase for Palladio's genius; and Roman-built Verona, a city infused by the legacies of dynastic rule and love.

# At a glance

A whistle-stop tour of Venice & Veneto

The Dolomite mountains.

Veneto is the proud and prosperous northeast shoulder of the Italian state. Wedged between the border region of Friuli-Venezia Giulia to the east, the Dolomite mountains to the north, the powerhouse of Lombardy to the west, the marshes of Emilia-Romagna to the south and, of course, the Venetian lagoon to the southeast, Veneto offers visitors a marvellous multiplicity of things to see and do.

### Venice

It is, of course, **Venice** that draws most visitors to the region. This unique city on water is steeped in the past. Its artistic treasures, architectural wealth and reliance on boats to move around, all hark back to an age when it was at the vanguard of Western civilization. Venice is not like the rest of Italy. Undamaged by the bombing of World War II and unsullied (bar belching Marghera on the edge of the lagoon) by the industrialization that has encircled most other towns, it has an unreal quality that is part of its appeal. You cannot turn a corner in Venice without seeing something wonderful. It takes time to adjust to the fact you are on an artificial island, standing on lumps of Istrian stone and pine logs driven deep into the mud. Until you head off to the lagoon's other islands, it's hard to imagine that much of it was once a mosquito-ridden swamp. And, until you walk round the *calli* and get lost a hundred times over, you just don't realise how inspired the creation of this floating city is.

# The lowdown

### Money matters

Venice is probably the most expensive Italian city after Rome. Even if you buy a Venice Card (€73 for three days), which gets you free admission to many sights and free travel on the vaporetti, you'll still need €40-70 per person per day to cover your lunch and dinner. Build in a bit of comfort and joy – the occasional coffee, *Spritz* or gelato, say – and you're talking around €100-120 per person. And, if you really want to splash out on gondola rides, meals at top restaurants and a night at the opera at La Fenice, you can easily double or treble this amount. Cortina is similarly expensive during the high season but when the snow melts, prices can come down. The other cities are notably cheaper; you can lunch with water, wine and cover charge in Verona for €10.

### Opening hours & holidays

Shops, churches and a lot of sights close for a long lunch at around 1230 and may not open again until 1600, although the larger sights and some shops in Venice now stay open all day to accommodate the tourist hordes. Many places (particularly clothes shops) are closed on Sunday and/or Monday. Family-run restaurants or bars may also shut for a day during the week. Eateries will often stop serving after lunch (around 1400-1500) and sometimes as early as 2100 in the evenings, so don't expect to be able to order meals at any hour. Finally, the Italian holiday month is August. This means that shops, bars, restaurants and even some sights can be closed for a fortnight or longer. They'll also close for Christmas, New Year and some of January, too.

Gondola.

### Tourist passes

Each of the cities covered in this guide operates some kind of discount tourist pass, valid for a few days, which allows admission to some sights and often includes travel on the vaporetti, buses or trams. Children under 12 may be included in an adult ticket price. Check the various deals and bear in mind that it might not just be money you save with these but also time spent queuing and rummaging about in pockets for change.

### Tourist information

The following official tourist information websites are useful sources of information before your trip: turismovenezia.it; turismopadova.it; trevisotourism.com; cortina.dolomiti.org; vicenzae.org, and tourism.verona.it. If you're travelling by train, also check out trenitalia.it. Once you're there, the regional tourist offices have mounds of leaflets and flyers on places to see, stay and eat, as well as themed information on architectural trails, wine tours, local gastronomic delights and the like. However, you may struggle to get information about areas outside the immediate vicinity. Some offices will also help you to book accommodation, although the level of assistance you receive will depend on individual members of staff. Many sights, hotels and restaurants have their own websites which can be useful for gleaning extra information or exact locations, although not all of them will have an English version.

*Piccioni* in piazza San Marco: feed them and be fined.

Venice ruled over the surrounding region of Veneto for over 400 years. Although this influence is very apparent, the people of Veneto have a different personality from their former rulers. Yes, they share the same entrepreneurial gene and are as deeply conservative in many of their views, but they also tend to be more outward- and forward-looking.

### Padua & around

**Padua**, just 30 minutes from Venice on the train, seems to be a concrete jungle until you reach its Renaissance kernel. Its historic university, café society and rebellious past all contribute to making this a hugely sociable city, while Giotto's frescoes in the Cappella degli Scrovegni mean it scores off the scale as far as art is concerned. Padua is connected to the Venetian lagoon by the Brenta Canal, or Venetian Riviera, where rich Venetians built Renaissance villas to escape the heat and intensity of the city and to lay claim to the fertile land. South of Padua are the Euganean Hills, a protected landscape that is beloved of walkers and vinophiles.

Above: Masks at Venice's *Carnevale*.
Top: Verona's Arena.

### Treviso & the north

Just half an hour from Venice to the north is **Treviso**. This medieval, fortified and moated city knows how to make and to enjoy its wealth. It has a different pace of life from Venice and is a great place to rest, recoup, meander and eat well. Head north and you'll pass broad, green cultivated plains where the northeast's post-war economic boom is most obvious. But don't expect ugly sprawling industry: here, small, clean factories intermingle with cherry orchards, vineyards and maize fields. The most northerly part of Veneto, just over two hours from the lagoon, is dominated by the mighty Dolomite mountain range, as vertical and frozen as Venice is flat and watery. Here the chic town of **Cortina d'Ampezzo**, playground for the rich and famous, is flashier than Milan and a little less Italian, too: a Germanic influence is noticeable in the Tyrolese architecture and the guttural dialect.

Venice, certainly, is the ultimate chocolate box of never-ending delights: Gothic and Baroque churches, extravagant palazzi, bustling *campos*, moonlit canals and the entire history of art in its galleries. But, when you breathe in the air of the Dolomites, stand on the outer ring of Verona's Arena, shake your head in disbelief at the beauty of the vistas from Asolo or amble down the cypress-lined hill from La Rotonda, you will realise that Venice doesn't have everything, after all.

### Vicenza & around

Back down on the plains, on the route that links Venice with Milan, lies **Vicenza**. One of the wealthiest cities in Italy, it is also one of the smallest and the most architecturally rich. The handiwork of Palladio is all around you, from the palazzi and public buildings in the city centre to the villas in the surrounding countryside, where La Rotonda, considered his most perfect tribute to the principles of proportion, symmetry and pleasure, sits in absolute harmony with the landscape.

### Verona

And then there is **Verona**, suspended in fiction by an Englishman who had never visited and mobbed by tourists who come to see the balcony of a young girl who never existed. But the romance and drama of Verona is very real. The Roman legacy of its astonishing amphitheatre, *teatro* and other ruins under your feet has been complemented over the years by monumental churches and gracious palazzi to create a perfect stage set for an enchanting stay. Around Verona, the western Veneto is characterized by vineyards that cling to every hill and patch of fertile soil, fed by the Alpine waters of the Adige and its tributaries. The region stretches as far as the eastern shore of Lake Garda, where, in the summer, lakeside towns such as **Torri del Benaco** buzz with Veronesi escaping the heat and humidity of the city.

> **Venice is the ultimate chocolate box of never-ending delights: Gothic and Baroque churches, extravagant palazzi, bustling campos, moonlit canals and the entire history of art in its galleries.**

Piazza San Marco as seen from the Campanile.

# Best of Venice & Veneto

Top 20 things to see & do

**❶ Piazza San Marco**

For many visitors this piazza is Venice. The gold-covered Byzantine Basilica, the lavish Palazzo Ducale, the 99 m Campanile, the Torre dell'Orologio and the splendid Museo Civico Correr are its stand-out attractions. Napoleon called it "the finest drawing room in Europe". Page 89.

**❷ Santi Giovanni e Paolo**

The hulking brick of Gothic 'San Zanipolo' sits in a buzzing *campo* full of children playing and old men chatting. The resting place of many doges, its highly crafted tombs and art by Bellini and Veronese, to name but two, are magnificent. Page 99.

**❸ Gesuiti**

The first glimpse of this white, ornamental Baroque church in a down-to-earth, working-class *campo* takes your breath away. Inside, green marble, carved to make it look as if it is draped, and epic paintings by Titian and Tintoretto seal its status. Page 107.

1 Piazza San Marco.

### ❹ Madonna dell'Orto

On the edge of town, the young Tintoretto filled his local church with art, just for the price of some paint and brushes. Full of fear, passion and tenderness, it is an astonishing insight into his prodigious talent. His humble tomb is within the church. Page 110.

### ❺ Ghetto

The original Jewish ghetto dates from the 16th century, when the movements of the city's Jewish population were tightly controlled. The Museo Communità Ebraica offers social history tours of the area, finishing at the poignant Holocaust Memorial. Page 112.

### ❻ Santa Maria Gloriosa dei Frari

This colossal Franciscan Gothic church holds some of Venice's most extraordinary and moving art works, from the mournful lion on Canova's pyramidal tomb to the vivid splendour of Titian's *Assumption*. Page 118.

### ❼ Accademia

Walk though the history of art in just two hours, from the stylized faces and ubiquitous halos of Byzantine art to the Renaissance, when Lotto, Titian, Tintoretto and Veronese gave light, colour and meaning to art. Page 121.

### ❽ Peggy Guggenheim Collection

Women don't really feature in the official history of Venice. That is, until Peggy came along with the shock of the new and took over a palazzo on the Canal Grande to show her unrivalled collection of surrealist and abstract art. Page 125.

### ❾ San Sebastiano

Veronese ran wild in this small, neighbourhood church and covered every surface with colour and life. His architectural illusions change the whole internal dimensions of the church so you don't know what is painting and what is relief. Page 129.

3  Gesuiti.          4  Madonna dell'Orto.

10  San Giorgio Maggiore.

17 Palladio and Scamozzi's Teatro Olimpico in Vicenza.

### ⑩ San Giorgio Maggiore

A white beacon of beauty and hope in the Bacino di San Marco, Palladio's monumental church transformed this island into one of the symbolic images of La Serenissima. Also here are dreamy cloisters and the half-moon Teatro Verdi. Page 132.

### ⑪ San Lazzaro degli Armeni

Byron used to swim here to spend time with the Mekhitarist fathers, learn Armenian and study the books in their library. Now a vaporetto will take you to the beautiful church and monastery, where a tour gives an enthralling insight into life then and now. Page 134.

12 Torcello mosaic.

### ⑫ Torcello

On this rugged, barely inhabited island in the lagoon stands the honourable Cattedrale Santa Maria Assunta, a Byzantine church festooned with spectacular mosaics of the Seven Sins and the Last Judgement. Page 136.

### ⑬ Cappella degli Scrovegni

Enrico Scrovegni built this chapel in Padua and commissioned Giotto to adorn it in an attempt to assuage the sins of his father. Giotto's unsurpassed frescoes breath stunning colour and life into the stories of Mary and Jesus. Page 170.

### ⑭ Università

Established in 1222, Padua university has attracted some of the finest minds in history to study and teach here. Its grandness is testament to the status such seats of learning had in both late Medieval and Renaissance periods. Page 173.

### ⑮ Possagno

Canova's home town has his tomb, designed by himself and built by the locals, and a stirring museum where the models and casts for his most famous sculptures can be found. Page 198.

### ⑯ Villa Barbaro

In the lush countryside of Maser stands one of Palladio's most delightful residences, which houses some of Veronese's finest frescoes. Built in 1580, Villa Barbaro epitomizes the vision and ideals of the Renaissance. Page 199.

### ⑰ Teatro Olimpico

Palladio may have designed this semi-circular tiered theatre in Vicenza but it is Vincenzo Scamozzi's stage set that draws gasps of wonder. Still in use, it is the only surviving Renaissance theatre in Italy. Page 220.

### ⑱ La Rotonda

This is considered by many architects to be the perfect building. Palladio himself took great pride in the way the landscape, materials, location, symmetry and mathematical precision came together in such beauteous harmony. Page 224.

### ⑲ Arena

Verona's Roman amphitheatre is in amazingly good condition, despite having been built 2000 years ago. It is now the setting for Verona's famous opera season; a performance here is a spectacle never forgotten. Page 238.

### ⑳ Teatro Romano & Museo Archeologico

Verona's Roman theatre is still used as a performance venue and has held on to its ancient allure. The Museo, housed high on a hill in the former convent of San Girolamo, offers the most majestic views of the Teatro and of Verona itself. Page 249.

18  Palladio's La Rotonda, just outside Vicenza.

19  Verona's Roman Arena.

# Month by month

## A year in Venice & Veneto

### January & February

The Veneto in January can be breathtaking, literally, with amazingly clear skies and a dazzling brightness, especially in the mornings. However, temperatures can hover around freezing and the wind chill, with gusts from Siberia, make it feel Arctic. In Venice, the days when the canals froze over seem to have passed but the sheer quantity of water around the island and the icy winds that race through the *calli* make the city feel desperately cold and certainly damper than the mainland at

Rain in piazza San Marco.

times (*acqua alta*, or high tide, is a regular occurrence). That said, if you are in rude health, this can be a beautiful time to visit, particularly if there's a blanket of snow, either crisp against the blueness of a clear sky or subdued by the watery light. Elsewhere in the Veneto, snowfall is to be expected. This is not considered the *very* best time for skiing in the Dolomites but there's usually a bit of action up there.

After Christmas and New Year, Epiphany celebrations and the welcoming of the witch Befana (see page 58) extend the festive spirit for a little longer. The winter sales are held in January, with Treviso, Padua and Verona perhaps the best places to pick up bargains. However, lots of places are closed in January, as family-run businesses recover from the long summer season and gear up for the next one.

February means Carnevale, famous in Venice but also across the region, when locals partake in serious pre-Lent overindulgence. Celebrations last for ten days up until Shrove Tuesday, climaxing on the last weekend. This is an enormously busy time for the city, so if you want to visit, book ahead and prepare to pay high season prices (see page 58). Those with a sweet tooth will love the sweet fritters, *frittole* and *galani* served across the Veneto during Carnevale.

Enjoy Venice's *Carnevale* from behind a mask.

## March & April

Spring in the Veneto sees warmer temperatures, reaching the low 20s in Venice. However, there can also be lots of rain throughout the region, so visitors to Venice should be prepared for *acqua alta*, when the low-lying areas of the city are flooded. March is the month of the Venice International Boat Show meaning hotels are busy, while the Venetian equivalent of our St Valentine's day, Festa di San Marco on the 25th sees the best restaurants booked up. The first *castraure* (early buds of the purple artichoke) are harvested in Sant'Erasmo and are available in Venice's markets and restaurants.

In Verona, Vinitaly, the biggest wine fair in the country, runs for five days in late March/early April, putting the city's accommodation under a bit of strain, so make sure you have booked in advance. Up in the Dolomites, Cortina is at its busiest and best for skiing and people watching. It's also one of the best places to celebrate Easter with the 40-strong polyphonic choir, Schola Cantorum, filling Chiesa di Santi Filippo e Giacomo with song throughout Holy Week.

## May & June

With temperatures ranging from 15 to 25 degrees and eight to nine hours of sunlight a day, this might be the best time to visit Venice. Local festivals, such as the La Sensa celebrations and the Voga Longa (see page 59), create a buzz, while the start of the Biennale (see page 104) in June brings the artistic or architectural elite to the city. However, accommodation prices rise to high season rates at this time and there is very little left over at an affordable price during the Biennale's first week.

This is also a great time to see the other cities and towns of the Veneto. It's the season for cherries and white asparagus, which are readily available across the region. Padua's Sagra di Sant'Antonio (13th June), celebrating the city's patron saint, is a very sociable affair and a good excuse to stay in the city. Vicenza has a gold fair around this time so hotel accommodation is very hard to secure. Verona's opera season (see pages 238-239) begins in mid June and lasts until August. It livens up the city no end but happens during high season when prices and demand for accommodation is high. However, those who can find somewhere to stay will enjoy the Festival Shakespeariano, which runs until August in the open-air Teatro Romano.

## July & August

This is peak season which, in Venice, means high temperatures (mid to late 20s by day; in the late teens by night), mosquitos, huge crowds and a shortage of places to eat and stay. And as for the prices! If you are determined to visit at this time, book everything possible (including entrance to the Palazzo Ducale and the Basilica) before you come and combine a few days in the city with a trip to other parts of the region. Verona is incredibly humid in July and August (air conditioning is a must) but these are excellent months to visit either the Dolomites for hiking and mountain biking or the outlying hill towns of the Veneto to *asolare* (do not much). The third Sunday in July is the Festa del Redentore in Venice (see page 60), which ends with an amazing firework display and is one of the best nights of the year to be in the city.

August is holiday month in Italy and one of the most unbearable heatwise. Many businesses pull the shutters down and head to the coast. You'll need to check that the places you want to visit will be open. Late in the month, the Venice Film Festival (see page 155) takes over the city. It's great for cinema goers but, again, book in advance.

## September & October

These months can be the most pleasant to visit the region, as it can still be sunny and warm but not blisteringly so: the average temperature is around 20 degrees during the day but can drop to 10 degrees at night. Towards the end of September Venice quietens down and the prices drop. It's a great time to come to the city, as the Biennale (see page 104) is in full swing. There are also rowing competitions in September, during Venice's Regata Storica and Burano's Sagra del Pesce. All over the region small food festivals take place to celebrate the harvest; one of the biggest is on the island of Sant'Erasmo in the lagoon.

*Above: A night at the opera in Verona's Arena.*
*Opposite page: The fireworks at Festa del Redentore.*

## November & December

The weather becomes a whole lot more unpredictable in the last two months of the year, with a distinctly chill wind from the north. November is one of Venice's wettest months with regular *acqua alta*, so bring your wellies, but December is, on average, one of the driest. Either way, this is when Venice is handed back to the Venetians, so there is a very different vibe across the city. If you're coming for the art and the food and to understand something of the people, this is by far the best time to visit, The Festa della Salute on the 21st November is the last significant festival of the year before Christmas. There are a few more food festivals to be enjoyed across the region; December's Radicchio in Piazza in Treviso being one of them but, in general, the atmosphere is much more low key at this time of year.

# Screen & page

Venice & Veneto in film & literature

## Films

### Senso
**Luchino Visconti, 1954**
This was Visconti's first use of Venice as a backdrop. Alida Valli plays a Venetian countess who falls in love with an Austrian officer during the Italian-Austrian war in 1866.

### Summertime
**David Lean, 1955**
Katharine Hepburn plays a spinster from Ohio who falls in love while on holiday in Venice. During filming, Hepburn was required to fall into a canal beside campo San Barnaba in Dorsoduro; it left her with a permanent eye infection.

### Romeo & Juliet
**Franco Zeffirelli, 1968**
This famous film version of the tragic love story has an innocence that is missing from Baz Luhrman's more violent and knowing 1996 adaptation. It was not filmed in Verona but some of the props and costumes can be found in the Casa di Giulietta.

### Death in Venice
**Luchino Visconti, 1971**
Based on the Thomas Mann novella, this film stars Dirk Bogarde as an old composer, Gustav von Aschenbach, who is obsessed with a young Polish boy holidaying in the same Lido hotel (Grand Hotel des Bains). There is a cholera outbreak in Venice at the time and an air of death hangs over the film. The old man's humiliation and tragic end are played out to a Mahler soundtrack.

### Don't Look Now
**Nicholas Roeg, 1973**
Donald Sutherland and Julie Christie star in this Daphne du Maurier thriller about a couple who, having just lost their daughter, go to stay in Venice where the husband renovates the church of San Nicolò dei Mendicoli in Dorsoduro. Hotel Baur (where the sex scene was filmed) and San Stae (the funeral) are just some of the other locations you'll spot.

### Everyone says I love you
**Woody Allen, 1996**
A musical set in New York, Paris and Venice. There seems little reason for the action to move to Venice but, of course, the city doesn't let the movie down.

### Merchant of Venice
**Michael Radford, 2004**

Al Pacino plays the embittered Jewish moneylender Shylock determined to get his "pound of flesh" from a loan defaulter (Jeremy Irons). Radford and Pacino succeed in showing the abuse and bigotry Shylock experiences as a Jew in Christian Venice. You'll spot scenes around the city.

### Casanova
**Russell T Davies, 2005**

This BBC mini series, starring David Tennant, was filmed entirely in Venice, with the interiors of Scuola San Rocco, Palazzo Ducale and other buildings providing luscious stage sets. The fabulousness of the city is enhanced (and cleaned up) by the profuse use of Photoshop and computer graphics. It's worth comparing Tennant's performance with Heath Ledger in the film of the same name and year.

### Wings of the Dove
**Hossein Aminin, 1997**

An excellent film adaptation of the novel by Henry James, starring Helena Bonham Carter, playing a baddy, for once, who manipulates an ailing young American visiting Europe. There are some wonderful shots of piazza San Marco and the cemetery on San Michele.

### Italian for Beginners (Italiensk for Begyndere)
**Lone Scherfig, 2000**

Italian for Beginners is a surprisingly cheery Danish Dogme 95 film (think hand-held cameras and natural lighting). Six people, all unknown to each other and all miserable, start an Italian class in a dreary Danish village. When their teacher dies of a heart attack, they decide to go to Venice as a tribute to him, where some of them fall in love.

### Bread and Tulips (Pane e Tulipani)
**Silvio Soldini, 2000**

A bored housewife, separated from her family and friends at a service station, takes her chance and jumps on a bus to Venice. There she meets Bruno Ganz, a pedantic bachelor, and they fall in love but are pursued by a blundering crime-fiction addict, who has been hired by her husband to find her. Hilarious but sweet, this shows more of the poorer side of Venice than most films.

## Literature

### Fiction

#### Divine Comedy: Inferno
#### Dante, 1308 to 1321

Dante describes a journey through the vividly imagined circles of Hell. Dante was a deeply aggrieved man when he wrote it, having been exiled from Florence and stripped of his possessions. The Inferno is populated by the poet's enemies, each of whom suffers a grisly fate which is described in fascinating detail.

#### Secretum
#### Francesco Petrarca, 1347 to 1353

Petrarch lays bare his woes, insecurities and failings in this achingly honest and beautifully written conversation with St Augustine.

#### Beppo, a Venetian story
#### Lord Byron, 1818

Written during Byron's residency at Palazzo Mocenigo, the story tells of a Venetian woman who takes a *cicisbeo* (chivalrous lover), after her husband is lost at sea. The husband returns and all live happily ever after: not a great plot but it is clever and evocative of the era.

#### Epilogue to 'Asolando'
#### Robert Browning, 1889

A great poem about love and optimism, published the day he died in Ca' Rezzonico on the Canal Grande (12 December 1889).

#### Wings of the Dove
#### Henry James, 1902

The story of Milly Theale, a rich but dying heiress, and the friends and parasites she attracts during a trip to Venice.

#### Death in Venice
#### Thomas Mann, 1912

The book that inspired Luchino Visconti's film. Mann's characterization goes that bit deeper than the film, providing more of a background to the character of Gustav von Aschenbach and making his conceit and attempts to fool himself all the more wretched and painful.

#### Commissario Guido Brunetti Mysteries
#### Donna Leon, from 1990 onwards

These detective books involve a Venetian cop who knows the dark underbelly of the city, fights crime and eats very well. His favourite place for coffee is Rosa Salva (campo San Luca, San Marco 4589).

#### Miss Garnet's Angel
#### Sally Vickers, 2000

An ever-so-slightly twee but still very readable tale of a buttoned-up spinster who becomes fascinated with Chiesa di San Angelo Raffaele on a trip to Venice. There are some great descriptions of the city and its art.

#### The Floating Book
#### Michelle Lovric, 2004

Set in 17th-century Venice, just as the first printing presses were in operation, the plot of this novel jumps between various characters and back to the life of Catullus in the first century BC. Two German brothers (based at the Fondaco dei Tedeschi) want to print some of Catullus' erotic verse, much to the revulsion of the Venetian authorities.

Lovric's other books also have a Venetian theme: *Carnevale* (2002) is set in the 18th century and is about a lover of Casanova, while *The Remedy* (2006), set around the same time, moves from the medical world of London to that of Venice.

### Venice: A documentary history 1450-1630
**David Chambers and Brian Pullan, 1992**
This may be a university text book but its collection of source documents regarding the development of the Venetian government, the persecution of the Jews, the Venetian Inquisition, the Sumptuary Laws and much more, is utterly absorbing.

### The Virgins of Venice: Enclosed Lives and Broken Vows in the Renaissance Convent
**Mary Lavin, 2003**
You won't believe what went on in Venetian convents in the 15th and 16th centuries. This volume explains what happened to hundreds of Venetian girls whose father couldn't afford to marry them off. It makes shocking reading but is entertaining, nonetheless.

### The Treasures of Venice
**Antonio Manno, 2004**
The best art guide to Venice ever written: beautifully thought out, carefully researched and composed, and superbly photographed. It's perfect for anyone wanting to go that bit deeper into the architectural and artistic wealth of the city.

### Francesco's Venice: The dramatic history of the world's most beautiful city
**Francesco da Mosto, 2007**
Only a Venetian whose family had been intimately involved with the crumbling bricks of the city could have written with such genuine passion and enthusiasm. The photographs by John Parker are striking, stolen moments.

### A Venetian Affair
**Andrea di Robilant, 2004**
This books charts the failed, clandestine love affair between di Robilant's great, great, great, great grandfather, Andrea Memmo, and a half-Greek, half-English woman called Giustiniana Wynne in the 18th century. The book is based on the couple's original love letters, many written in code, which were discovered by di Robilant's father.

### Non-fiction
### The story of my life (Histoire de ma vie)
**Giacomo Girolamo Casanova, 1894**
The memoirs of this very Venetian traveller, spy, gambler, escaped convict, womanizer and finally, librarian (1725-98). Casanova tells his own story in explicit but insightful detail and is as harsh a critic of himself as he is towards the many characters he comes across.

# Contents

About the region

The *Buccintoro* at Venice's Museo Storico Navale.

# History

The lion, Venice's calling card, at Musei Eremitani in Padua.

Architectural fragments at Torcello, on the Venetian lagoon.

## Roman Veneto

Veneto was populated by various tribes, including the Veneto Eugeni, the Rhaetians and the Veneti around the sixth century BC. They settled near the lagoon and on the banks and tributaries of the Adige and Brenta rivers. The people who located here had migrated from numerous territories, including Greece (some Venetians still consider themselves to be descendents of Troy), Gaul and Illyria. Scientists recently carried out tests on the people of Posina, a small village near Vicenza, and those from Barco di Pravisdomini, a village near the lagoon. These people look the same, speak the same dialect and would both consider themselves as indigenous but they have totally different mitochondrial DNA. This is highly unusual and shows the ethnic melting pot that Veneto once was.

Around 300 BC the Romans came, saw and conquered Veneto. Romanization of the area was completed in 89 BC when the cities of Tritium (Treviso), Patavium (Padua), Vincentia (Vicenza) and Verona became *municipia* and their male inhabitants were made Roman citizens, with the right to vote, stand for office, make binding contracts including those with foreigners, get married, move around the Roman Empire and enjoy a host of civil liberties. Roman mercantile tradition encouraged great prosperity in Veneto. The saying, '*omnes vias pecuniae norunt*' (they know all the ways of money) is most often said of the Venetians but was true of all those living in this thriving region.

The ambition and wealth of the Roman Empire can best be seen in Verona. The city was a strategic gateway to the Alps and lay between the key Roman cities of Genoa and Aquileia. Its humungous Arena (see page 238), built in AD 30, is one of the

## Around 300 BC the Romans came, saw and conquered Veneto.

## About the region

three best preserved amphitheatres in Italy (behind the Coliseum and the arena in Capua) and the only one that is still regularly used for performances. The Roman *decumanus* grid layout of the streets is still apparent in the modern city and the ruins of the Forum, conduits and other Roman buildings are visible under your feet. Verona's Teatro Romano (see page 249), built in the first century BC, is less complete than the Arena. However, the Museo Archeologico has a model of the theatre that reveals its original size and splendour.

The region also fathered two of the Roman era's most famous writers. Gaius Valerius Catullus, playboy, author of erotic poetry and inspiration to Ovid and Virgil, was born in Verona in 84 BC. Some 25 years later Livy (Titus Livius) was born in Padua and, after moving to Augustus, wrote *Ab Urbe Condita* (From the Founding of the City), one of the definitive texts on the history of Rome.

Christianity was awarded official status in the Roman Empire by Emperor Constantine in AD 313. The creation of a state religion and the recognition of a more absolute, natural law above that of the state and its figureheads is considered by some to be the beginning of the end of the Roman Empire. What's more, the increasing urbanization of the Empire through the building of fortified cities meant that peripheral areas were constantly at risk of attack by barbarians. Unprotected by Roman leagues, who were focused on progressing their eastern boundaries, these areas became depopulated and Rome's grasp on many parts of its empire started to weaken. In AD 331 Constantinople became capital of the Roman Empire and, over the following decades, power shifted eastwards. The fifth century saw the Visigoths and Ostrogoths making significant gains in the northern territories, including Veneto, which was taken by Theodoric the Ostrogoth in AD 489. Rome had fallen a few years earlier in AD 476, when Romulus Augustus, the last Roman Emperor, was displaced by Odoacer, a Germanic barbarian. This signalled the end of the Roman Empire and classical antiquity and the beginning of the Middle Ages and the Byzantine Empire.

### The rise of Venice & the Golden Age

It was the marauding barbarians who ran amok in Veneto in the fourth and fifth centuries who provided the catalyst for the creation of Venice. Refugees, fleeing the violence and chaos, headed to the islands of the Venetian lagoon, which provided a safe, naturally defended haven. The first settlements were rough wooden huts suspended on stilts, which were built on some of the myriad marshy mudflats. The supposed date for the founding of Venice was 25 April 412 (St Mark's Day) but there is no real evidence to support this.

Attila the Hun is known to have plundered Veneto in AD 452 (a stone chair, alleged to be his throne, can be seen at Torcello, see page 137), followed by Total the Goth in AD 552 and then the Lombards in AD 570. Each successive incursion saw ever greater numbers of people migrating to the lagoon. By the seventh century AD Venice's major settlements were Heraclea (now Cittanova), on the mainland coast of the lagoon, Malamocco on the Lido, which had direct access to the Adriatic, Olivolo (now the Sant'Elena area of Castello) and the more sheltered Rivo Alto (which became Rialto). It is claimed that Venice's first doge, Paoluccio Anafesta, was elected in AD 697 and ruled from Heraclea, although the first officially recorded doge

Above: A gold coin from the reign of Constantine the Great.
Opposite page: The Rialto Bridge at sunset.

was Orso Ipato in AD 726 whose seat was Malamocco. As the population increased, so did Venice's status. In AD 776, Olivolo was awarded a bishop's seat by the Pope on the site of San Pietro.

Around this time Venice found itself caught up in the scuffles between the Eastern Byzantine Empire (ruled by Nicephorus) and the Western Empire (ruled by Charlemagne). Charlemagne's son, Pepin, seized Chioggia and Palestrina in AD 810 and was only kept out of the Venetian settlement by the narrow channel of water between the mainland and Malamocco. After this close call, Venice's administrative functions and many of its noble families moved to the Rivo Alto area, thus consolidating the city. It quickly developed a distinct identity and, significantly, a maritime presence.

In 828, two Venetian merchants stole the body of St Mark from Alexandria and took it back to Venice. Doge Giustiniano Participazio was delighted: securing the relics of such a significant Apostle was a major boon for the city, giving it a divine status and ensuring a constant stream of paying pilgrims. Within four years the first basilica in San Marco had been built (see page 90). This burned down in 976 but was rebuilt soon after and consecrated in 1094.

The first symbolic marriage of the city to the sea took place in 1000 with Doge Pietro Orseolo taking the vows in a tradition that continues to this day on the festival of La Sensa (see page 59). Venice's location, its growing population and its maritime dominance contributed to the city's niche as a trading post between East and West. As trade grew so did Venice's interest in affairs beyond the lagoon. Venice sought the assistance of Constantinople to deal with Slavic pirates who pestered and plundered the goods on Venetian ships working the Mediterranean. In return, Venice lent its support against Muslim Saracen forces that were seeking to conquer strategic positions in the eastern Mediterranean. A number of Venetian ships were involved in the First Crusade in 1095, although this was not a political intervention but a private venture by merchants who sought to curry favour and protect their trading routes.

Meanwhile, more of the lagoon's marshland was drained and cultivated or developed as the city expanded. Huge logs, 7.5 m long, were forced into the sandy clay then packed with stone from Padua or elsewhere in the region before stone foundations were laid. Single storey houses with courtyards were typical of the age, with wells dug into them for drinking water. Bridges were built over the network of canals. In 1171 the six *sestieri* of San Marco, Castello (formerly Olivolo), Cannaregio, San Polo, Santa Croce and Dorsoduro were created for administrative purposes and, in 1173, the first Rialto Bridge was erected (see page 117). This was of wooden construction with a drawbridge in the middle to allow sailboats to pass through. The city also began to enjoy its position as the well-paid middleman in the trade of silks, spices and jewels.

Venice helped in the Fourth Crusade (1199-1204) and was able to expand its territory into Dalmatia and Corfu. As Constantinople's power crumbled away, Venice took control of trading routes in Asia and the Far East and Doge Enrico Dandolo was given the catchy title of 'Lord of a Quarter and a Half Quarter of the Empire'. Four bronze horses were taken as booty from the Hippodrome in Constantinople and flaunted on the roof of the Basilica San Marco.

In 1295 Marco Polo returned after 17 years in China (and seven years travelling there and back) laden with gems and stories of exotic lands and treasures. The taste for Eastern pleasures became something of a hobby amongst the Venetian nobility, as artefacts in both the Museo Storico Navale (see page 103) and the Museo Orientale at Ca' Pesaro (see page 118) bear out. By this time, Venice had transformed itself into a rich, influential city, protected by its natural boundaries. There seemed no end to its desire for wealth and

Above: Palazzo Ducale. Opposite page: Basilica di San Marco.

Above: Villa Pisani on the Brenta Canal.
Opposite page: Detail from Francesco Colonna's *Hypnerotomachia Poliphili*, the first book published in Venice in 1499.

In 1308 the pope threatened to excommunicate Venice, following the Republic's attempt to snatch the river Po from Papal Ferrara. This irritated the Venetian authorities who didn't like the church interfering in its affairs. However, the biggest threat to Venice's dominance came in 1348-9 when the plague, supposedly brought by boats carrying Middle Eastern goods, ravaged the city. Almost 80,000 lives were lost: more than half the population. This had a terrible effect on the navy which, without Venetian men to enlist, had to hire mercenaries from Greece and Dalmatia who were not necessarily loyal to the Republic. Frequent scuffles with Genoa over trade culminated in the 1380 Battle of Chioggia at which the Republic regained control of the Adriatic, at least for a while.

supremacy. Furthermore, it wasn't prepared to share its power or influence with anyone.

The late 13th and early 14th century saw a number of moves by Venice's ruling class to entrench their privileged position and to ensure that the title of Doge was restricted to just a few families. In 1297 membership of the Greater Council was made permanent and hereditary. The building of Palazzo Ducale (see page 93) began in 1309, followed a year later by the creation of the Council of Ten. The council was established specifically to deal with an attempt to overthrow the Doge and was intended to provide greater security for the Republic's administration but it soon ended up running all of the Republic's diplomatic and military affairs, passing laws and managing the intelligence services, which sought to thwart rebellion or corruption. The compilation of the *Libro d'Oro* (Golden Book) in 1325, an official list of the Venetian nobility, determined who could vote or hold office in the Republic. No matter how rich and successful they became, those Venetians who weren't on the list could not break through this impregnable, if extravagantly gilded, glass ceiling. However, in later years, as the costs of constantly going to war mounted, it became possible to buy your way in to the Venetian nobility – for a hefty price, of course.

## As the challenge to Venice's domination of the seas increased, the Republic looked landwards to see how it could augment its power.

As the challenge to Venice's domination of the seas increased, the Republic looked landwards to see how it could augment its power. In 1339 Venice had seized Treviso from the powerful Scaligeri family (see page 243). It took Vicenza in 1404 and Verona a year later, along with Padua from the Carraresis family. This expansion into terra firma encouraged noble families to build villas in the Veneto, famously along the Brenta Canal (see page 178) but also in the fertile hinterland, where they sought to cultivate profits from agriculture. This proved to be a canny move by the Venetians. The loss of Constantinople to the Turks in 1453 and the discovery of the New World by the Portuguese at the end of the 1400s shifted maritime power away from Venice. And, as the world's focus turned to the west, the value of spices, for so long a cash cow for the Venetians, dropped.

## The Renaissance

The 1500s marked the beginning of the decline of Venice's naval and trading dominance but you would never have known it. The Renaissance took hold of 'La Serenissima' – as the Republic's government rather vaingloriously called itself – and the city flourished like never before. The spread of new ideas in art and literature was facilitated by the advent of printing, which allowed for the production of small, portable books. The first printing press in Venice was set up by Teobaldo Mannucci (also known as Aldus Manutius), who published *Hypnerotomachia Poliphili* by a Dominican monk, Francesco Colonna, in 1499.

Venice's ambition and dedication to beauty created a fertile ground for artists such as Bellini, Titian and Tintoretto who imbued painting with realism, feeling and colour. But Venice struggled a little with new architectural ideas. While Vicenza, the home of Andrea Palladio (see page 50), was sold on the new classicism, Venice took time to let go of the old and fuddled Gothic and to sign up to the new precise and intellectual style. However, by this time, the city needed better infrastructure to support its large population, which was bigger than Rome's and Florence's put together, and the nobility were keen to display their growing power and wealth in grand building projects. Jacopo Sansovino (1486-1570) was employed as the city's *Proto* (chief architect) and set about restyling piazza San Marco. Palladio, meanwhile, was commissioned to design the façade of San Francesco della Vigna (see page 103) in 1572. Renaissance architecture in Venice triumphed with the completion of Palladio's San Giorgio Maggiore (see page 132) in 1580.

## About the region

Venice came under increasing foreign pressure during the 16th century. The League of Cambrai saw Pope Julius II, the Holy Roman Emperor, France and Spain joining forces to limit Venetian influence in northern Italy. Although the Pope later switched sides, the continued external threat created instability within the city, causing the Republic to turn in on itself. One of Venice's least glorious legacies was the creation of the Jewish ghetto in 1516. Although the persecution of the Jewish people was commonplace in Europe at that time, herding them into a designated area, restricting their movements and making them pay for the administration of such a policy was a new approach. The authorities became increasingly suspicious of internal conflict, establishing the State Inquisitors in 1540, who spied on prominent members of the ruling classes in an attempt to uncover plots and treachery. The state also sought to control the behaviour of its citizens. A series of laws were introduced between 1460 and 1543 to regulate prostitution, going so far as to stipulate what a prostitute could and couldn't wear, so that members of the public could distinguish a lady from a lady of the night. The Venetian Sumptuary Laws, passed in 1515 and 1562, prohibited displays of wealth and ostentation and even determined how much fish could be served at a banquet.

Vice, sodomy and the flaunting of riches were considered by the sanctimonious to be the cause of Venice's plague of 1575, when it lost one quarter of its population (50,000 people). So prolonged and dreadful was the experience that Pope Gregory XIII revoked all the Vatican's interdicts against the Republic. In 1577 the authorities agreed to build Il Redentore (see page 133) to mark the end of plague and Palladio was commissioned to design it. However, this did not prevent the plague from striking again in 1630, in turn spurring the building of Santa Maria della Salute (see page 126) by Baldassare Longhena. In 1591 another iconic Venetian structure was built: the ponte di Rialto (see page 117), designed by Andrea da Ponte.

## Decline & fall

In 1669 Crete fell to the Turks and in 1718 the surrender of Morea was the last nail in the coffin of Venice's maritime empire. The Republic had no significant trading power and lost its *stato da mar*. However, back home, the Venetians were still having a rare old time. Vivaldi, Brunello and Goldoni were the showbiz names of the age. In 1703, Antonio Vivaldi became choirmaster of Ospedale della Pietà, an orphanage and music school for abandoned and deformed children. Recitals were held to fund the good works and many of the children went on to become accomplished musicians, even if they did have to play behind a grille so as to not offend the audience. Caffè Florian, with its resident orchestra, opened in 1720, filling piazza di San Marco with melody, followed in 1755 by Caffè Quadri. And, in 1790, La Fenice staged its first opera.

It was around this time that gambling became commonplace in the city, with fortunes and palazzi regularly changing hands. Excess was the order of the day and any excuse for revelry and feasting was indulged to the full. In 1725 Venice's most decadent and immoral ambassador, Giacomo Girolamo Casanova was born. After a stint at Padua University and a failed attempt at a monkish existence, he took to writing. He famously caroused, gambled, swindled, amused and seduced his way around the *calli* of the city, before being sent to jail in 1755. He escaped, of course, and fled to France, where he did more of the same on an international scale. The Venetian authorities eventually pardoned him and allowed him to return but, despite his celebrity status, he was poor and had to work as a lowly spy for the state just to get by. He fell foul of the authorities after mocking a member of the nobility and fled to Bohemia where he worked as a librarian for Count Joseph Karl von Waldstein until his death in 1798.

Revolution in France sent shockwaves around the European ruling elite. Initially, the ripples weren't noticed in Venice, a city that still believed in its own pre-eminence. However, when Napoleon, at war

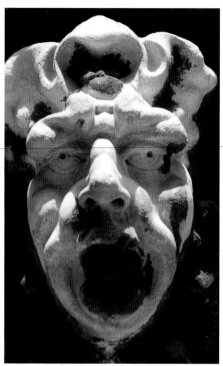

Above: A fountainhead.
Opposite page: Basilica di San Marco.

with Austria, began to encroach on Italian territories in 1797, Venice had to take notice. Napoleon took Verona, Vicenza, Padua and Mestre in quick succession and the fall of Venice became inevitable. On the 12 May 1797 Doge Ludovico Manin resigned and power was transferred to Napoleon. The French sailed into Venice a few days later, selected the treasure they wanted, then handed the city over to the Austrians. The Republic of Venice was at an end. Napoleon briefly sought to retake Venice to complete his portfolio as King of Italy but the Congress of Vienna in 1814-15 returned it to Austria's rule. The Venetians, at first bewildered by the turn of events, soon developed a simmering resolve to seize back control of their city.

## About the region

### The 19th & 20th centuries

In the 1800s the rest of the world finally caught on to Venice's treasures and it developed a reputation as a good-time city for monied visitors who sought a cultural haven like no other. Lord Byron came to Venice in 1818, staying with a menagerie of pets at Palazzo Mocenigo and using the library at San Lazzaro degli Armeni (see page 134). Robert Browning bought a house in Asolo (see page 195) before returning to Venice to visit his son at Ca' Rezzonico, where he died in 1889. John Ruskin visited with his new wife Effie in 1848 and wrote *The Stones of Venice* while staying at the Palazzo Gritti. Henry James came in 1869 and set his 1902 novel *The Wings of the Dove* in the city. Richard Wagner visited many times in his life before dying of a heart attack in Palazzo Vendramin in 1883. Venice's status as a tourist destination was facilitated by the opening of the railway bridge to the mainland in 1846. This hugely controversial development turned the once independent state into a mere peninsula of mainland Italy.

Veneto's resentment towards its Austrian rulers turned to revolt in 1848 with uprisings across the region, most significantly in Padua. The resistance surrendered the following year and the Risorgimento's student leaders in Padua were hanged. However, the Second War of Independence in 1859 showed more promise, with Giuseppe Garibaldi garnering popular support across the country. In 1866 the Third Italian War saw the liberation of Venice and Veneto from Austrian rule. Venice didn't go back to being an independent Republic, however, but instead became part of a unified nation.

At the turn of the 20th century, Venice's popularity among foreign visitors was augmented by the development of the Lido as a chic seaside resort and by the staging of the first Venice Biennale showcasing international contemporary art. However, the advent of World War I saw the region once more at war with Austria, with bombing raids across Veneto. The Alpini regiment of the Italian army fought the fiercest battles in the Dolomites and around Monte Grappa. Post-war humiliation and the economic collapse that ensued led to the rise of Italian nationalism. Benito Mussolini gained power in 1923 and Italy became a Fascist state.

At the start of World War II, Italy was an ally of Nazi Germany: the Jews of Veneto were sent to concentration camps and many cities in the region were shelled by Allied forces, with Padua, Treviso and Verona suffering the most; Venice was let off lightly. However, in July 1943 the Italian government withdrew its support for Mussolini and, on 8th September, an armistice was signed between Italy and the Allies. The Italian army began to fragment: some soldiers remained Fascists and continued to support the Germans who occupied the north of Italy; some went into hiding but many others became partisans, fighting against the Fascists and the Nazis. Mussolini was shot by partisans while attempting to flee the country in April 1945.

Surviving *acqua alta* requires resourcefulness.

Gondolas are for tourists only: you'll rarely hear of a Venetian using one.

## What the locals say

On 26 September 1944, 31 young partisans, one of whom was just 16 years old, were hanged by the Germans in Bassano del Grappa, under each of the trees which are still visible on viale dei Martiri. It happened towards midnight and the following morning the whole town awoke to this terrible scene. The bodies of the young men were left hanging for 20 hours so that everybody could see them. It was such a cruel act that it affected the whole population of Veneto for decades; my parents, who were 11 and nine at the time, still talk about it. Those responsible were never punished but Karl Franz Tausch, the German official in charge, killed himself on the 26 September 2008, the 64th anniversary of the hangings. The trees on viale dei Martiri tell a terrible story but one that it is important to know and to not forget.

*Miriam Duravia*

Bullet holes, a constant reminder of WWII, visible from the ponte degli Alpini in Bassano del Grappa.

The end of the war signalled a new beginning for Veneto, which was transformed from Italy's second poorest region to one of the most agriculturally and industrially rich in the country. However, the intensification of industry around the Venetian lagoon at Marghera and increased levels of water traffic were contributing factors in the devastating floods experienced by Venice in 1966, which spoiled artworks and damaged buildings. The clean-up continued well into the 1970s, with international organizations such as Save Venice and Venice in Peril set up to raise funds. The floods had another unforeseen effect: thousands of Venetians, unwilling to suffer the increasingly high tides, moved to the mainland town of Mestre. The impact of heavy industry, the depopulation of the city and the deluge of tourists who descend on this floating island each year continue to put Venice's very existence at risk.

# Art & architecture

❺ *Tempest* by Giorgione, Gallerie dell'Accademia.

The wealth of the Venetian Republic and its desire to be beautiful created a fertile environment for the city's hugely influential artistic Renaissance. Its watery beauty tested the ingenuity of artists who sought to decorate and celebrate the city, its nobility and its ambitions. What's more, the Venetians' self-confidence in their city's pre-eminence gave painters the freedom to express themselves and provided the patronage to support them. During the Renaissance there was a fundamental shift in the role of art, from a means of invoking awe and fear of God, to a medium that expressed more personal responses to beauty and ideas. The following 10 works of art illustrate the development of Venetian art from the Middle Ages to the fall of the Republic; for a more comprehensive account, visit the Gallerie dell'Accademia (see page 121).

**❶** *The Last Judgement* mosaics
(ninth century) – artist unknown
**Cattedrale Santa Maria Assunta, Isola di Torcello**
The Byzantine mosaics of the Last Judgement in Torcello's seventh-century cathedral are considered some of the best in the world. Not quite as flamboyant as those in the Basilica di San Marco, they were created by an unknown craftsman who had studied in Salonica in the eighth and ninth centuries. Rudimentary yet rich in colour and gold leaf, they show Christ's crucifixion, his descent into limbo and a doomsday portrayal of fiery hell, with sinners being poked at with sticks and swallowed up, legs still kicking, by dog-like beasts. Artists at this time were agents of the church who sought to instil awe and fear in the congregation by reinforcing the messages of hell, fire and damnation for sinners.

**❷** *Coronation of the Virgin* polyptych (1325) – Paolo Veneziano (born before 1321, died before 1362)
**Gallerie dell'Accademia, Venice**
Wholly religious in nature and stylistic in composition, medieval art in the early 1300s was all about inspiring awe in the viewer. However, Veneziano was one of the first to create works that were intended to be viewed at eye level rather than on high and out of reach. This hugely complicated and elaborate altarpiece, with its extravagant use of gold, shows the crowning of Mary as mother of God, the church and the heavens. Particularly noteworthy is the painstaking depiction of the sumptuous fabric that adorns the majestic subject matter. The eastern style of the painting reflects the role of Venice as a crossing point between the Orient and the Occident.

Icons like this were painted with egg tempera (egg mixed with pigment), applied with a brush on to a wood panel. Details were picked out in gold leaf and a varnish was applied to the whole to increase the vibrancy of the colours: the lapis-lazuli blue on this painting is fantastically brilliant. Veneziano's use of colour to convey magnificence is something that Venetian artists would develop throughout the Renaissance.

**❸** *St Christopher*, part of the St Vincent Ferrer polyptych (1464) – Giovanni Bellini (1430-1516)
**Santi Giovanni e Paolo, Venice**
Bellini worked with the same materials that had been available to Veneziano but he pushed tempera to its limits and started to play with light, mood and colour. This early painting on a wood panel is one of six that make up the polyptych. It is remarkable for its depiction of human emotion, something that Bellini would develop further in his studies of the Madonna with infant and of the dead Christ. This St Christopher is shown not as a bearded vagrant, as was the usual portrayal, but as a devoted, hopeful young man, firm of muscle, steadying himself and the baby Jesus on his shoulders with his staff. This realistic portrayal of flesh and strength is one of the first in Venice.

**❹** *Meeting of St Ursula and St Etherius* (1495) – Vittore Carpaccio (active 1490-1523)
**Gallerie dell'Accademia, Venice**
Like Bellini's brother, Gentile, Carpaccio championed huge narrative paintings featuring crowds, architecture and activity on a horizontal plane. This rather phantasmagorical depiction of

## About the region

Venice painted on canvas was part of a cycle created for the Scuola di Sant'Orsola (located where Santi Giovanni e Paolo now sits). Carpaccio unleashed his imagination in a desire to show the multiplicity of the city and evoke its grandeur. The painting's composition, luxurious colours and referencing of aspects of the real Venice demonstrates the new taste of the Venetian nobility for art that was still religious but also conveyed their class and their ambitions. The Bible and the lives of the saints were still considered the greatest stories ever told but Venice, its rulers and its God-given riches could now be part of the picture.

**❺** *Tempest* (1507) – Giorgione aka Giorgio da Castelfranco (c1477-1510)
Gallerie dell'Accademia, Venice
Giorgione, a contemporary of Bellini, Titian and Tintoretto, lived a short but potent life. This painting, created just three years before his death from the plague, demonstrates an altogether darker undercurrent in Venetian art and the Venetian mindset. It depicts a woman, disrobed, breastfeeding her child while a man stands near by and a storm brews on the horizon. Who is the man? Is she in danger? In fact, the human characters are of little importance; what matters is the poetry and the ambiguity of the painting, created by the interplay of darkness and shadows. Giorgione's use of *sfumato*, the technique of graduation from light to dark, gives the painting sensuousness and mystery. Hung next to it in the Accademia is his *La Vecchia* (1505) showing a shattered old woman looking careworn and almost accusing as she holds a paper saying '*col tempo*' (in time). Despite our worldliness and sophisticated tastes, Giorgione's paintings still evoke feelings of uncertainty, as they did then.

**❻** *Assumption* (1518) –
Tiziano Vecelli aka Titian (1487-1576)
Santa Maria Gloriosa dei Frari, Venice
The death of Giorgione in 1510 and Bellini in 1516 created opportunities and creative space for Titian. After he had completed the unfinished commissions of these artists and secured his reputation, Titian began a series of paintings

that have come to define the Venetian High Renaissance. This epic painting was one of them. It shows the moment before Mary ascends into heaven and is crowned. The inhabitants of Earth and Heaven are at once identifiable as witnesses to this sacred event. There is an overpowering sense of movement in the painting that seems to swirl around the Virgin as she soars upwards. She is resplendent in swooshing coral robes that are so rich and velvety, you want to touch them. It is the depth and vibrancy of the colour, created by layer upon layer of oil paint, and Titian's mastery of light – falling, illuminating and dignifying – that makes this painting so remarkable. Religious scenes like this had been painted before but never with such emotion, such realism and such skill. Looking at this painting, it is as though you are experiencing such a divine physical moment yourself.

**❼** *Portrait of a young gentleman in his studio* (1530) – Lorenzo Lotto (1480-1556)
Gallerie dell'Accademia, Venice
Titian was the pre-eminent portrait painter of the age but the portraits of young men by Lorenzo Lotto are more psychological. This one, which hangs alone in a room in the Accademia, is one of his finest. Lotto sought to reveal what was going on in the head of his perfectly composed sitter. There is skill in obtaining a true likeness, which comes from being able to paint what you see, but Lotto could also paint what his subject felt, just through their eyes, their hands and the setting of their lips. The intensity of the repressed emotion in this painting creates a dark, frustrated subtext.

**❽** *The miracle of St Mark freeing a slave* (1548) – Jacopo Robusti aka Tintoretto (1518-94)
Gallerie dell'Accademia, Venice
Many of Tintoretto's paintings defy the artistic conventions of the age in which they were created but it was this painting that put Tintoretto on the map. Despite only being Titian's apprentice for a few days, Tintoretto copied the master's technique of fashioning little wax or clay models and assembling the scene he wanted to paint. The resulting image is

❸ *St Christopher*, part of the *St Vincent Ferrer polyptych* by Giovanni Bellini, SS Giovanni e Paolo.

like a still from an action movie: the confusion of bodies, along with the dynamism of the saint swooping down, mean that you have to study this painting for a good few moments before you can understand what is happening. If Tintoretto had been alive today he might have been a film director, less interested in reality than in capturing a sudden turn of events in a breathtaking image.

⑨ Frescoes (c1560) – Paolo Veronese (1528-99)
Villa Barbaro, Maser

Veronese was perhaps the most humorous of the Renaissance fresco painters and had a run-in with the Inquisition over his inappropriate composition in *Feast in the House of Levi* (1573). Apparently, Palladio was none too pleased with Veronese's frescoes in Villa Barbaro, either, which he felt contorted the simplicity and classicism of his perfectly symmetrical rooms. He's not entirely wrong. Veronese's ability to paint architectural features such as columns and balustrades using perspective create a 3-D effect that redraws the rooms' internal dimensions whilst his trademark palette of pastel tones make them look like coloured marble. But Veronese's 'windows' and 'views' add life to Palladio's precision and order and many visitors to the villa would argue that he perfects Palladio's almost-perfect building.

⑩ Frescoes (1757) –
Giambattista Tiepolo (1696-1770)
Villa Valmarana ai Nani, Vicenza

Obviously inspired by Veronese, Tiepolo worked during the swinging, decadent last century of the Venetian Republic. As a fresco painter he did paint liturgical scenes but it was his allegorical works that were in demand: the *Allegory of Merit between Nobility & Virtue* (1758), a ceiling fresco in Ca' Rezzonico in Venice, has angels soaring through the air with such momentum that you think they may fall on your head. The Villa Valmarana frescoes are similarly symbolic, painted in warm hues and wild with movement but their domestic setting means you can get closer to them. You may find yourself almost lost in the dreamlike scenes of angels, Romans, farmhands and old women taking in the harvest.

⑨ Frescoes by Paolo Veronese, Villa Barbaro, Masèr.

## About the region

To those who know or care little about the history of architecture, Venice is just beautiful: an appealing scene that combines an exotic-looking Basilica with grand if crumbling palazzi on the Canal Grande and monumental marble churches with big domes. But Venice wasn't built in a year or even in a century; its development took place across four periods of architecture.

### Byzantine

The relocation of the heart of the Roman Empire to Byzantium (later known as Constantinople) in the late fourth century marked the start of the Byzantine era, which lasted for nearly a thousand years. While the rest of Veneto had been part of the Roman Empire and had the architecture to prove it (most notably the Arena and Teatro in Verona), Venice was born into the new world order and developed its own idiosyncratic style, influenced by its status as the crossing point between East and West.

Byzantine architecture is characterized by the use of Doric, Ionic and Corinthian columns, semi-circular arches, Moorish domes, geometric patterning and mosaics. Torcello's **Cattedrale Santa Maria Assunta** (see page 136) dates from AD 639 and is the oldest building in the lagoon. It follows the Roman Basilica model but its internal arches, complex patterned floor tiles and rich mosaics reveals the eastern influence.

The most glittering version of a Byzantine building in Venice is **Basilica di San Marco** (see page 90). Originally built in the ninth century, it was altered in the 11th century to imitate Constantinople's Church of the Six Holy Apostles, with five domes each placed on a point of its new Greek cross plan. **Fondaco dei Turchi**, although rebuilt, and **Ca' da Mosto** are good examples of non-ecumenical Byzantine buildings.

Below: Basilica di San Marco.

# Architectural glossary

**Columns** the Greeks had three orders of columns: the **Doric** order, characterized by straight up-and-down plainness is meant to symbolize man (the grooves are called fluting); **Ionic**, characterized by scrolls, symbolizes women, and **Corinthian**, which has a bell-shaped top (or capital) and is adorned with acanthus leaves and volutes, symbolizes virgins. The Romans added the **Tuscan** order, which is without decoration, while the **Composite** order is a mish-mash of the three Grecian orders.

**Aedicule** A frame around a doorway or window made up of columns or pilasters and an entablature on top. It can also be a mini decorative structure housing a statue. It is used in both Classical and Gothic architecture.

**Arcade** A row of columns that support arches.

**Architrave** The lower part of an entablature, which meets the capitals of the columns.

**Baldachin** A canopy over a tomb, supported by columns.

**Campanile** Bell tower.

**Capital** The crown of a column adorned with scrolls (Ionic) or acanthus leaves (Corinthian).

**Cloister** Usually part of a church, this is a covered passage around a courtyard, lined with columns or arches.

**Choir** The chancel of a church, which is used by the clergy and the choir; it is occasionally separated from the nave by a screen.

**Colonnade** A series of columns.

**Cornice** A horizontal ledge or moulding. Practically, it's a gutter, draining water away from the building; aesthetically, it's a decorative feature.

**Cupola** A dome on a roof.

**Entablature** The upper part of an order that is held up by the column and includes the architrave, frieze and cornice.

**Frieze** The centre of an entablature; often decorated.

**Loggia** A recessed open gallery or corridor on the façade of a building.

**Nave** The central body of the church, between the aisles.

**Narthex** A long porch along the entrance wall of a church, before the nave.

**Pilaster** A rectangular column that only slightly protrudes from a wall.

**Pinnacle** A small often ornate turret, popular in Gothic architecture.

**Plinth** The lower part or base of a column.

**Portico** A roofed space that serves as an entrance to a building.

**Sacristy** A room off the main or side altars in a church or, occasionally, a separate building that houses the sacred vessels, vestments and records.

**Tracery** Ornamental stonework that supports the glass in Gothic windows.

# About the region

## Gothic

The 1300s saw many of the city's Byzantine buildings knocked down to make way for new Gothic structures. The Republic's confidence was bullish at this point: it had just trounced Genoa for control over trading routes and was expanding its territories on land and at sea. Venice's appetite for buildings that showed off its strength and power fitted perfectly with the Gothic style, which was all about soaring masonry, characterized by the use of ogee arches, which rise to a point resembling the keel of a ship. Originating from Islamic architecture, they are used for doorways and windows and are often embellished by tracery and mouldings, and pinnacles all made of white marble or stone to provide contrast with the reddish brick used for the rest of the building.

Santi Giovanni e Paolo (see page 99) and Madonna dell'Orto (see page 110) are classic examples of Gothic architecture. The Frari (see page 118) has all the immensity of a Gothic building but none of the adornment, while the pink-hued Palazzo Ducale (see page 93), although it is more delicate and elaborate, is also true to the Gothic style. On the mainland, excellent examples of Gothic architecture include the vast Chiesa di San Nicolò, which looms large on the Trevigani skyline (see page 193), and the overblown baldachin of Arche Scaligeri in Verona (see page 243), which takes Gothic decoration to the absolute limit.

## Renaissance

Venice remained stuck in a Gothic timewarp well into the 1400s, much longer than the rest of Italy, which scoffed at its infatuation with a style that was so out of fashion. However, the principles and fundamentals of Greek and Roman architecture – symmetry, proportion, and the use of columns, pilasters and entablatures – did gradually begin to permeate Venetian style, resulting in some architectural confusion. The struggle to marry the 'old' Gothic and the 'new' Renaissance architecture is well illustrated by the church of San Zaccaria, which has a lower section by Antonio Gambello dating from 1458 and an upper façade (1483) by Mauro Codussi (1440-1504). Codussi's Chiesa di San Michele in Isola (see page 134) from 1469 is considered the first real Renaissance building in Venice. He also built Santa Maria Formosa in 1492 (see page 100) and completed Pietro Lombardo's confection of a church, Santa Maria dei Miracoli (see page 108). Most significantly, he started to design the Procuratie Vecchie on piazza San Marco and, along with Bartolomeo Buon, built the Torre dell'Orologio (see page 89).

Following the sacking of Rome in 1527, architects of repute, including Michele Sanmichele (1484-1559) and Jacopo Sansovino (1486-1570), arrived in Venice. Sanmichele was deployed in mainland Veneto building imposing fortifications,

The Ospedale and SS Giovanni e Paolo.

Above: Procuratie Vecchie, piazza San Marco.
Opposite page: San Zaccaria.

# Andrea Palladio (1508-1580)

Andrea di Pietro della Gondola was born in Padua on St Andrew's Day (30 November) 1508, the year Michelangelo began painting the Sistine chapel. Aged 13 he began an apprenticeship with a stonecutter in Padua before moving to Vicenza in 1524 where he worked for masons to the Vicentine nobility. He had mastered his craft by the time he met Count Giangiogino Trissino in 1537. Trissino became his mentor and introduced him to the liberal arts and classical Roman architecture. It was also Trissino who gave him the nickname 'Palladio', after the Greek goddess of wisdom, Pallas Athene.

Palladio's first significant project was Villa Godi in Lonedo, just outside Vicenza (1540). It was clearly inspired by the new rules and principles Palladio had studied and proved popular with those who would become future patrons. In 1541 he began the first of his visits to Rome to study its ancient buildings. His big break came in 1545, when, aged 38, he beat off competition from Sansovino and Sanmichele to win the prestigious contract to refurbish the Basilica in Vicenza. Here he effectively wrapped a two-storey neoclassical loggia around the older Gothic core. This was such a huge project that it was only completed in 1614 by his protégé Vincenzo Scamozzi. Scamozzi began working for Palladio in the 1560s and finished many of Palladio's designs after he died in 1580.

After the Basilica commission, demand for Palladio increased, with commissions in Udine (Palazzo Antonini, 1581), Vicenza (Palazzo Thiene, completed by Scamozzi in 1593) and in Venice: the impressive façade and cloister of San Giorgio Maggiore (started in 1566). In 1567 Palladio began designs for La Rotonda and in 1570 wrote and illustrated his *Quattro libri dell'architettura* (The Four Books of Architecture), which became a bible for architects. His final works were Il Redentore in Venice (finished in 1610 by Scamozzi) and Teatro Olimpico in Verona (completed by Palladio's son, Silla, and Scamozzi in 1583).

So, what did Palladio do for architecture? He was a great fan of Vitruvius whose mantra was '*firmitas, utilitas, venustas*' (strong, useful, beautiful). Palladio did not blithely copy Greek and Roman styles but instead used his craftsmanship and understanding of his clients to take classical principles and harness them in a modern way, creating harmonious buildings that were practical, comfortable and so very satisfying.

such as the **porta Nuova** and **porta Palio** in Verona which served as gates of glorification rather than defence. Sansovino, meanwhile, was made *Proto* or chief architect and superintendent of properties to the Procurators of San Marco. He was largely responsible for the revamping of San Marco, building both the **Loggetta** of the Campanile (see page 89) in 1549 and the **Biblioteca Nazionale Marciana** (see page 89), which was completed in 1591 by Vincenzo Scamozzi.

However, if there is one architect that revolutionized architecture in the Renaissance, it was Andrea Palladio (1508-1580). His mathematical approach to dimensions made for 'perfect' buildings that were balanced and pleasing to the eye. His main works in Venice include **Il Redentore** (see page 133), **Chiesa di San Francesco della Vigna** (page 103) and **San Giorgio Maggiore** (see page 132). But this is only part of the Palladio story. The city of Vicenza is the architect's showcase, with

## If there is one architect that revolutionized architecture in the Renaissance, it was Andrea Palladio.

Above: Baldassare Longhena's Baroque beauty, Santa Maria della Salute.
Left: Villa Barbaro. Opposite page: San Giorgio Maggiore.

highlights including the **Basilica Palladiana** (see page 216), **Palazzo Thiene** (see page 219) and his acclaimed summerhouse, **La Rotonda** (see page 224). Palladio's work can also be seen throughout rural Veneto in the luxurious villas of the Venetian nobility. His idea of incorporating the agricultural buildings alongside the main residence produced beautiful but functional villas, such as **Villa Barbaro** in Maser (see page 199) and **Villa Foscari** on the Brenta Canal (see page 179).

Palladio died when many of his designs were still just drawings or building sites but his protégé, Vincenzo Scamozzi (1548-1616), continued his work, finishing the **Teatro Olimpico** in 1583 (see page 220) and numerous other buildings in Vicenza, as well as designing his own buildings, such as the **Procuratie Nuove** in Venice (completed by Baldassare Longhena in 1650, see page 89).

## Baroque

The skyline of Venice was completed in the 17th century, when, in line with the excesses of its inhabitants, the city desired a little more ornamentation. The simple lines and understated elegance of the Renaissance gave way to the flamboyant use of sculpture, lavish embellishment, layered structures and artistic effects, such as trompe l'œil.

Baldassare Longhena (1598-1682) was the *Proto* (official city architect) and chief adorner in this period. His towering triumph was **Chiesa di Santa Maria della Salute** (1680), an octagonal structure encrusted with statues and crowned by a monumental dome (see page 126), but he also designed **Chiesa di Santa Maria di Nazareth degli Scalzi** (see page 111), next to the train station, and **Ca' Rezzonico** (see page 128), which were both finished by other architects.

After this flourish, there was a brief return to neo-classicism in the mid 18th century before the fall of Venice in 1797. Napoleon demolished 12 churches across the city, including San Geminiano, which was flattened to make way for his **Ala Napoleonica** on piazza San Marco. This was built in 1814 by Giuseppe Maria Soli in the style of the Renaissance Procuratie Nuove and now houses the **Museo Correr** (see page 96).

# Venice & Veneto today

An advertising hoarding shrouds the Biblioteca Nazionale Marciana.

## The 'Disneyfication' of Venice

Tourism brings at least 15 million visitors a year to Venice and is worth €12 billion to the local economy but although it's the city's main employer and source of income, the Venetians aren't exactly thrilled to live in the most visited city in Italy. Venice's popularity comes at a real cost.

During the city's heyday in the 15th and 16th centuries, its population was around 200,000; today, it is just 62,000. Most Venetians have moved out of the city and commute daily into work. Those who have stayed tend to be older, wealthier residents (the average age is 50 and 25% of the population is over 64) and, although they may live in the most beautiful city in the world that doesn't make their lives easy. The cost of property is so prohibitive that to get a house you need to fork out a Doge's ransom or rely on inheriting one from your family. If you want to buy a washing machine, you have to go to Mestre, then get it delivered by boat. There are still great neighbourhoods with a spirited community atmosphere and, yes, there are still shops like butchers and bakers where you can buy daily essentials but there are also an awful lot of mask

Now one of Venice's biggest exports: masks for tourists.

The huge cruiseships leave in the evening.

makers and glass ornament sellers. And if you live in San Marco and want to send your kid to the local nursery you can't: it was recently turned into a hotel.

That said, for most Venetians, it is the daily barrage of tourists that makes life so difficult. During peak season 50,000 tourists are in the city each day. Add the workforce from the mainland, another 50,000, plus 15,000 students and you have 115,000 additional people on the island: almost double the city's resident population.

Around 80% of those who visit the city are daytrippers. Many sail into the lagoon on a cruise liner, pile off the boat and, led by a guide carrying a little flag, jam the *calli* in the 'Bermuda Shorts Triangle', around piazza San Marco, the ponte di Rialto and the Accademia. Then, come sunset, they traipse back to the boat and sail out of the lagoon. Others only come for a day because they just can't afford to stay overnight. Venetians much prefer the other 20%, the residential tourists, who are booked into a hotel, B&B or apartment because they contribute financially to the city.

Venice might make a mint from the tourist industry but it also needs a mint just to keep functioning as a city. The regular dredging of the canals means Venice no longer smells so bad in hot weather but this upkeep, along with the constant renovation of historical buildings, the endless maintenance of pavements and bridges, the removal of waste and the introduction of recycling are all major challenges and hugely costly for the city.

The struggle to achieve a balance between the demands of tourism and a quality of life for the locals is the job of the city's Mayor, currently Massimo Cacciari, a liberal intellectual who's not afraid to push a non-populist line. But in rising to the challenge he's taken on both the residents, who enjoy many of the benefits of unfettered tourism, and the tourists themselves.

In order to fund the never-ending programme of renovation and structural improvements, Cacciari has made it clear that he will speak to anyone who is prepared to bankroll some of the bigger renovation projects. Visitors to Venice very quickly see what this means in practice, as tarpaulins that swathe the renovation works are sold as advertising space. The Mayor has even suggested renaming the wooden crossing over the Canal Grande from San Marco to the Accademia, 'Gates Bridge', should Bill want to help pay for its renovation. Far from welcoming this sponsorship of their city's heritage and landmarks, locals are appalled at the idea that Venice is for sale.

And tourists are being challenged too. It can be expensive to dine out in Venice but be careful if you decide to have a picnic instead or you'll find a 'hostess' threatening you with a €50 fine for eating in a public place. The city will also no longer issue licenses for new bathrooms within residences of a certain size thereby curtailing the growth of the B&B sector. B&Bs were introduced in 2001 to make overnight accommodation more affordable for cash-strapped visitors but now the city wants to

ensure that reasonably priced homes are kept for Venetians rather than being turned into accommodation for tourists; it won't stop big palazzi being converted into posh hotels, however.

The Mayor is criticized for avoiding other issues. Will he stop the big cruise liners coming in to the lagoon or would the lost revenue from docking charges make this too unpalatable? Should the city introduce incentives for tourists to stay overnight, such as gratis passes for sights or vaporetto tickets? Some have even suggested there should be a charge to get in to the city itself, as there is for theme parks.

The 'Disneyfication' of Venice is a phrase often used by commentators to describe how Venice is becoming a living museum or historical theme park. To avoid this fate, Venice must have a viable living and working population; it must be a functioning city, with an infrastructure that meets the locals' needs first and the tourists' needs second. It is most likely that visitors to Venice will be expected to pay for this. Is that such a bad thing?

**Left: Souvenir caps for sale, Venice.**
**Below: Riva degli Schiavoni.**
**Opposite page: Vicenza, city of Palladio and site of a controversial US military base.**

## No dal Molin : People power in Vicenza

Vicenza is one of Italy's smallest, richest and most perfectly formed cities, with a building by Andrea Palladio around every corner. However, it is in the midst of a furious battle that spans the council, the courts and the Italian government.

Take an early morning stroll down the corso Palladio and you'll come across noisy huffing, puffing US servicemen out for their morning run. The city is home to several US military installations, including Camp Ederle, which has tripled in size since it was established in 1955. There are now plans for a new bigger base to be located at the quiet civilian airport of Da Molin just one mile from the *centro storico* of Vicenza. Berlusconi, famously accommodating to the US government, and local officials have approved the new base but local people – worried about the militarization of their city, the environmental impact and the risk of becoming a terrorist target – are growing increasingly vocal in their opposition to the scheme. When protestors' demands for an environmental assessment were not met, something unusual started to happen in this traditionally conservative part of the world.

The '*No Dal Molin*' movement, a highly articulate grassroots campaign against the new base, has grown in support and stature to become a national cause with people all over Italy demonstrating against the government's failure to consult with local communities. Their political figurehead, Cinzia Bottene, stood in the 2008 *comune* (council) elections and not only won a seat but convinced the frontrunner for the mayoral contest, Achille Variati (who went on to win), to stand on a '*No Dal Molin*' platform and seek a local referendum on the matter. Berlusconi, described the referendum as "seriously inopportune". His party colleague, Roberto Cattaneo, leader of the opposing '*Si Dal Molin*' campaign, former employee of the base and a member of the Vicenza comune, managed to kickstart the notoriously slow Italian judicial system and won immediate hearings that put an end to a referendum. The protesters went ahead anyway on an unofficial basis and in September 2008 an astounding 95% of Vicentini voted '*No Dal Molin*'.

By the end of 2008 it was still unclear how events would unfold but the campaign has exposed not only the lack of transparency and due process in the way national and local government works, but a new fighting spirit amongst the once apathetic Vicentini.

## A watery end?

If you arrive in Venice by train, you'll see the silvery chimneys of Porto Marghera belching black smoke on the western side of the Venetian lagoon but you won't see the factories quietly drawing water out of the lagoon and pumping waste back in. Take a vaporetto up the Grand Canal and you'll see the wake from speed boats slapping relentlessly at the walls of the already crumbling palazzi. Visit Venice in December, when the *acqua alta* is at its highest, and you'll hear the klaxons shriek and see the water gush round the duckboards you have to walk on. The threat of a watery ending to Venice is very real.

The Venetian lagoon covers 500 km². Just over 90% of this is water, which is, on average, only 1 m deep (and no more than 5 m); the rest is made up of low-lying sandbanks and marshy islands. The tides gush in from the Adriatic through three inlets at Chioggia, Malamocco and Porto di Lido, swilling the lagoon with fresh seawater that supports a wide variety of fish and birdlife. Since the first settlers arrived in the fourth century the lagoon has been key to the identity and survival of the city, yielding food and the basis for its economy. As Venice rose up from its watery surroundings, it provided a sheltered and secure port for the Venetian fleet, giving the city an advantage not enjoyed by those it sought to dominate. Building such an influential city state on what was just a

**Building such an influential city state on what was just a few mud flats required vision, ingenuity and a great deal of resources.**

few mud flats required vision, ingenuity and a great deal of resources; sustaining Venice's future in the age of global warming and other man-made challenges will require even more.

In the 19th and 20th centuries the construction of petro-chemical factories brought new wealth to the area. Their goods were shipped out by huge tankers that needed special channels cut out of the lagoon bed to stop them running aground. This activity also brought spills, fires and effluence, upsetting the balance of the lagoon's ecosystem. At the same time, the construction of the rail and road bridge turned what was an island, only accessible by boat, into a peninsula. Improved transport caused a surge in tourism, which, like the factories, brought wealth to the city but at an environmental cost.

Industrial damage to the lagoon peaked in the decades following the Second World War. As Marghera expanded so did the incidence of *acqua alta*, defined as when the tide rises 1 m above its 'zero' level, and piazza San Marco was often flooded 40 times a year rather than the usual seven or eight. The city's worst flood came in 1966 when the *acqua alta* rose 194 cm, causing severe damage to the city.

Over the last 10 years in November, December, February and April tides have risen over 1 m once a day, sometimes twice, putting enormous pressure on the city's foundations. If sea levels increase by 50-60 cm as a result of global warming between now and 2100, the chances of saving Venice from inundation seems hopeless. Already, warmer temperatures in the lagoon have allowed new species of bivalve, clam and algae to move in, altering the natural balance of the aquaculture and putting indigenous species at risk.

In an effort to protect the city, the Consorzio Venezia Nuova (a private consortium of Italian builders and engineers) has decided to raise the height of *fondamenta* (canalside pavements), dredge the canals more often, reinforce the sea walls and limit the number of petrol tankers on the lagoon. In the mean time, Mayor Massimo Cacciari presses on with the construction of MOSE (Modulo

Above and opposite: *Acqua alta* in Venice.

Sperimentale Elettromeccanico). Despite its name, this is not something a kid would make in his bedroom but rather a mechanized and mobile barricade to be located at the three inlets at Chioggia, Malamocco and Porto di Lido.

In 2008 it was 37% complete and projected to cost €3.7 billion. The politicians, worried about the spiralling costs, have stopped then started the project more than once, whilst Venetians and environmentalists in the 'no MOSE' camp are hugely sceptical and suggest that a better and cheaper scheme could have been put in place. Will MOSE turn back the tide? Only time will tell.

# Festivals & events

## January

**Festa Nazionale della Befana** (6th)
To celebrate Epiphany Italian children receive presents from Befana, a good witch who leaves honeycomb candy for good children and coal (or biscotti died black) for naughty children. In Venice they hold a regatta, so expect to see witches in gondolas showering children with sweets.

## February

**Carnevale** (10 days before Ash Wednesday)
Carnevale, literally 'farewell to meat', lasts for 10 days (it used to be two months!) and ends on Shrove Tuesday. This masked festival was first celebrated in Venice in the 11th century and was traditionally a hugely decadent and debauched affair. Napoleon put a dampener on things when he handed Venice over to the Austrians and Mussolini banned mask-wearing in the 1930s but, in 1979, Carnevale was revived and nowadays the whole city seems preoccupied with revelry.

There are events in nine *campos* across the city including numerous over-the-top *sfilata delle mascheri* (mask processions). Special sweet *fritole* are served in the *patisserie* and a party atmosphere pervades throughout. However, getting a ticket for one of the *mascheranda* (masked balls) can be difficult and expensive, and some preparation is required if you want to hire an elaborate costume. Do some research on the Carnevale website (carnivalofvenice.com or carnevale-venezia.com) to ensure you know what is happening and when. Events start on the first Friday of the carnival with the **Festa delle Marie** (an unpious celebration of the Virgin Mary) and the **Gran Corteo Storico** (Great Historic Parade). On the Sunday is the **Volo dell'Angelo** (Flight of the Angel), in which a woman dressed as an angel 'flies' from the Campanile to the balcony of the Palazzo Ducale.

Verona has its equivalent, **Becanal del Gnoco**, on the Friday before Shrove Tuesday, which is a bit more democratic in spirit.

## March

### Salone Nautico
The Venice International Boat Show, showcasing every kind of seafaring vessel, is held at Stazione Marittima. The Arsenale – usually closed to the public – is open for this event so it is worth visiting for this delight alone (festivaldelmare.com).

### Easter
Celebrations, including processions and hugely popular church services, take place throughout Venice and Veneto.

### Su e zo per i ponti
'Up and down the bridges' is a fun, non-competitive run held in Venice on a Sunday in April. It starts at the Colonna on piazzetta San Marco and heads east through all of Venice's *sestieri* before ending back at piazza San Marco for some festivities. The runners cross a total of 45 bridges and cover 9.8 km, while the walkers cross 32 bridges and cover just over 5 km (tgseurogroup.it).

### Festa di San Marco (25th)
This festival to remember the city's patron saint is the Venetian equivalent of St Valentine's Day. The tradition involves buying a rose for your true love and eating *risi e bisi* (rice and peas). There is also a gondola race across the Dogana to Sant'Elena.

### Vinitaly
The biggest wine fair in the country runs for five days in Verona (vinitaly.com).

### La Sensa (Sunday after Ascension)
This is when Venice renews its marriage vows to the sea in a millennium-old ceremony. Today, in the absence of a doge, the Mayor of Venice stands aboard a ducal galley and says, *"We wed thee, O sea, in a sign of true and perpetual dominion, asking God to protect those who travel by sea"*, before casting a ring into the watery depths off the Lido (sevenonline.it/sensa).

### Voga Longa (Sunday after La Sensa)
The 'Long Row' is a colourful rowing competition in which teams race from piazza San Marco to Sant' Erasmo, Burano and back down the Grand Canal.

### La Biennale
The world's largest non-commercial art exhibition is held from early June until early November every odd-numbered year. It is centred round the Giardini Pubblici but takes over the whole of Venice, opening up an otherwise self-obsessed city to create a truly international vibe (labiennale.org). See also page 104.

Carnevale.

The fireworks at Festa del Redentore in July.

### Venezia Suona
Street music of every genre fills the *calli* and *campos* of Venice on a single Sunday in June. Dixieland on the ponte dei Rialto, anyone? Weird but wonderful (veneziasuona.it).

### Sagra di Sant'Antonio (13th)
Padua celebrates its patron saint with processions and food stalls in the city's beautiful public park, the Prato della Valle.

### Festival Lirico all'Arena di Verona
Verona's opera season begins in late June and runs until September at the Arena. Rotating classics, including *Aida* and often *Tosca*, are played out in this most awesome of venues. See also page 238.

### Festival Shakespeariano
The Shakespeare festival in Verona starts late in the month and runs until early August with performances in the Teatro Olimpico.

July

### Festa del Redentore (third Sunday)
Moored boats create a pontoon across the Giudecca canal in Venice to allow VIPs and Venetian citizens to process from San Marco to Il Redentore. The festival commemorates the end of the plague in 1576 and ends with an amazing firework display over the Bacino di San Marco.

### Sognando Shakespeare
From July until September this theatre company dresses in full Renaissance garb (including tights for the chaps) and stages impromptu Shakespearian performances across Verona.

## August

### La Biennale
The architecture exhibition lasts from August until early November and is held every even-numbered year. It centres round the Giardini Pubblici but there are pavilions and events across the city (labiennale.org). See also page 104.

### Mostra del Cinema di Venezia
The Venice Film Festival in late August and early September sees the city overtaken by helicopters, paparazzi and, of course, movie stars and their entourages. The Lido is where it all happens, with big screens showing trailers for forthcoming movies, interviews and press conferences (labiennale.org).

## September

### Regata Storica (first Sunday)
Dating back to the 13th century, the regatta is a colourful parade of gondoliers and other boatmen. There are four rowing competitions: the *gondolini* for elite rowers; the *caorline* for those who don't qualify for the elite race; the *mascarete* for women, and the *pupparini* for young rowers aged 14 to 18.

### Partita a Scacchi (second Sunday in even years)
This faux medieval festival is held in the town of Marostica and involves residents dressing up in costume to watch a game of human chess on Vicenza's main piazza. See page 225.

### Sagra del Pesce (third Sunday)
Burano's fish festival is a chance to gorge on plates of fried fish and polenta and cups of white wine before viewing a rowing competition.

## October

### Festa del Mosto (first weekend)
The lagoon island of Sant'Erasmo, known as the garden of Venice, celebrates the harvest.

### Venice Marathon
The Venice marathon is restricted to 7000 participants. It begins at Stra, continuing through Mestre, across the bridge into Venice, along the Zattere, across a specially made floating bridge and then on to the finish line in piazza San Marco.

### Ombralonga (third weekend)
Treviso's food and wine festival involves merrymaking in the streets and festivities around the Fontana delle Tette.

## November

### Festa della Salute (21st)
Although it has a similar format, this festival is more compact and arresting than the Festa del Redentore. The pontoon of boats stretches from piazza San Marco to La Salute and commemorates all those who died of the plague in 1630.

## December

### Raddichio in Piazza (weekend before Christmas)
Treviso celebrates one of its famous local foodstuffs, with plenty of food, drinking and general revelry.

### Natale (25th)
The run-up to Christmas is celebrated with Christmas markets, sparkling lights, nativity scenes, processions and fabulous concerts in churches and basilicas across the region. Midnight mass, be it under the glittering Byzantine mosaics of Venice's Basilica San Marco or in front of the carved choir of Verona's Santa Maria in Organo, is heart-stirringly beautiful. The Frari in Venice hosts a free Santo Stefano (Boxing Day) concert in the late afternoon which is hugely popular with both locals and visitors.

### Capo d'Anno (31st)
The residents of Venice and Veneto tend to over-indulge on food rather than drink on New Year's Eve.

# Sleeping

Finding a good, affordable hotel in Venice that's not too far from a vaporetto stop, not up too many stairs and is close to the best restaurants, bars and shops can be a bit of a challenge. Actually locating the hotel in Venice's labyrinthine *calli*, especially late at night, can be even harder.

The six *sestieri* all have different characters. Most of the top hotels are located in **San Marco**. It's the heart of the city but can be noisy and choked with tourists, not to mention the fact that it is notoriously expensive. **Castello** and **Cannaregio** feel more like local neighbourhoods, are less crowded and have some great apartments to

rent out as well. However, the eastern part of Castello, in particular, can feel a bit far away from the action and is a long trek from the train station. **Santa Croce**, **San Polo** and **Dorsoduro** have the widest range of accommodation, restaurants and bars, as well as interesting shops and a boho vibe.

Venice has a huge mix of hotels, from historical old palazzi on the Canal Grande (such as **Locanda Sturion**, see page 142) and good old-fashioned *pensione* (**Pensione Accademia**, for instance, see page 144), to a new wave of boutique and contemporary hotels (such as **Ca' Pozzo**, see page 141, and **Ca' Pisani**, see page 143) that eschew the typical Venetian look of swags and tiebacks and go for edgier modernism. In the last few years a number of B&Bs have sprung up in the city (such as **Fujiyama**, see page 144) but the population crisis means that the authorities are cracking down on the development of B&Bs: they'd rather these kinds of houses were used for resident families.

Those on a budget who want to spend as much time as possible in Venice should consider renting an apartment. Some of these (owned by Brits or Americans) are advertized in quality newspapers in both the UK and the US. For a wider selection there are a few Venetian agencies (such as **Venice Apartments**, veniceapartments.org) that offer a good range of properties and prices. If you are on

Opulence comes at a price.

a really tight budget, you could stay in a convent. These are basic and operate curfews but, since the city turns the lights off pretty early, you may not miss that much (see page 143).

Throughout the rest of Veneto accommodation is less plentiful but generally more affordable than in Venice; Cortina d'Ampezzo in the Dolomites is the exception to this rule, especially in ski season. There is a variety of accommodation on offer, including B&Bs (such as **Villa Pasini** outside Vicenza, see page 228), *agriturismo* (**Al Morer** in Asolo, see page 206) and apart-hotels (**L'Ospite** in Verona, see page 252). It's always easiest to stay in or close to the *centro storico* of a city but those who don't mind taking buses or taxis or who are renting a car will find some great villas amongst the vineyards and cypress trees on the outskirts or beyond.

On arrival in Italy you used to have to register with the local police station. Now, when you check in (be it at a hotel, B&B or even to pick up apartment keys), hand over your passport and staff will take down the details to pass on to the police.

## Tip...

While most hotels have air conditioning, B&Bs and some apartments may not. It gets unbearably hot in this area during July and August, so bear this in mind when you choose your accommodation. The alternative is to sleep with the windows open, which is undesirable in a ground-floor room or beside a noisy thoroughfare.

Don't leave your windows open at night unless you *want* to be ravished by mosquitos.

# Eating & drinking

## What to eat

The Venetian lagoon yields fantastic seafood and fish, best seen at the city's Pescaria (fish market; see page 117): look out for huge *tonno* (tuna), *branzino* (sea bass), *capesante* (scallops), *polipetti* (baby octopus) and *granseole* (spider crabs). Ease of transportation means that fresh seafood is popular and readily available throughout the Veneto but the further inland you go the less of it is to be found in traditional regional cooking. In winter particularly dried fish was traditionally used, as in the Vicentine dish of *baccalà alla Vicentina* (dried cod braised with onions, milk and cheese).

## Tip...

Like all Italians, the Venetians love popping in and out of bars all day to have a little coffee or an *ombra* (a small glass of wine). *Cicchetti* are small portions of fish or fried/grilled vegetables that are served in osterie (or *bacari* as they are called in Venice) and are popular with those wanting a bite to eat with their drink. If you're hungry, however, ordering portion after portion of these tasty snacks can be a pricey way to eat.

Pescaria, Venice.

While Venice is fishy, the further inland you go the meatier it gets. Although *fegato alla Veneziana* (calf's liver served with onions) is a Venetian speciality, in general, meat dishes are not served in the city in the same quantity and variety as you'll find in the rest of Veneto. In Verona popular dishes include meat stewed with Amarone wine and *bollito con la perà* (boiled meat with bread sauce). The Sottosalone market in Padua has the most impressive assortment of cured meats, including Montagnana ham from the Colli Euganei and special local sausages: *tombolo cotechino* and *sopressa*. The Trevigani snack of *panino porchetta* (a roast pork sandwich), meanwhile, keeps these industrious people on their toes. Diners from the UK and US may be perturbed to find *caval/cavallo* (horse) and *asino* (donkey) on the menu in Veneto. It is often served shredded with olive oil and balsamic vinegar (*sfilacci di cavallo*), cooked in a stew (*pastissada de caval*) or in a pasta sauce (*bigoli con ragu d'asino*).

Regional pasta varieties include *bigoli* (fat spaghetti, often wholewheat) and, towards the Dolomites, *casunzie* (large stuffed pasta parcels). Veneto is where gnocchi (small potato dumplings) were invented and, in the mountainous parts of the region, you'll find *canederli*, a super-sized version. Two of Italy's most heart-warming dishes also originated here: polenta (served as a maize porridge or left to harden, then fried) and risotto: try risotto with cuttlefish ink in Venice; risotto with *radicchio rosso di Treviso* in Treviso and *risotto dell'Amarone* in Verona.

Although a vegetarian dining in Venice may struggle to find much on a typical menu, even the fussiest diner can eat like a doge by employing some charm and persuasion. Beyond Venice, the food becomes a little more *contandino* (peasant), which means a greater use of vegetables in pastas, risottos, pizzas and flans. The quality of the vegetables in Veneto is splendid: a simple plate of *melanzane e zucchini grigliate* (grilled aubergine and courgette) served with a lump of *mezzanello di monte* (a local cheese) is a dream dish. Be sure to try the local delicacies of *castraure* (spring buds

of the purple artichoke), grown on the lagoon island of Sant'Erasmo, *radicchio rosso di Treviso* (bitter red chicory) and Bassano del Grappa's famous *asparago bianco* (white asparagus), available in May.

## Where to eat

Italians famously love to eat and to eat out and there is a range of venues to cater for their needs. Technically and historically **ristoranti** are posher than **trattorie**, while **osterie** are primarily wine bars. However, you'll soon notice that these names are little help in telling you the price or salubriousness of an establishment. In Venice a **bacaro** is like a pub, serving wine and *cicchetti*, as well as beer, coffee and soft drinks.

Venice suffers from a bad reputation when it comes to eating out. The unremitting hordes of tourists mean restaurants don't have to try hard to make a living and don't really care if you never come back: there's always some other tourist looking for a table. Keep your wits about you and seek out those places that genuinely take pride in their food and service. Steer clear of restaurants with point-and-pick menus (those with pictures), which tend to be situated near the main sights and are aimed exclusively at tourists. Unless it's early in the evening and their patter is genuinely good, you should also ignore waiters positioned outside some restaurants trying to lure you in. And remember, first impressions count: if the reception is taciturn and the vibe generally unpleasant, why stay a minute longer?

## Tip...

You'll find a selection of picnic spots listed throughout the guide. However, if you're planning a picnic in Venice, be careful: the Office of Decorum will fine you €50 if you are seen to "sit or linger on the street to eat picnic lunches" in piazza San Marco. You have been warned.

# Food glossary

*anguilla alla veneziana* eel cooked in a tangy sauce

*aragosta* lobster

*asino* donkey meat

*asparago bianco* white asparagus from Bassano del Grappa

*baccalà* dried salted cod, often creamed (*mantecato*) and served on polenta slices

*baccalà alla Vicentina* Vicentine dish of cod cooked very slowly with onions and parmesan cheese, then served with soft polenta

*bigoli con l'anatra* thick tubes of pasta with duck bolognese (duck from Thiene is the most celebrated)

*bigoli con ragu d'asino* thick tubes of pasta with donkey sauce

*bigoli con le sarde* thick tubes of pasta with sardine sauce

*bisato in tecia* roasted eel with bay leaf and tomato sauce

*bollito con la peará* a Veronese dish of boiled meat served with bread sauce

*branzino* sea bass

*brodetto* fish soup/stew

*bussolai buranelli* butter biscuits that you dunk in sweet vin santo

*canederli* liver-stuffed dumplings, popular in the Dolomites

*capretto sullo spiedo* roasted goat

*carpaccio* thin slices of raw cured beef, usually served with *rucola* (rocket), lemon juice and *grana padana*

*casatella* local creamy cheese

*castrato con risi e bisi* rice and peas from Lumignano, served as a broth rather than a risotto

*castraure* artichoke buds from Sant'Erasmo, beautiful dipped in olive oil and salt; at their best in June

*casunzie rossi* pasta parcels stuffed with beetroot

*caval/cavallo* horsemeat

*chiocciole* (aka *scios*) little snails

*cicchetti* Venetian tapas: bite-sized portions of anything fishy or fried

*fegato* calf's liver cooked in onions

*formaggio imbriago* a sharp cheese aged amongst grapes, giving it a sweet, dark red rind

*frittura mista* mixed small fried fish and vegetables

*granseole* spider crab; at its best from October to December

*moeche frite* small soft-shelled crabs dipped in egg and fried; available in March/April and November/December, when the crabs shed their shells

*moscardini* baby octopus stewed and served with polenta

*orata* bream

*pane con l'aciugheta* bread with anchovy paste

*panino porchetta* a speciality in Treviso: a pork-filled sandwich

*pappardelle con finferli* large pasta ribbons with tiny mountain mushrooms

*pappardelle alle lepre* large pasta ribbons with rabbit sauce

*patatine frite* chips

*radicchio rosso di Treviso* red chicory that is bitter but very tasty

*risotto all'Amarone* rice cooked in the richest of the Veneto's red wines

*risi e bisi* a creamy pea risotto fit for a doge

*sarde in saor* fried sardines in onions, marinated in a sweet vinegary sauce with raisins, pine nuts and some sweet spices like cinnamon and nutmeg

*scampi crudi* raw langoustines, halved and drizzled with olive oil

*sfilacci di cavallo* shredded horsemeat

*sogliola* sole

*sopa coada* pigeon broth

*sopressa* a salame from the Pasubio and Recoaro valleys, generally eaten with a slice of grilled polenta

*spaghetti al nero di seppia* spaghetti cooked in the black ink of the cuttlefish

*spaghetti alle vongole* spaghetti with clams

*tagliatelle e intingolo di lepre* tagliatelle with hare sauce

*tiramisù* locals say this creamy, spongy, coffee concoction was invented in Treviso

*zucca* pumpkin

## When to eat

**Colazione** Breakfast usually consists of nothing more than a cappuccino and a *cornetto* – a pastry filled with *crema* (custard), marmalade or Nutella – and is consumed on the go in a bar, any time from 0600 until the *cornetti* run out. Expect to pay upwards of €2 to much more in Venice, especially if you sit down. Larger hotels tend to offer a buffet breakfast of eggs, cheese, ham, cakes, yoghurts, etc.

**Pranzo** Lunch is served between 1000 and 1400 but can go on for a bit longer than that. The sequence of an Italian menu is: *antipasta* (starter); *primo piatto* (first dish), which is usually pasta or risotto; *secondo piatto* (second dish), which is meat- or fish-based and often served with or before *contorni* (vegetables) or salad, and, finally, *dolce* (dessert). Don't think for a minute you have to order all of this: you can have as much or as little as you want. Likewise, you can order a glass of wine, instead of a whole bottle, or just have water or even beer (in some places). In Venice, expect to pay from €15 for a plate of pasta and some water and coffee, but be prepared to pay anything from €35 up to hundreds for the full works. Prices are lower in the rest of Veneto: you can have a *primo*, a *secondo* and some wine for €10 in **Pane e Vino** in Verona, for example, see page 253.

**Cena** Dinner is served between 1900 and 2200, although some places will stop taking orders at 2100. It follows the same format as lunch and should cost the same.

## Tip...

The cover charge should be stated on the menu and can be anything from €2 to €8. There might also be a service charge of 10%. If you're on a tight budget, it's wise to calculate the real cost of your meal, including charges, before you sit down.

## Where to drink

Venice is at its most vivacious at aperitivo time (from 1700 to 2000), when families out for the *passeggiata* fizz round bars and cafés kissing each other and chattering loudly. The hot spots are campo Santa Margherita in Dorsoduro, the relatively new bars at Fabricche Vecchie in Rialto and the long-standing favourites along fondamenta della Misericordia, but all neighbourhoods have their own scene. Venice has a great drinking culture, centred around the *bacari* (Venetian pubs). It is not unusual to see Venetians on a *giro di bacari* (pub crawl) going from *bacaro* to *bacaro*, drinking and eating *cicchetti*. Cafés tend to close at 2000, with bars staying open until 2200, midnight or later.

In the rest of Veneto aperitivi can last until well after midnight. The places to go are the streets off via Calmaggiore in Treviso; around piazzi dell'Erbe and dei Signori in Padua; the streets off corso Palladio in Vicenza, and Sottoriva and piazza Bra in Verona. Bars are open later on the mainland, closing any time between midnight and 0200.

# Coffee

If you ask for *'un caffè'* in Italy, you will be served an espresso in a very small cup. It's strong in taste with a creamy froth known as *crema*. Some suggest that ordering a cappuccino after 1030 in the morning will earn derisive looks from the locals. Poppycock! Order whichever coffee you want, whenever you want; as long as you pay, they'll not care a jot.

*caffè Americano* weaker coffee made with more hot water.

*caffè latte* coffee made with lots of hot milk and a touch of foam on top.

*cappuccino* espresso with hot milk and a thick foamy top.

*cappuccino chiaro* weaker cappuccino but not yet a caffè latte.

*cappuccino scuro* strong cappuccino.

*corretto* espresso 'corrected' by a slug of grappa.

*doppio* double espresso.

*latte macchiato* steamed milk 'marked' with a shot of espresso.

*lungo* longer, weaker coffee made with more hot water.

*macchiato* espresso 'marked' with steamed milk on top.

*ristretto* strong espresso made with less water.

## Tip…

There can be a whole range of prices for the same cup of coffee, depending on whether you stand at the bar, sit inside or sit outside on the piazza. If you need a coffee but refuse to pay €4 for the piazza price stand at the bar: it's much cheaper. You can't hang about though.

**Valpolicella** This red wine has a poor reputation in Britain but is enjoyed by those in the region and, at its best, by wine lovers in the know. It's a soft, cherryish, easy-to-drink wine made from Corvina, Rondinella and Molinara varieties that are grown in the Negrar and Adige valleys. There are two types: Superiore, which has aged for a year, and Classico, which comes from the Valpolicella area north of Verona. Top producers include Allegrini, Tedeschi and Quintarelli.

**Recioto della Valpolicella** The *rece* (ears) are the grapes on the outside of a bunch and are the ripest and most mature. They are laid out on mats to dry before being used to make this sweet, rich wine.

**Amarone** This is essentially Recioto della Valpolicella that has undergone at least 25 months (but often five to ten years) fermentation in oak barrels to produce a dry but robust dark red wine, reminiscent of bitter chocolate. Amarone is considered by many to be the best wine from the Veneto.

**Bardolino** Grown on the eastern shores of Lago di Garda, Bardolino uses the same grapes as Valpolicella but in different proportions: less Corvina and more Rondinella. It can include a small percentage of local varieties, too. There's a Superiore (aged for at least one year and with a higher alcohol content); a rosé, known as Bardolino Chiaretto, which has a shorter fermentation period; a lightly sparkling *frizzante,* and a *novello* (similar to a Beaujolais Nouveau).

**Soave** Hailing from an area east of Verona, this white wine is made from Garganega and Trebbiano grapes. It has a deservedly mixed reputation in the UK but it is celebrated by locals who love its freshness. There's a *reciot* version made in the same way as Recioto della Valpolicella.

**Prosecco** Grown and produced in the area between Conegliano and Valdobbiadene, just north of Treviso, this white wine comes in three varieties: dry sparkling (*spumante*), semi-sparkling (*frizzante*) and still. It is served by the glass in all bars (€1.50-4 depending where you are) and can also be mixed to create classic cocktails. A Bellini, inspired by the pinky hue from a Bellini painting, is prosecco mixed with white peach purée and a spot of raspberry juice.

## "Vorrei due spritz, per favore"

At aperitivo time in Venice you'll soon notice that most of the adults are consuming a bright orange drink called a Venetian *spritz* (pronounced 'spriss'). As the name suggests, this was one of the few legacies of Austrian rule that the Venetians appreciated and wholeheartedly adopted. Spritz is served in all bars in the city all day long, although it is most popular drunk as an aperitivo. It may be served bitter or sweet, so be sure to ask if you have a preference. It is made from two parts dry white wine or prosecco; one part Aperol (for sweet Spritz) or Campari (for bitter); a splash of soda, tonic water or fizzy mineral water; some ice and a slice of orange for a sweet Spritz or a green olive for a bitter (or both). It is usually accompanied by *spuntini* (crisps or little nibbles). *Cin cin!*

Spritz.

# Entertainment

Those who think they are coming to a city of revelry and debauchery will be sorely disappointed by Venice's nightlife. Although the university ensures a supply of thrill-seeking youngsters, a disproportionate number of the city's 60,000 inhabitants are over 50. What's more, the younger workers who commute into the city each day want to catch the last train home to Mestre and elsewhere, so you'll not see many of them clubbing or propping up the bars late at night. When it comes to high culture, however, Venice hits the high notes with a profusion of classical music, opera, dance and theatre venues and events. Verona is another cultural hotspot with music and theatre festivals and, of course, its world-famous opera season at the Arena. The productions tend towards Verdi rather than Wagner but if it's entertainment and colour on a balmy evening you're after, you cannot fail to be captivated.

## Cinema

Most English-language films are dubbed into Italian, so cinema-going tends not to be a pleasurable experience in Italy, even for Italian speakers. However, the **Venice Film Festival** in late August/ early September is a chance to see forthcoming releases on huge screens, some outside, and to do some celeb-spotting (see page 155).

## Classical music

Opera lovers will be in their element in Veneto, thanks to prestigious venues like **La Fenice** in Venice and the **Arena** in Verona. La Fenice stages opera, classical concerts and ballet throughout the year and its programme is complemented by **Teatro Malibran**. The Verona opera season runs from June to August (see page 238). In Padua the **Teatro Verdi** hosts classical music and dance performances and a solid programme of drama.

For classical music buffs, Venice is associated with **Antonio Vivaldi** (1675-1741), who wrote *Le Quattro Stagioni* (The Four Seasons). He was a former priest who became the director the Conservatorio at the Ospedale della Pietà on the Zattere in Venice (otherwise known as Santa Maria della Visitazione). This wasn't a hospital but a forward-looking

orphanage that gave the children intensive music lessons, allowing them to pursue musical careers as adults. Recitals of Vivaldi's work are given by the Orchestra Collegium Ducale (in Palazzo delle Prigioni) and the Interpreti Veneziani (in Chiesa di San Vidal), as well as in Santa Maria della Visitazione itself.

**Richard Wagner** (1813-83), the German composer, may only have spent a short time in Venice but the Venetians hold him in high regard and consider him as *almost* one of their own. His friend Franz Liszt wrote *La lugubre gondola* (1883) in memory of the black funerary gondola that took Wagner's body down the Canal Grande from Palazzo Vendramin, where the composer died. Wagner's operas are regularly performed at La Fenice and Teatro Malibran.

Below: La Fenice.
Opposite page: Venice Film Festival.

### Contemporary music

Venice is awash with classical recitals but contemporary music doesn't figure much due to the lack of large venues and an elderly population that complains about the noise. There are plenty of bars featuring DJ sets, however, and **Ancora** and the **Venice Jazz Club** hold small-scale gigs. Padua has a jazz festival in November and its Fishmarket venue has a year-round programme fusing art, live music and DJs. For bigger gigs, Verona has a buzzing live music scene with **Teatro Romano**, the **Arena** and **Interzona** ensuring everyone from Björk to Pink Floyd tribute bands have a platform.

### Gay & lesbian

Machismo is still very much to the fore in Italy but this is also a nation that excels in turning a blind eye to other people's business: *vivi e lascia vivere* (live and let live). There isn't much of a gay scene in Venice; Padua and Verona are the places to go for the best clubs and theme nights. However, Carnevale is becoming increasingly popular with the gay crowd.

### Theatre & dance

The Venetian playwright, **Carlo Goldoni** (1707-1798) is credited with reviving popular Italian theatre by hauling it out of the confines of *commedia dell'arte* into theatrical storytelling and creating a new genre, *opera buffa* (comic opera), along the way. His tales from the wrong side of the canal are written in the Venetian vernacular and are still performed in the **Carlo Goldoni Teatro**, which also stages work by the likes of Shakespeare, Voltaire and Chekhov. The edgiest drama can be seen in Padua at the **Teatro Comunale Verdi**, while Vicenza's **Teatro Olimpico** is a must for lovers of classical theatre. Shakespeare enthusiasts should head for Verona, where a Shakespeare festival (June-August) and the on-street, improvised Sognando Shakespeare (August-September) make the most of the city's dramatic locations.

Venice's **Festival Internazionale di Danza Contemporanea** (see page 156) is held in even years for two weeks in June. Directed by a celebrated choreographer, this is one of the most cutting-edge dance festivals in the world. Venues include the charming Teatro Malibran, the open-air Teatro alle Tese and other industrial units in the Arsenale. For other dance events, including information on visiting companies performances at La Fenice and Teatro Malibran, check out hellovenezia.com.

# Shopping

## Tip…

If you are not an EU citizen and have spent more than €155 on a purchase from a shop that is affiliated to the 'tax free for tourists' scheme, keep your receipt (*scontrino*), ask for the requisite form and get it stamped at the point of sale. This allows you a sales tax rebate of 20% at the airport or on your return.

Although it's no longer a trading super-power, Venice is still a great place to shop; you can buy almost anything you want here – for a price. However, it would be a mistake when shopping in Venice to think you'll pop back later to make your purchase, as there is a good chance you'll spend hours vainly trying to relocate the right shop; if you see something you want, buy it on the spot.

Shoe makers, mask makers, *stamperie* (old-fashioned printers), model makers, bead threaders and paper makers are still common and you'll find a lot of shops dealing in antiques, art and old books. There are plenty of places selling Murano glass and Burano lace. However, if you want to buy the authentic articles, a trip to Murano or Burano should ensure you don't end up with something made in China. Fashion is dominated by international designer labels but there are also unique boutiques selling handmade, one-offs by unknown designers and even a few vintage clothes shops. And then, of course, there are food shops selling gastronomic delights from sweet treats like *croccante* (sticky nut nougat) to marinated *cozze* (mussels).

The best areas for shopping in Venice are: from Rialto through campo San Polo to the Frari, and from campo Santa Margherita through campo San Barnaba towards the Accademia, with a few more good shops along the stretch from the Accademia

Above: Murano glass, beware of imitations. Opposite page: You can buy – or hire – anything in Venice.

to the Peggy Guggenheim Collection. As for San Marco, it could take you a week to get round all the shops there; you'll find the usual mix of high-street names but amongst them are some wonderful little emporia selling everything from reclaimed Venetian door knockers to Fortuny scarves.

There is great shopping in Treviso, Padua, Vicenza and Verona, too. Treviso is the home of Benetton and its superstore has the complete range, as well as some cracking bargains. Padua's Sottosalone (under Palazzo delle Ragione) is a food lover's heaven with artisan shops selling the very finest local specialities. Vicenza's corso Palladio is crammed with fashion and shoe shops while Verona's fabulous antique shops along via Sottoriva and corso Santa Anastasia provide a real insight into the past lives of the Veronese. It is also worth looking out for the antiques markets that are held around the region; you'll be surprised by the cornucopia of delights (and, admittedly, tat) that can be picked up for a few euros.

Generally, shops are open Monday to Saturday from 0900 until 1300 and then again from 1530 to 1930. Big supermarkets may stay open all day and

on a Sunday, as might shops in tourist areas. However, clothes shops are often closed on a Monday morning and food shops on a Wednesday afternoon. Some smaller shops also close for a holiday during August.

## Wine

Airport restrictions on fluids in hand luggage make it trickier than in the past to take a few bottles of wine home with you. You can still buy alcohol and other bottled liquids after security at the airport itself but it is likely to be much pricier than in the shops. Any bottles in your hold luggage should be covered in bubble wrap, sealed in a zip-lock bag and padded out with towels or clothing to prevent breakages. Shipping is an option if you're planning to take home a case of wine or more, although you will need to prove to Customs that the wine is strictly for personal consumption and you should bear in mind that the shipping price per bottle may be more than the wine itself. For the best advice, ask the Enoteca or dealer when you buy the wine.

# Activities & tours

## Boating & watersports

The Venetian lagoon has an almost eerie, otherworldly quality to it that seems far removed from the flurry of the city. A number of companies take tours round the wetlands of the lagoon in a *bragozzo* (€200 for up to four people). If you'd rather propel yourself, you can have a go at *voga veneta* (Venetian rowing), *canotaggio* (regular rowing) or sailing for approximately €40 per hour. Or why not make a total fool of yourself and try to learn the craft of a gondolier for a day (€240)?

Heading inland, boats ply the Brenta Canal between Venice and Padua, stopping at the famous villas en route. Companies charge €71 in high season for a day tour, which includes entrance to the villas and the services of a guide. For watersports, head to Lago di Garda: just north of Torri del Benaco where you can windsurf, enrol on sailing courses or hire out boats.

## Cultural tours

The experience of being stuck behind a large group shambling behind a squawking guide can make the idea of going on a guided tour distinctly unappealing but, in fact, a good guided tour is a great way to see a city. Each local tourist office will be able to provide you with a list of well-qualified and experienced guides who can take you on a two-hour walk around San Marco, say, for €30 per person. The Secret Itinerary tours in the Basilica di San Marco and Palazzo Ducale are also well worth the euros, as they ensure you get to spend more time in these tourist hotspots than a normal visit allows.

A walking tour of Palladio's palazzi and public buildings in Vicenza is an excellent way to introduce yourself to the work of this visionary architect. In more rural areas, sights such as Villa Barbaro and Asolo are difficult to reach by public transport, so, if you don't have access to a car, consider hiring a local guide and driver who can ensure a packed day visiting outlying sights. Prices start at €200.

## Cycling & hiking

Veneto encompasses all sorts of terrain from the outlying islands of the Venetian lagoon to the lush Euganean Hills and from the undulating villa-strewn countryside around Vicenza to the more challenging and lung-bursting ascents of the Dolomite mountains. Consult the local tourist

Out and about in the mighty Dolomites.

websites for information on walks and bike routes around these areas. Bike hire is a little pricier than in other parts of Italy (around €25 a day) but these places are magnets for enthusiasts, so you're bound to get some great advice about routes and pizza stops thrown in.

### Food & wine

The increasing popularity of cookery courses has created a whole new arm of the tourist industry out here. You can learn all about fish and how to cook it at the Rialto market in Venice (from €135), master bread-making in Asolo (€100) or discover how to make the perfect risotto in Verona (from €50).

One of the big draws of this region is the wine. Verona and Treviso tourist offices offer helpful maps and information about guided and self-directed wine tours for those who like to toddle around vineyards and cantinas at their own pace. Alternatively there are a number of companies offering wine-tasting events that examine the process and the history of winemaking (from €50). However, by walking into a *bacaro* or osteria and chatting to the bar staff, you are likely to learn just as much. For those who are really into their wines, **Vinitaly**, the biggest wine fair in the nation, is held in Verona for five days in April and includes lots of tastings and events around town.

### Snowsports

Cortina d'Ampezzo in the Dolomites is the playground of the wealthy and one of the chicest ski resorts in Europe. It has 49 lifts (including seven cable cars) and 140 km of piste, ensuring that skiers and boarders are in heaven here.

# Contents

Venice

Baby face.

# Introduction

## What to see in...

...one day

Created out of a mosquito-ridden swamp, the Most Serene Republic of Venice grew in size and status, becoming a superpower of the Middle Ages with influence that went far beyond the lagoon. Its fight to secure and expand its commercial interests and trading routes, and its adornment and enjoyment of its riches has left the most mesmerizing legacy. The fall of the Republic at the end of the 18th century seems almost academic: the political power may have been lost but the physical manifestation of its brilliance is still there to be admired.

Defined by its epic history and deeply conservative, Venice rests on its laurels. But, such are the abundance and quality of its past glories, Venice can dine out on its history for many more years to come. John Ruskin, who stayed here in 1848 and wrote the *Stones of Venice*, said the city has as much chance of surviving as "a lump of sugar in hot tea". Yet, today, Venice is doing rather nicely. Yes, it's overwhelmed by tourism and losing its population because Venetians can't afford to live in the city anymore but the tides of visitors continue to bring prosperity. It is still the most awe-inspiring city on the planet with breath-catching beauty across every bridge.

Begin with a visit to the **Rialto** bridge and markets. Then take a *traghetto* across the Canal Grande in order to explore the **Ghetto**, **Madonna dell Orto**, the **Gesuiti**, and **Santi Giovanni e Paolo**. In the afternoon head to **piazza San Marco** and try the queues for the **Basilica** or the **Palazzo Ducale**. Alternatively, cross over to **San Giorgio Maggiore**. Spend the hours around dusk at **La Salute** or make for the great bars on **via Garibaldi** in Castello. A night-time cruise up the **Canal Grande** is an excellent end to the day.

**...a weekend or more**
On your second day, get up early and see **piazza San Marco** before the tourists descend, then cross the wooden bridge to the **Accademia** or the **Guggenheim**. In the afternoon visit the **Frari** and **San Rocco** and then do some shopping in **San Polo** and on the **Ruga Rialto**. In the evening, make for campo **San Giacomo dell'Orio** to enjoy an aperitivo.

Ponte dei Sospiri – the Bridge of Sighs.

# Essentials

**❶ Getting around** The **vaporetti** (water buses) and **traghetti** (gondola-style ferries that cross the Canal Grande) are the favoured forms of transport around Venice. The price of one hour of travel by vaporetto is €6 but there are also passes (€22/33 for 36/72 hrs). The traghetti cost just 60 cents. **ACTV** (T041-2424, actv.it) runs these services as well as bus services to Mestre and Marco Polo airport. Route maps are available from the ACTV website, ticket offices and tourist information offices. If money is no object you can go from door to door by **water taxi** with **Consorzio Motoscafi** (T041-522 2303, motoscafivenezia.it) or **Veneziana Motoscafi** (T041-716922). It will cost around €70 for up to four people from Santa Lucia train station to most hotels and €95 from the city to Marco Polo airport. Always agree the price beforehand and be prepared to pay extra for every piece of baggage. **Gondolas** are now only used for pricey tourist excursions (see page 127).

**❷ Bus station** **Piazzale Roma**, Dorsoduro. ATVO (T041-383672) runs buses to Marco Polo airport via Mestre (€3 one way, 20 mins), Treviso airport and Treviso Centrale train station (€5 one way, 1 hr). **ACTV** (041-2424, actv.it) runs a cheaper if slower service to Mestre and Marco Polo airport (€1 one way, 30 mins).

**❸ Train station** **Ferrovia Santa Lucia**, Cannaregio, T848-888088, bookings through **Trenitalia** T89-2021, trenitalia.it.

**❹ ATMs** Cash machines are available at Marco Polo airport, Santa Lucia train station, in piazza San Marco, along the Zattere and in most large *campos*.

**❺ Hospital** **Ospedale SS Giovanni e Paolo**, Castello 6777, T041-529 4111, has a casualty (*pronto soccorso*) department.

**❻ Pharmacy** For information on the rota of night pharmacies (*farmacie di turno*) ask your hotel or check the local newspapers (*Il Gazzettino*, *Leggo*,

## Finding your way

Venice uses some unique terms for its streets and waterways; these can seem rather bewildering until you have spent a few hours exploring.

*campo/campiello* Venetian piazza or piazzetta
*corte* court or cul de sac
*fondamenta* the road beside a canal
*parrochia* parish neighbourhood
*rio* canal
*rio terrà* filled-in canal
*riva* wide *fondamenta*
*ruga* street with shops
*salizada* main street
*sottopassaggio/sottoportego/sottoportico* covered underpassage

Venetian addresses also take a bit of getting used to. Each house in a *sestiere* has its own number, eg San Polo 2750. Most addresses for restaurants or shops – but not all – will also give the name of the street.

*Nuova Venezia e Corriere del Veneto* or *Il Venezia*) or the magazine for tourists, *Un Ospite di Venezia*.

**❼ Post office** **Fondaco dei Tedeschi**, San Marco 5554 (next to ponte di Rialto), T041-271 7208, Mon-Sat 0830-1830.

**❽ Tourist information offices** There are **APT** offices (T041-529 8711, turismovenezia.it) in the Arrivals hall of Marco Polo airport, at Santa Lucia train station, in piazza San Marco, in piazzale Roma (for those who arrive by bus or car) and at Santa Croce. There's also an information point in the Venice Pavilion, San Marco. For visitors with disabilities, **Informahandicap Venezia** (T041-274 8144, commune.venezia.it) provides information on accessible routes, sights, hotels and, handily, how to get hold of the keys that operate the chair lifts on the bridges.

**Tourist Passes** The **Venice Card** is pricey (€73, €66 children for three days; €96, €87 children for seven days) but, if you want to see the museums on the list and make plentiful use of the vaporetti, it is probably well be worth it, as it includes the following: unlimited use of the vaporetti; free admission to

Palazzo Ducale, Museo Correr, Biblioteca Nazionale Marciana, Museo Archeologico Nazionale di Venezia, Palazzo Fortuny, Ca' Rezzonico, Palazzo Mocenigo, Casa di Carlo Goldoni, Ca' Pesaro, Museo del Vetro and the Museo del Merletto; free admission to the 15 churches on the Chorus Circuit; free admission to the Querini Stampalia Foundation and the Jewish Museum; reduced entrance to temporary exhibitions and cultural initiatives; discounts and other concessions at the main car parks; recommendations for excursions and leisure time; free use of the city's supervized toilets and baby-changing facilities.

Alternatively, if you're not planning a sightseeing marathon and only want to visit a few places, one of the other tourist passes and cards might be more suitable. These are all available from the sights mentioned or from the tourist office.

- **Museum Pass** (€18, €12 under 15s, students under 29 and over 65s, valid for six months)

One free visit to each of the Accademia, Biblioteca Nazionale Marciana, Ca' d'Oro, Ca' Pesaro, Ca' Rezzonico, Casa di Carlo Goldoni, Museo Archeologico Nazionale di Venezia, Museo Correr, Museo del Vetro and the Museo del Merletto on Burano, Palazzo Ducale, Palazzo Fortuny, Palazzo Mocenigo. The Museum Pass and the Museo di Piazza San Marco Card are only available at veniceconnected.com

- **Museo di piazza San Marco Card** (€12/6.50, valid for three months) Free admission to the Biblioteca Nazionale Marciana, Doge's Palace, Museo Archeologico and Museo Correr.
- **Chorus Pass** (€9, €6 under 15s and students under 29) Free admission to 15 churches (see page 102).
- **Vaporetto Pass** (€23/33 for 36 or 72 hrs; reduced rates are available on some passes for under 15s and students under 29).

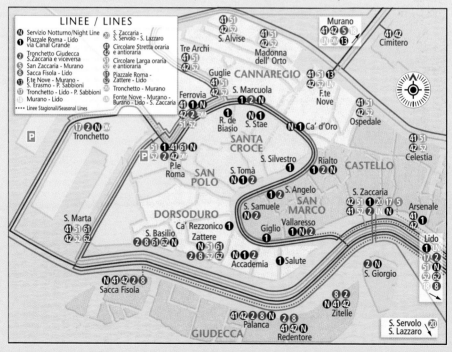

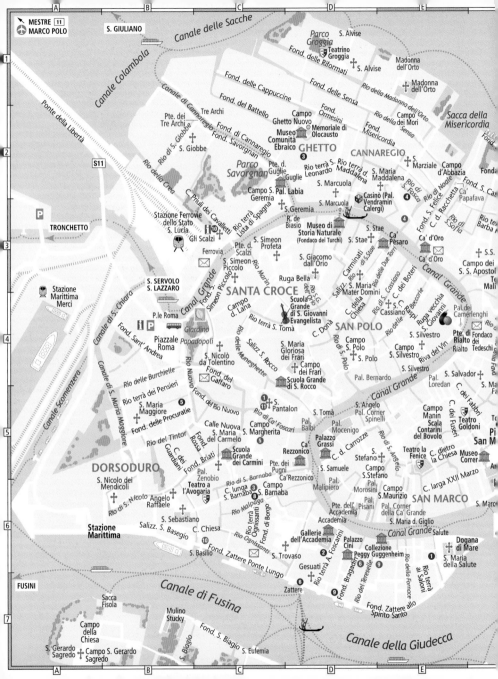

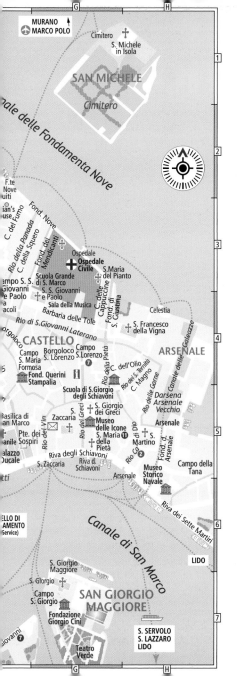

# Venice listings

### ● Sleeping

1 **Ca' Maria Adele** *fondamenta di Salute, Dorsoduro 111*, E6
2 **Ca' Pisani** *rio Terrà Antonio Foscari, Dorsoduro 979*, D6
3 **Ca' Pozzo** *sottoportego Ca' Pozzo, Cannaregio 1279*, D2
4 **Ca Vendramin di Santa Fosca** *fondamenta De Ca' Vendramin, Cannaregio 2400*, E2
5 **Casa Caburlotto** *fondamenta Rizzi, Santa Croce 316*, B5
6 **Centro Culturale Don Orione Artigianelli** *fondamenta Zattere ai Gesuati, Dorsoduro 909/A*, D7
7 **Cipriani & Palazzo Vendramin** *giudecca 1*, F7
8 **Fujiyama** *calle Lunga San Barnaba, Dorsoduro 2727A*, C6
9 **La Calcina** *fondamenta Zattere allo Spirito Sante, Dorsoduro 780*, D7
10 **La Locanda di Orsaria** *calle Priuli dei Cavalletti, Cannaregio 103*, C3
11 **La Residenza** *campo Bandiera e Moro, Castello 3608*, H5

### ● Eating & drinking

1 **Caffè Blue** *calle dei Preti, Dorsoduro 3778*, C5
2 **Corte Sconta** *calle del Pestrin, Castello 3886*, H5
3 **Fujiyama Tea Room** *calle Lunga San Barnaba, Dorsoduro 2727a*, C6
4 **La Cantina** *campo San Felice, Cannaregio 3689*, E3
5 **Osteria ai Carmini** *campo Santa Margherita, Dorsoduro 2894a*, C5
6 **Osteria Vecio Forner** *campo San Vio, Dorsoduro 671B*, D6
7 **Pizzeria 84** *salizzada San Giustina, Castello 2907Aa*, G4
8 **Puppa Roberto** *calle del Spezier, Cannaregio 4800*, F4
9 **Ristorante Ai Gondolieri** *ponte del Formager, Fondamenta Zorsi Bragadin, Dorsoduro 366*, E6
10 **Suzie Caffé** *campo San Basegio, Dorsoduro 1527*, C6
11 **Tonolo** *calle San Pantalon, Dorsoduro 3764*, C5

# Canal Grande

**Vaporetto: 1 from Ferrovia to San Zaccaria, €6 single.**

Can there be a more impressive high street than Venice's Grand Canal? This 4-km stretch of water that snakes through the heart of the city is said to follow the curves of an old river bed. It measures 30 m across at its narrowest point, just before the ponte di Rialto, and 90 m at its widest, at punta della Dogana, with a depth of up to 6 m.

A trip down the 'Canalazzo', as the Venetians call it, is not only a chance to admire great buildings but also to learn about the human history of the Venetian empire or, at least, that of the rich ruling class. You'll see grand palazzi flaunting the tremendous wealth and power of patrician families, as well as the faded remains of their greatness and their falls from grace. The changing fashions in architecture are on show too, from the pointed windows of the Gothic to the rounded arches and plentiful columns of the Renaissance. The authorities have passed laws to slow the water traffic down and limit the detrimental effect of the boats' lashing wakes

and greasy residue on these grand buildings. Meanwhile, those owners who can afford it are involved in a continual cycle of renovation to fight the crumble.

Many of the palazzi on the Canal Grande are *casa fondaco*: that is, homes that were also workplaces and so were well suited to the needs of rich trading families. You'll see a small gate or door on the canal that is the entrance to a loading bay where goods were disembarked and stored. Round the back would be an entrance from the calle and, probably, a small courtyard with a well.

A mezzanine would have housed the offices of the business, while the first floor (*piano nobile*) was used to receive clients and show them the wares. A hall (*portego*) ran from front to back with rooms on either side. The upper floor or floors would have been the living quarters where the family resided.

If you only have one day in Venice, a vaporetto ride down the Canal Grande (or a water taxi, if you're feeling flush) will open your eyes to the breathtaking creation that is Venice. This is a city not just built on muddy flats but on pots of wealth, masses of ego and limitless imagination.

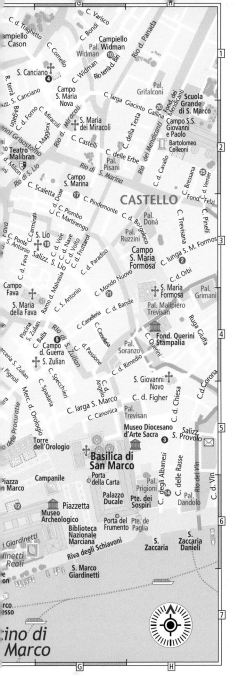

# Canal Grande listings

### ❶ Sleeping

1 **Al Ponte Mocenigo** *calle dei Preti, San Croce 2063*, C1
2 **Antica Locanda Sturion** *calle del Sturion, San Polo 679*, D3
3 **Ca' dei Dogi** *corte Santa Scolastica, Castello 4242*, H5
4 **Corte Gherardi** *corte Gherardi, salizada San Canzian, Cannaregio*, G1
5 **Istituto San Giuseppe** *ponte della Guerra, Castello 5402*, G4
6 **La Villeggiatura** *calle dei Botteri, San Polo 1569*, C2
7 **Locanda Orseolo** *corte Zorzi, San Marco 1083*, E5
8 **Novecento** *calle del Dose, campo San Maurizio, San Marco 2683/84*, C7
9 **Pensione Accademia** *fondamenta Bollani, Dorsoduro 1058*, A7
10 **Residence Corte Grimani** *corte Grimani, San Marco 4404*, E5

### ❶ Eating & drinking

1 **Ai Nomboli** *calle dei Noboli, San Polo 2717*, A4
2 **Al Mascaron** *calle Lunga Santa Maria Formosa, Castello 5225*, H3
3 **Al Pesador** *campo San Giacomo di Rialto, San Polo 126*, E2
4 **Al Prosecco** *campo San Giacomo dell'Orio, Santa Croce 1503*, A1
5 **Alla Botte** *calle della Bisa, San Marco 5482*, F3
6 **Alla Madonna** *calle de la Madonna, San Polo 594*, E3
7 **Ancora** *campo San Giacomo di Rialto, San Polo 120*, E2
8 **Bacaro Jazz** *salizada del Fontego dei Tedeschi, San Marco 5546*, F3
9 **Bistro de Venise** *calle dei Fabbri, San Marco 468*, E5
10 **Boccadoro** *campo Widmann, Cannaregio 5405*, G1
11 **Caffè dei Frari** *fondamenta dei Frari, San Polo 2564*, A3
12 **Caffé Florian** *piazza San Marco, San Marco 56/59*, F6
13 **Centrale** *piscina Frezzaria, San Marco 1659b*, E6
14 **Da Bonifacio** *calle degli Albanesi, Castello 4237*, H6
15 **Easy Bar** *campo Santa Maria Mater Domini, Santa Croce 2119*, C1
16 **Il Refolo** *campo San Giacomo dell'Orio*, A1
17 **Italo Didovich** *campo Santa Marina, Castello 5909*, G3
18 **La Patatina** *calle Saoneri, San Polo 2741/A*, B3
19 **L'Olandese Volante** *campo San Lio, Castello 5658*, G3
20 **Osteria al Ponte** *calle Larga Gallina, Cannareggio 6378*, H2
21 **Osteria Alle Testiere** *calle del Mondo Nuovo, Castello 5801*, G4
22 **Osteria Al Vecio Fritolin** *calle della Regina, Santa Croce 2262*, C1
23 **Osteria Da Fiore** *calle del Scaleter, San Polo 2202*, B2
24 **Osteria La Zucca** *calle del Tentor, Santa Croce 1762*, B1
25 **Rosa Salva** *campo SS Giovanni e Paolo, Castello 6799*, H2
26 **Ruga Rialto** *ruga Rialto, San Polo 692*, D3
27 **Torino@Notte** *campiello San Luca, San Marco 4592*, D4
28 **Trattoria da Fiore** *calle delle Botteghe, San Marco 3461*, B6

# San Marco

The political and administrative centre of Venice, San Marco is the *sestiere* to which tourists throng. The iconic images of Venice can be seen here: the grand hub of piazza San Marco with its outdoor cafés and warring orchestras; the showers of flapping *piccioni*; the basilica with its five domes, gleaming horses and glittering pinnacles, and the Doge's Palace, which despite being 700 years old, still looks like a cake that has just been iced. Venice's most expensive shops, elegant restaurants and lavish hotels are also squeezed into this corner of the island. Beyond the piazza, there are buzzing little *campos* to discover, where you can stop to enjoy a *piccolo bibita* (little drink).

Piazza San Marco.

Vaporetto: San Marco.
Map Canal Grande, F6, p87.

Napoleon called it the finest drawing room in Europe and Gentile Bellini's painting *Procession in Piazza San Marco*, which hangs in the Accademia, shows just how little it has changed since the 15th century.

Crowning the piazza on its eastern side are the **Basilica di San Marco** (see page 90) and to the south, towards the quayside, the **Palazzo Ducale** (see page 93) but there are fine buildings all around its boundaries. Going round the piazza anti-clockwise from the basilica is the **Torre dell'Orologio** (known as the Moor's clock tower), designed by Mauro Codussi and completed in 1499. Above the large clock face, the lion of St Mark is depicted against a night-time sky. Two Moors stand on top and ring the bell on the hour. Like the basilica, the clock tower shows Byzantine influence and boasts some rich mosaics.

The north and south sides of the square are lined by the *procuratori*, originally administrative buildings that provided office space (below) and accommodation (on the top floors) for the procurators of San Marco. These were the highest-ranking state-appointed magistrates, chosen from among the wealthiest patricians, and they had enormous influence and status. One of their most important roles was to commission and maintain the buildings of the entire Republic.

The original **Procuratie Vecchie**, on the north side, dating from the 12th century, was destroyed by fire in 1512. The chief architect at the time, Bartolomeo Bon, along with Guglielmo De' Grigi worked to replace it with a multi-arched Renaissance façade using designs by Giovanni Celestro; 42 arches were completed before Jacopo Sansovino took over in 1529 and finished the last eight. Today these buildings are still used as administrative offices but the arcaded street level now houses posh shops and the famous **Caffè Quadri**, which served its first coffee in 1638.

The western side of the piazza was once the site of the Chiesa di San Geminiano. The church was demolished in 1810 and a grand palace, the **Ala Napoleonica**, was built in its place (c1814) using Vincenzo Scamozzi's designs for the Procuratie Nuove. This now houses the **Museo Civico Correr** (see page 96).

The **Procuratie Nuove**, on the south side, is home to the **Museo Archeologico** and the **Biblioteca Nazionale Marciana** (also known as the Libreria Sansoviniana), which sit directly across from the Palazzo Ducale; both are accessible through Museo Correr. In 1553 Sansovino sought to create a building reminiscent of a Roman forum: the lower level has Doric porticos; the middle has Ionic arches with graceful windows punctuated by Roman friezes; while on top sits a balustrade decorated with pagan gods. Following Sansovino's death in 1570, work continued under Vincenzo Scamozzi (Palladio's protégé) and Baldassare Longhena, who finished the Renaissance elevation in 1640. Following the fall of Venice, the Procuratie Nuove became Napoleon's royal palace. Today, like the Procuratie Vecchie, its lower level houses swanky shops and **Caffè Florian** (1720), Quadri's rival.

The tallest building on the piazza and one of the most distinctive landmarks on the Venetian skyline is the **Campanile**. Known as *il paron di casa* (head of the house), it was first built around AD 900 as a watchtower, then, after being struck by lightning, was rebuilt as a bell tower, reaching its full height of 99 m. It totally collapsed in 1902 (the only fatality being the church cat) and was rebuilt in 1912 as a faithful, if not sturdier, copy of the original. The ornate **Loggetta** below was built by Sansovino in 1540 and reconstructed after the collapse of the campanile.

South of the main square is the **piazzetta San Marco**. Here, facing the lagoon, are two columns symbolizing the gateway to Venice. Possibly plundered from Greece, they are crowned by the lion of San Marco and by San Teodoro (the also-ran saint of the city) standing on a crocodile. When such displays of brutality were fashionable, this is where executions took place.

## Basilica di San Marco

*Piazza San Marco, T041-522 5205,
basilicasanmarco.it.*
Vaporetto: San Marco. Map Canal Grande, G5, p87.

The basilica is the heart and the history book of
Venice. It symbolizes the former republic's ambition,

power, wealth, self-importance and its interface
between the Occident and the Orient. The basilica
originally served as the doge's private chapel,
although it was also used for state occasions. It did
not become the city's cathedral until 1897, taking
over from San Pietro at the far end of Castello. The
basilica was also the city's showcase for the spoils
of war, containing loot such as the horses and the
tetrarchs plundered from Constantinople and
Alexandria following the sacking of these cities.

The first church on the site was built following
the arrival of St Mark's relics in 829. The basilica was
commissioned by Doge Domenico Contarini and
was consecrated in 1094. During the 12th and 13th

## Basilica essentials

**Basilica**  Easter-Oct Mon-Sat 0945-1700,  Sun 1400-1600,
Nov-Easter Mon-Sat 0945-1700, Sun 1400-1600, free.

**Treasury**  Easter-Oct Mon-Sat 0945-1700, Sun 1400-
1700, Nov-Easter Mon-Sat 0945-1600, Sun 1400-1600,
€3, €1.50 under 15s.

**Pala d'Oro**  Easter-Oct Mon-Sat 0945-1700, Sun 1400-
1600, Nov-Easter Mon-Sat 0945-1600, Sun 1400-1600,
€2, €1 under 15s.

**Museum**  Easter-Oct Mon-Sat 0945-1645, Sun 1400-
1545, Nov-Easter Mon-Sat 0945-1645, Sun 1400-1345,
€4, €1 under 15s.

**Campanile**  Easter-Jun & Oct daily 0900-1900,
Jun-Jul daily 0900-2100, Jul-Sep 0900-1200,
Nov-Easter daily 0930-1545, €8, €4 under 15s.

**Tours**  Apr-Oct Mon-Sat 1100 in the Basilica's atrium;
check the noticeboard for tours in English and other
languages; must be booked in advance, T041-241 3817,
Mon-Fri 1000-1200 or at venetoinside.com.

**Services**  Mon-Sat 0700, 0800, 0900, 1000, 1100, 1200
(Sep-May only), 1845; Sun and holy days as before but
also 0645 and 1730; sightseeing limited during mass.

**Note**  Modest dress required (no bare shoulders or
knees); leave bags/luggage free at the Ateneo San
Basso beside the Basilica, free.

## Tip...

After queuing for an hour or so you may be
devastated to learn that you are only allowed 10
minutes inside the basilica. Some guidebooks
advise you to avoid queues by coming early in the
morning but this is now one of the busiest times. It
can be quieter in the afternoon but you'll miss the
illumination of the mosaics (except on Sunday). If you
are really keen to explore the basilica properly and to
see the illumination, the best advice is to book a tour.

Above: One of the three horses taken
from the Hippodrome in Constantinople.
Opposite page: The goldon lion of Venice
atop the Basilica di San Marco.

centuries, as the empire grew, it was remodelled, expanded, covered in marble and decorated with mosaics and columns. Built on the Greek cross plan, it has five cupolas: one large central dome (the Ascension dome) and four smaller domes on each arm of the cross.

The façade shows Romanesque, Byzantine and Gothic features, with five lower arches under a balcony and five higher arches ornamented with golden pinnacles between each. The four **horses** that stand on the balcony above the central doorway are copies of those that were stolen from the Hippodrome in Constantinople in 1204. The originals, later plundered by Napoleon, can be seen in the basilica museum in the Loggia dei Cavalli. Weighing 897 kg each and made of gilded bronze, they are thought to have been made in the second or third centuries AD and appear to have been harnessed to one another. Above the horses is the **Golden Lion** (the Latin on his book reads 'Peace to you, oh Mark, my evangelist'), a statue of St Mark and six angels with golden wings.

# St Mark

The city's principal patron saint, Mark had always been an important Apostle for the people of the Veneto: during the eighth and ninth centuries they used his gospel, which recorded the teachings of St Peter. Mark was martyred in Alexandria on the 28 April AD 68.

In AD 828 two Venetian merchants, Buono da Malamocco and Rustico da Torcello, on business in Alexandria saw their chance, allegedly, to prevent the saint's relics falling into Muslim hands and took the relics back to Venice. They were received by Doge Giustiniano Participazio on the 31 January 829 who declared St Mark to be the patron saint of the city. The relics were housed in a specially erected chapel on piazza San Marco that would, in time, become the basilica. Having such a significant Apostle's relics was politically and commercially beneficial for Venice, as it meant status, protection and a steady stream of paying pilgrims.

St Mark is often represented as a winged lion, a symbol that became the calling card of the Venetian Republic and can be seen all over northern Italy.

# Basilica highlights

❶ **Illumination of the mosaics** (Mon-Fri 1130-1230, Sat 1130-1600, Sun 1400-1600)  The golden mosaics on the domes and arches are like nothing you'll have ever seen before. Depicting the stories of Joseph, Moses, Abraham, Genesis and the Ascension, they radiate with colour when the lights are on.

❷ The 13th-century Gothic **Rose window** in the right-hand transept sits under the vaulted gold dome of St Leonard. It is best admired from room five of the museum.

❸ **Pala d'Oro** Although its best stones were picked out by Napoleon as booty to bring back to Paris, this gold and enamel altarpiece still glistens as it depicts the lives of Christ and the Virgin Mary. The lower part was crafted by Paolo Veneziano in 1105, while the upper section was looted from Constantinople in 1204; the two halves were joined together in 1343.

❹ **Tesoro** The Treasury is full of opulent Eastern booty, including a thorn from Christ's crown. The Icon of Archangel Michael, though toy-like, is delightful.

❺ **Museo** Here, you'll find the original four horses as well as the altarpiece, Pala Feriale (1345) by Paolo Veneziano and his sons, and some religious tapestries. The balcony offers the most impressive views of piazza San Marco.

As you enter the atrium, the entrance to the Cappella Zen is on the right and the nave is straight ahead. The inclination is to look up to admire the golden glory of the Pentecost and Ascension domes but make sure you also look down: the mosaic floor stretches out like a rich Arabian carpet and is one of the finest in the world. Along the walls and vaults are Eastern-influenced ground-gold mosaics telling stories from the Old Testament. To the left is the Mascoli Chapel and Sta Isadore's chapel, which holds her remains looted from the island of Chios. To the right is the entrance to the baptistery (closed to the public) and the treasury. In front of you (from left to right) are the altar of the Madonna of Nikopeia, the sanctuary of St Peter, the magnificent Pala d'Oro altarpiece and

Detail from the Basilica's façade.

St Clement's chapel. Behind the presbytery is the locked sacristy and St Theodore's church.

The story of St Mark is told throughout the basilica. As you enter, look up at the main portal to see him dressed in his liturgical robes. The north wall shows him being consecrated as a bishop by St Peter, healing a leper and baptizing followers, while the south wall and the main façade tell the story of the saint's relics and their journey from Alexandria to Venice: look out for the beautiful mosaic, *The Translation of the Body of St Mark to Venice*, above the north door. There are more graphic scenes from his life and death, including his strangulation, in the Cappella Zen.

As you leave the basilica, look out for the statue of the **Tetrarchs**, near the exit, or porta della Carta, of the Palazzo Ducale. The tetrarchs were the four men appointed to rule the Roman Empire at the turn of the third century AD and this contemporary statue shows them all richly attired and identical in size to symbolize the equality of their rule. They are made of Egyptian red porphyry marble and were taken following a raid on Constantinople. This was confirmed in 1965 when archaeologists excavating Philadelphion square, found the missing left foot of the left-hand figure.

## Palazzo Ducale & Ponte dei Sospiri

*Piazza San Marco, T041-271 5911.*
Apr-Oct daily 0900-1900, Nov-Mar daily
0900-1700, last admission 1 hr before closing
(if time is short book in advance),
€12, €6.50 concessions.
Vaporetto: San Marco. Map Canal Grande, G6, p87.

All of the economic, military, political and
cultural decisions that led to the rise and fall of
the Venetian empire took place here, in the Doge's
Palace, which remained the seat of the Republic's
power until 1797.

A palace of sorts has stood here since the ninth
century but as the empire and its administration
grew, so did the palace. The delicate pink wedding
cake we now see was the vision of the Venetian-
Gothic architect Filippo Calendario (c1315-55).
Encased in Istrian limestone and pink Verona marble,
the two lower stories are arcaded, making it look
quite fragile; it is only when you get to the inner
courtyard, with its stockier colonnaded loggias,
that you appreciate its robust marble structure.

The tour of the palace follows a defined route
that is fairly comprehensive in its inclusion of the
major rooms, although restoration work can
sometimes mean the route may be diverted. You
enter the palace on the lagoon side, through the
**Porto del Frumento** (where the grain came in) and
go across a small patio to reach the main courtyard.
This is dominated by the **Scala dei Giganti** (the
Giants' Staircase), adorned with statues of Mars and
Venus by Jacopo Sansovino. It was at the top of
these stairs that the new doge was sworn in.
Visitors are not permitted to climb this staircase
and, instead, reach the first-floor loggia via the
**Scala dei Censori** (Censors' staircase), from where
you can view the scale and shape of the palace.

**First floor** Here you'll find the Doge's opulent
apartments, the **Sala degli Scarlatti**, where the
doge's right-hand men would meet and the **Sala
Grimani**, with its carved wooden ceiling, where he
received visitors. If these visitors were foreign, the
audience was observed by a member of the minor
*Consiglio*. Also on this floor is the **Sala delle Mappe**,
which contains two huge globes and is adorned

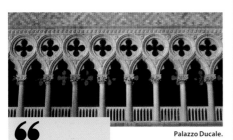

Palazzo Ducale.

> 66
>
> A realist, in Venice,
> would become a
> romantic by mere
> faithfulness to what he
> saw before him.
> 99
>
> *Arthur Symons*

## Building the dream

A visitor's first impression of Venice is always one of
wonder. It's not just the splendour of the buildings, their
happy union with the lagoon and the ways light falls on
the water and stone, it's also the logistics of the city: so
compact and so complete (bar the constant renovation
work), it's hard to imagine how Venice was built.

When settlers arrived around AD 450 they began
to make their home on some of the 117 small islands
in the lagoon, little more than muddy flats protected
by the stretch of land now known as the Lido. The
building techniques they developed have stood the
test of time and tide. They drove densely packed
pinewood logs (from the forests of the Veneto) 7.5 m
deep into the clay at the bottom of the lagoon and
then filled in the gaps with stone chips. The base
was further stabilized by foundations made of Istrian
stone, which could withstand corrosion by sea water.

Venice was originally divided into 38 *parrochiali*
(parishes), which were formed around the city's
churches. From 1171 these *parrochiale* were
grouped into six *sestieri* (administrative districts):
San Marco, Castello, Cannaregio, San Polo, Santa
Croce and Dorsoduro.

Palazzo Ducale and La Zecca at night.

## Tip...

The **Secret Itineraries Tour** (T041-520 9070, Sep-Jun daily 0955, 1045 and 1135, Jul-Aug 0955 and 1135, €16/10) takes visitors beyond the lavish public rooms to reveal the day-to-day dirty work of the palace. It lasts one-and-a-half hours and is worth every penny. You will visit the **Cancellaria**, which was used by pen pushers by day and converted into an antechamber for the adjoining **Camera del Tormento** at night. And, you'll see the *bocca della verità* (the mouth of truth) where citizens could tell tales on their fellows by posting anonymous accusations: this system became discredited after over-use and abuse. The tour also takes you to the *piombi* (cells) and shows you Casanova's escape route. Tours are available in English but places must be booked in advance.

with maps of the seas conquered and lost. Look out for the 17th-century map of the New World, showing Boston, beside the door.

**Second floor** Sansovino designed the next staircase, the **Scala d'Oro** (Golden staircase) which takes you to the second floor. The **Sala delle Quattro Porte** was the meeting room of the *Collegio*, the cabinet of the Republic. It houses a painting by Andrea Vicentino depicting the lavish reception of Henry III of France to the palazzo (c1593) and Giambattista Tiepolo's *Venice receiving*

*the gifts of the sea from Neptune* (1750). In the **Sala dell'Anticollegio** you'll see the marvellous *Rape of Europa* (1580) by Paolo Veronese: the bull may seem docile but he's Zeus in disguise and soon to carry her off to Crete to ravish her. You'll also go through the armoury where weapons and shiny arsenal are displayed. The **Sala del Collegio** is a slender meeting hall with a raised tribune at one end where the doge and his counsellors sat. The walls and wood-carved gold-leaf ceiling are decorated with a series of classical allegories by Paolo Veronese (c1580), representing chastity, vigilance, fortune, meekness, prosperity, moderation and industry. The **Sala del Consiglio dei Dieci** (room for the Council of Ten) and the **Sala della Bussola**, an antechamber for those waiting to see the Council or the Inquisitors, complete the governmental part of the second floor.

**First floor** Down the stairs and to the left you'll find the **Sala della Quarantia Civil Vecchia** and the **Sala del Maggior Consiglio** (the Great Council room), considered by many to be the most awesome room in the Palazzo. It looks like a opulent ballroom but was, in fact, built to accommodate the enlarged council of 1412 which consisted of up to 2622 patricians. It was damaged by the fire of 1577 and rebuilt in 1605. Tintoretto's *Paradiso* (completed posthumously by his son, Domenico, and a horde of assistants in 1592) is reputedly the largest oil painting in the world and fills one end of the chamber; above it is Veronese's *Apotheosis of Venice* (1579). A frieze depicts portraits of the first 76 doges, although a black curtain covers the shame of Doge Marin Falier who was beheaded for treason in 1355.

Next door is the **Sala della Quarantia Civil Nuova**, where the magistrates of the new council sat in judgement, and next door to that the **Sala dello Scrutinio** where all the internal elections were held. Along the corridor you are lead to the **Sala del Magistrato alle Leggi**, which is notable for its paintings by Hieronymus Bosch (c1500), his only works in Italy, including one of his famous depictions of hell, with devils spewing fire, etc.

While the lavish surroundings of the doge's quarters and meeting rooms inspire awe, it is the interrogation rooms, prisons and **ponte dei Sospiri** (Bridge of Sighs) that illicit visible glee from visitors. On the same level as the Sala del Maggior Consiglio were the criminal courts (the **Sala della Quarantia Criminale**) and the **Camera del Tormento**, the torture room. You can still see the dangling rope, which was used to hang the accused from his wrists. Prisoners were then taken to the ground floor of the palace where the Republic's old prison was located. The *pozzi* was used for the riff-raff, while the cells under the roof (*piombi*) were for upper-class criminals and were much more comfortable. (This is where Casanova was held and from where he escaped; see page 37.) The rise in crime, or perhaps the rise in accusations of crime, led to the **Prigioni Nuove** (new prisons) being completed in 1610 on the other side of rio di Palazzo della Paglia, connected to the main palace by the Bridge of Sighs. The bridge was started by Antonio Contino and completed in 1601 by Bartolo di Alessandro di Venezia and is split into two levels: one took prisoners in; the other took prisoners out.

# Governing Venice

**Il doge**  The doge was originally elected for life (until 1528 when the tenure was restricted to two years) and was like the monarch and figurehead for the Republic. The system for electing him was hugely complicated to ensure against political carve-ups. The honour of being the doge in Venice came at a hefty price: he couldn't leave the city without permission, carry on his own business, receive foreign visitors alone or accept gifts (except flowers, herbs and balsam) and all his letters were read (even his *billets-doux*). None of his family could hold senior positions whilst he wore the *beretta* (the doge's red hat, also called the *zoggia* or *corno* – horn) and, if he seriously displeased the Maggior Consiglio, he could be removed from office himself. The position of doge was originally the most influential in the city but over time the role was eroded in to a mere civic, hand-shaking, swishing-about-in-robes position. Yet there was always a queue of 72-year-olds (the average age for a doge) keen for the honour. The first doge is said to have been Paoluccio Anafesta in AD 697, although the first recorded Doge was Orso Ipato, elected in AD 726. In total, 120 men of Venice wore the *beretta* until 12 May 1797 when the last doge, Ludovico Manin, surrendered to Napoleon.

**Maggior Consiglio** (Great Council)  Created in the 13th century, the Republic's parliament had 500 members who elected the doge and the following officials:

**Minor Consiglio** (Lesser Council)  A six-man team of advisors to the doge, who oversaw his work and sat in on his meetings.

**Senato** (Senate)  The upper house of the parliament.

**Savii** (Wise Men)  Selected by the Senato, this group advised on foreign and home affairs and maritime policy.

**Consiglio dei Dieci** (Council of Ten)  These were spies who kept an eye on all of those involved in government. They were later assisted by the Venetian Inquisition.

**Quarantie**  Elected by the Senato to sit on the supreme courts.

**Pien Collegio** (Full College)  In the 1600s, the Minor Consiglio and the Collegio dei Salvi came together to administer the Republic.

# Around the city

## Museo Civico Correr

*Procuratie Nuove, piazza San Marco 52,*
*T041-240 5211.*
Apr-Oct daily 0900-1900,
Nov-Mar daily 0900-1700, €12, €6.50 concessions.
See p 81 for more info about cumulative tickets.
Vaporetto: San Marco. Map Canal Grande, F6, p87.

Abbot Teodore Correr's bequest to the city has some rare treasures. The famous Italian architect Carlo Scarpa created the exhibition spaces in 1953 and 1960, giving this historic collection a contemporary environment. The first floor of the Napoleonic Wing houses some of Antonio Canova's earlier work, including *Orpheus and Eurydice* (1776), which he completed when he was just 19. Fascinating artefacts from Venetian history are also on display here, including the doge's ceremonial robes and objects from the Arsenale (the Republic's maritime sweatshop), as well as maps, armour and coins.

The Pinacoteca gallery on the second floor is hung chronologically, allowing you to see how access to the best materials and the challenge of the damp environment led to technical advances in Venetian art. Look out for the attention to light on the skin of Giovanni Bellini's *Pietà and Two Angels* (c1460) and the lucidity of the flesh in the *Pietà* (c1475) by Antonella da Messina. Ham-fisted restoration has erased much of the expression from the angels' faces but you can still see how using oil and varnish allowed a deeper, multi-layered approach. This gallery is also famed for Vittore Carpaccio's *Two Venetian Ladies* (1490, also known as *The Courtesans*). Both the amount of cleavage and the nonchalance displayed by these two finely attired subjects means no one knows if they were well heeled or well paid. This painting is actually the bottom half of another painting, *Hunting in the Lagoon*, which hangs in the John Paul Getty Museum in Los Angeles. Fashion lovers should look out for the *chopine* (displayed in Room 50 on the first floor), which are depicted in Carpaccio's painting. These were wooden platform shoes (some of which reached 20 inches) that Venetian ladies initially used to keep their frocks off the filthy streets but soon were worn to give the wearer extra status: you needed to employ someone to help you along the road.

From the first floor you can access the **Museo Archeologico Nazionale di Venezia** established in 1926. This impressive collection of Greek, Egyptian, Assyrian, Babylonian and Roman statuary and archaeological fragments was once kept in the Palazzo Ducale. A door in Room V of the Museo Archeologico leads to the **Biblioteca Nazionale Marciana** or Libreria Sansoviniana, a must for bibliophiles. It holds a stunning collection of classical texts and historical documentation about the city. It's worth popping in to see Titian's huge fresco, *Wisdom* (1560) alone.

## Beyond piazza San Marco

## Museo Fortuny Palazzo

*Pesaro degli Orfei, campo San Beneto,*
*San Marco 3780, T041-520 0995.*
Tue-Sun 1000-1800, €8.
Vaporetto: Sant'Angelo.
Map Canal Grande, C5, p86.

Fashion and style lovers will appreciate this celebration of the Spanish fashion icon's fabrics and dresses. A forerunner to Issey Miyake, Mariano Fortuny (1871-1949) is famous for creating pleated fabrics that clung to the body.

## Teatro La Fenice

*Campo San Fantin, San Marco 1965,*
*T041-2424, teatrolafenice.it.*
Vaporetto: Santa Maria del Giglio.
Map Canal Grande, D6, p86.

The Phoenix: never has a name been so fitting. The story of La Fenice theatre is as dramatic as anything that has ever been staged there. The first theatre on this spot opened in 1733. In 1774 it was burned to the ground, immediately rebuilt and renamed La Fenice by the Venier family. The beginning of the 1800s were opera boom time in Italy and La Fenice saw debuts by Rossini, Bellini and Donizetti.

## Palazzo Contarini del Bovolo

*Corte Contarini del Bovolo,
San Marco 4299, T041-271 9012.*
Apr-Oct daily 1000-1800,
Nov-Mar Sat-Sun 1000-1600, €4.
Vaporetto: Rialto. Map Canal Grande, D4, p86.

Built for the wealthy and influential Contarini family in the 1400s, this palazzo is tucked away in a rather insalubrious location: follow the yellow signs from campo Manin. The highlight is the splendid spiralling staircase, said to resemble a snail shell (*bovolo* in Venetian dialect).

## Fondaco dei Tedeschi

*Salizada Fondaco dei Tedeschi,
San Marco 5554, T041-271 7208.*
Vaporetto: Rialto. Map Canal Grande, F2, p87.

Now the post office, this huge Renaissance *casa fondaco* (completed in 1508) was the warehouse, offices and lodgings of the German merchants who plied their trade from this base until Napoleonic times. The immense internal courtyard seems somewhat undervalued and understated as a post office but it's been for sale since 2007, so is likely to become a hotel or commercial headquarters in the near future. From here it's a short stroll over the ponte di Rialto to the Rialto markets (see page 117).

In 1836 another fire razed the theatre to the ground. Again, it was hurriedly rebuilt and picked up where it left off as a showcase for new opera, showing premieres of Giuseppe Verdi's *Rigoletto* (1851) and *La Traviata* (1853). In 1996, it was consumed by fire once more and two electricians working on the building were convicted of arson. The embers were still glowing when the Mayor committed to rebuilding La Fenice for a third time. Three hundred craftsmen and hundreds of builders used photographs and footage from Luchino Visconti's film *Senso* (1954) to try to replicate the theatre's early 19th century glory and completed the project in 2003 at a cost of €90 million. Critics, among them the TV presenter, Francesco da Mosto, argue that the rush to rebuild has resulted in an inferior building but its lavish plasterwork, gold leaf, woodwork and Murano glass chandeliers are undeniably impressive. Productions at La Fenice remain as celebrated as ever and tickets, especially for first nights, are very pricey indeed. Audio guided tours are available during the day; dates and times vary, so visit the website for more information.

**Above: La Fenice.
Below: Palazzo Contarini del Bovolo.**

# Castello

East of San Marco, the district of Castello (originally called Olivolo) is one of the city's larger *sestieri*. Whilst its western fringes keep up with its neighbour, Castello's appeal lies in the fact that it is not San Marco but an altogether different neighbourhood. That's not to say it doesn't have its tourist honeypots: the Giardini Pubblici, home of La Biennale, and the Arsenale are two you don't want to miss. You'll find few tourists but plenty of Venetians hanging out in campo Santa Maria Formosa, campo Santi Giovanni e Paolo and via Garibaldi, which means prices are a little lower, menus are a little more typical and the pace is altogether slower.

Centro Sociale, Castello.

## Santi Giovanni e Paolo

*Campo Santi Giovanni e Paolo,*
*Castello 6363, T041-523 7510.*
Mon-Sat 0930-1800, Sun 1300-1800.
€3 or Chorus Pass.
Vaporetto: Ospedale.
Map Venice, G4, p83.

Venetians have a soft spot for 'San Zanipolo', as they call it. The *campo* outside is one of loveliest open spaces on the island and is always full of parents with their children running about. Dominican friars commissioned the Gothic building, which was begun in 1368 and consecrated in 1430. It has a brown-brick exterior with white tracery. Inside, the addition of three chapels on the south wall gives the immense nave a slightly unbalanced feel. Twenty-five doges are buried in the church: the elaborate tombs include monuments to a number of the Mocenigo family, Lombardo's tomb for Nicolò Marcello (c1474) and his monument to Andrea Vendramin (1478). (The latter was once adorned with saucy nudes but these were replaced with St Catherine and Mary Magdalene.)

The first chapel on the right holds the *St Vincent Ferrer Polyptych* (c1465) by Giovanni Bellini, which includes his painting of St Christopher. It is one of the few pictures of the Saint that doesn't depict him as hairy-faced vagrant but, instead, as an idealistic young man and its raw physical realism is quite overwhelming. The remains of St Catherine's foot are buried in the Cappella di San Domenico, which boasts Giovanni Battista Piazzetta's only ceiling painting, the *Glory of St Dominic* (1727). Also worth seeing is the Cappella del Rosario (rosary chapel) on the far left-hand side of the church, where Paolo Veronese's tender *The Adoration of the Shepherds* (c1560) hangs. The dominance of a big, biddable cow with a glistening wet nose so close to the holy infant is typical of Veronese but is unusual in a church painting. Indeed, his attention to non-essential characters in liturgical scenes was to get him into trouble with the Inquisition.

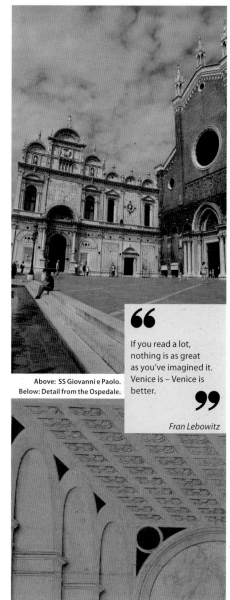

**Above: SS Giovanni e Paolo.**
**Below: Detail from the Ospedale.**

> **"**
> If you read a lot, nothing is as great as you've imagined it. Venice is – Venice is better.
> **"**
>
> *Fran Lebowitz*

## Scuola Grande di San Marco

*Fondamenta dei Mendicanti, campo Santi Giovanni e Paolo, Castello 6776.*
Library: T041-529 4923, Mon-Fri 0830-1400.
Church: T041-522 5662, Mon-Sat 0800-1200,
Sun 0900-1000.
Vaporetto: Ospedale. Map Canal Grande, H2, p87.

Part of the current hospital building, this is perhaps one of the lesser known *scuole* of Venice (see page 119) but one that is worth seeing. Architects and sculptors Pietro Lombardo, Giovanni Buora, Mauro Codussi and Antonio Rizzo rebuilt it in the late 15th century after an earlier fire and were responsible for the richly decorative ground and first floors. The library has a carved wooden ceiling, gilded and studded with the lion of St Mark.

Outside the *scuola* is a beautiful bronze equestrian statue of Bartolomeo Colleoni who led Venice's land forces in the 15th century. When Colleoni died in 1475 he requested a statue of himself to be erected 'in San Marco', in return for a significant legacy. The powers- that-be were keen to accept the money but keener still to avoid creating a precedent, so he was beautifully cast in bronze and erected in front of the Scuola Grande di San Marco instead. He and his powerful, sinewy mount were the last work of Florentine sculptor Andrea Verrocchio.

## Santa Maria Formosa

*Campo Santa Maria Formosa,*
*Castello 5267, T041-275 0462.*
Sep-Jun Mon-Sat 1000-1700, Sun 1000-1300,
Jul & Aug Mon-Sat 1000-1700.
€3 or Chorus Pass.
Vaporetto: Rialto. Map Canal Grande, H3, p87.

South of San Zanipolo, heading towards San Marco, you'll come across one of the liveliest *campos* in Venice. Campo Santa Maria Formosa is full of bars and restaurants and is also home to this oddly positioned church and campanile. With two 16th-century façades, one facing the *campo*, the other the canal, it feels as if it has been plonked in the wrong place.

There are lots of theories amongst the Venetians as to why it should be called '*Formosa*' (which means, er, buxom). Certainly, the two most

Santa Maria Formosa.

*Five of the best*

# Ways to get the most from your visit

**❶ Don't follow the herd**

The Basilica, Palazzo Ducale and the Accademia are wondrous sights but are not essential for a stimulating and authentic Venetian encounter. If you miss seeing them, don't despair. In high season they are so choked with tourists you might queue for ages to catch only a glimpse of something before being elbowed out of the way or hurried on. Instead, visit the sights in the outlying neighbourhoods, such as the churches of Santi Giovanni e Paolo, San Pietro and San Sebastiano or the Ghetto.

**❷ Get up early**

To avoid the crowds and to see Venice at its best, the golden hour that comes just after sunrise is by far the most magical time. The long shadows and fresh luminosity make the features and finery of the buildings more enchanting and the abandoned streets will make you feel as though you have the city to yourself.

**❸ See Venice by night**

Although you should always keep your wits about you and take care of yourself and your valuables, Venice is a great place for nocturnal meandering. It's one of the safest cities in Europe and its bars close early, especially out of season, which means your moonlit experience won't be spoiled by drunken revellers. Be careful you don't stumble into a canal, though.

**❹ Get lost**

As if you will be able to avoid it! The trick is not to bother following directions. If you need to find somewhere specific, use the churches as a general guide and look out for little yellow signs with arrows pointing to key locations (eg Rialto, Accademia, etc). You'll see a lot more this way than if your head is stuck in a guidebook, fretting about second lefts.

**❺ Visit out of season**

Venice in the summer is gorgeous but Venice in the winter is sublime. As the temperature and quality of light changes, the locals do too: the Venetians are far more laid back and engaging when they don't have to deal with high season's tourist masses. Even buying wellies to cope with *acqua alta* (high water) is a thrill.

important paintings in this church – Bartolomeo Vivarini's *Madonna of Mercy* (1473) and Palma Vecchio's *St Barbara and the Four Saints* (c1509) – both feature very shapely female subjects. Vecchio shows Barbara's quiet defiance in the face of her father's wrath for her new-found Christian faith; he went on to behead her.

The slightly wonky campanile is interesting for the gargoyle that crowns the door. John Ruskin described its face as *"huge, inhuman and monstrous, leering in bestial degradation, too foul to be either pictured or described..."*.

### Fondazione Querini Stampalia

*Campiello Querini Stampalia, Castello 5752, T041-271 1411, querinistampalia.it.*
Palazzo: Tue-Thu & Sun 1000-1800,
Fri-Sat 1000-2200. Library: Tue-Sat 1000-2400,
Sun 1000-1900, €8, €6 concessions.
Vaporetto: San Zaccaria.
Map Canal Grande, H4, p87.

This red building is tucked away at the south end of campo Santa Maria Formosa. Bequeathed by the Querini family in 1869 to the cultural foundation of the same name, this 16th-century palazzo is a peaceful sanctuary for those seeking silence and

## Tip...

If you're interested in Venice's churches, invest in a **Chorus Pass** (chorusvenezia.org, €9, €16 for a family or €6 for under 15s and students under 29), which will get you in to 15 of them, without having to pay €3 for entry to each individual church. The churches are open Monday to Saturday from 1000 to 1700 and you can purchase the pass at any of the participating churches: Santa Maria del Giglio, Santo Stefano, Santa Maria Formosa (see page 100), Santa Maria dei Miracoli (see page 108), San Giovanni Elemosinario, San Polo, Santa Maria Gloriosa dei Frari (see page 118), San Giacomo dall'Orio, San Stae, Sant'Alvise (see page 110), Madonna dell'Orto (see page 110), San Pietro di Castello (see page 104), Redentore (see page 133), Santa Maria del Rosario (Gesuati) (see page 107), San Sebastiano (see page 129), San Giobbe.

space. It houses a fine collection of paintings in the museum on the second floor, including work by Giovanni Bellini and Giambattista Tiepolo, a series by Gabriel Bella depicting Venetian life and *The Lion House* (1762) by Pietro Longhi, which shows dogs dressed up as aristocrats entertaining a lion. The lower rooms serve as an exhibition space, renovated and designed by the modernist architect Carlo Scarpa, who sought to mix the old and grand with the achingly modern. The library, popular with students and older Venetians alike, contains over 200,000 books and eschews computers and coffee in favour of a revered hush at all times.

### Museo Diocesano d'Arte Sacra

*Convento di Sant'Apollonia, ponte della Canonica, Castello 4312, T041-522 9166.*
Mon-Sat 1000-1800.
Vaporetto: San Zaccaria.
Map Canal Grande, H5, p87.

Located just behind the Basilica di San Marco, the Diocesan Museum of Sacred Art is where you find all the treasures, such as icons, crucifixes, paintings, sculpture and furnishings, from Venetian churches that are closed, deconsecrated or currently being restored. It also has a weird collection of robed Madonnas. Formerly a Benedictine monastery and then a criminal court, the building came under the control of the council's procuratie in the 1960s, who renovated it most sympathetically. The beautiful cloister has some unique (for Venice) examples of Roman tiles and mosaics, and its walls are lined with the Lapidario Marciano – Roman carvings dating from the first century AD – as well as remnants from the fifth to the 11th century of the original Basilica di San Marco.

## San Francesco della Vigna

*Campo San Francesco della Vigna, Castello 2787, T041-520 6102.*
Mon-Sat 0900-1700.
Vaporetto: Celestia. Map Venice, H4, p83.

Built by Sansovino in 1534, this neighbourhood church close to the Arsenale boasts a façade by Palladio (1572) that was his first work in Venice. It was bequeathed to the Franciscans and has a bronze statue of St Francis outside. Although it may seem as though you're in a forgotten corner of the city, this church feels well used and loved, and it's not without its riches: Paolo Veronese's fluid and colourful *Resurrection* (1584) and Giovanni Bellini's *Madonna with child and saints and donor* (1507) remind you that even the Franciscans used art to instil humility. Its foliage-filled cloister, visible from the *campo*, is one of the most enchanting in Venice.

## Arsenale

*Campo dell'Arsenale.*
Vaporetto: Arsenale. Map Venice, H4/5, p83.

The Venetian Republic didn't just have beauty, it had brawn too. From the 12th to the 16th century the naval shipyard, the Arsenale, grew in size and output, employing up to 16,000 men, known as *arsenalotti*. Despite the fact that each worker consumed up to five litres of free wine a day, they worked with such speed, efficiency and discipline that the Arsenale could construct, fit and arm an entire galley in 24 hours. It is claimed that in the face of war with Turkey at Cyprus in 1570, 100 ships were built in 60 days. The Arsenale was also where the Republic's firearms were developed and built. Four marble lions guard the porta Magna, the entrance gate on rio dell'Arsenale. The two bigger

### Tip...

Around the corner from San Francesco della Vigna to the south is the unusual colonnaded campo della Fraternità. It's a pleasant surprise to find it amongst the tightly-packed houses.

lions were plundered from Greece by Admiral Morosini in 1687 but by that time the roar of the Arsenale had begun to fade. However, it was back in business in the run-up to World War One.

Still a military base, the site is closed off to the public, although vaporetti 51 and 52 skirt round the outer perimeter. However, you can enjoy a great view of the Arsenale by visiting the **Corderie** as part of the Biennale (see page 104) or the Salone Nautico, Venice's International Boat Show, in March. This old rope factory stretches the length of the Darsena Grande, a huge quay inside the shipyard. It's hard to remember that this place once throbbed with sweaty, oily men toiling, shouting, banging and heaving huge planks of wood, the air thick with boiling tar. A visit to the Arsenale and the image of the bubbling, heaving black stuff inspired Dante to create the hell of the boiling pitch in Canto XXI of his *Inferno*.

## Museo Storico Navale

*Campo San Biagio, Castello 2148, T041-520 0276.*
Mon-Fri 0845-1330, Sat 0845-1330.
Vaporetto: Arsenale. Map Venice, H6, p83.

The Naval History Museum has four floors of maritime memorabilia, weaponry and war artefacts from across the decades. It is full of maps and models showing how the Republic's naval commanders planned their battles. For an interesting piece of war reportage, look out for

Arsenale.

## Around the city

Fernando Bertelli's *The Sea Battle of Lepanto* on the first floor, depicting the famous battle between Venice and the Ottoman Empire in 1572. There is a large section dedicated to Admiral Morosini, who plundered the porta Magna lions: it seems his spell as doge did nothing to interrupt his sacking and plundering fest. The highlight of the museum is the doge's ceremonial barge – the awesome golden Buccintoro. This is still used in the 'marriage of the sea' ceremony, La Sensa, which is held each May to symbolize Venice's union with the sea. Other treasures include a magnificent Chinese junk and other oriental crafts, and a collection of gondolas, including Peggy Guggenheim's.

Outside the museum is a stele by Antonio Canova dedicated to Angelo Emo, the last admiral of the Venetian fleet. When Canova's advance for the stele was not forthcoming, he threatened to replace Emo's face with that of his grandmother; fortunately the money came just in time...

### San Pietro di Castello

*Campo San Pietro, Castello.*
*Mon-Sat 1000-1700, Sun 1300-1700.*
€3 or Chorus Pass.
Vaporetto: San Pietro.

Towards the easternmost part of Castello, in the working class area of Sant'Elena, is this truly delightful church. It was the seat of the Bishop of Venice and served as Venice's cathedral until the Basilica di San Marco took the honour in 1887. The first church here was built in the seventh century on the remains of the Castel d'Olivio but, in the 16th century, it was rebuilt with a Palladian façade. It was heavily bombed during the First World War and has since suffered from poor maintenance. However, the American 'Save Venice Campaign' has set its sights on funding renovation work. Nearby **via Garibaldi** has a number of bars: Bar Garibaldi with its tables at the end of rio di Sant'Anna is the best, offering typical Venetian Spritz. There really is not much better in life than sipping a couple of aperitivi then strolling along to San Pietro to sit in the grassy square under the tilting campanile as they ring the evening bells.

# La Biennale

*Giardini Pubblici, Corderie and other locations around the city, T041-521 8849, labiennale.org.*
€15, €12 concession.
Vaporetto: Giardini or Arsenale.

What with all its rich history and bountiful assets, Venice can seem a rather inward-looking city that pays little attention to the outside world. However, all this changes during the Biennale when the city is imbued with a truly international atmosphere. The Venice Biennale is the world's greatest non-commercial art exhibition. It takes place from June to October every other year (2009, 2011, etc), with countries from all over the world taking part. Each country has a pavilion in which to profile a representative artist or artists. (The UK has been represented in recent years by Gilbert and George, Tracy Emin and, in 2009, will be represented by Steve McQueen.) The permanent pavilions are located in the Giardini Pubblici, an area of parkland to the east of the city centre that dates from the Napoleonic period. Palazzos, churches and other buildings around the city are also leased for the event. There is a curated exhibition at the Corderie (just beside the rio del Arsenale) and a big exhibition in the Italian pavilion in the Giardini. The opening week in June sees the worldwide art community and celebrity hangers-on descend on the city to network, party and be seen. And, as the world order changes so does the Biennale: it is now the stomping ground for a new breed of Russian and Chinese art collectors and dealers who come to find the next big investment and to promote their artists.

The first Biennale was held in 1895 and, from 1907 countries began to build some of the 30 national pavilions in the Giardini. Two world wars and the rise of Fascism served to give the Biennale renewed purpose: a music festival was introduced in 1930, followed by the film festival in 1932 and the theatre festival in 1934. However, it was in 1948, when Peggy Guggenheim arrived in Venice, that the Biennale began to gain its cutting-edge status. She showed her collection in the abandoned Greek pavilion before moving it permanently to Palazzo Venier dei Leoni in Dorsoduro, where it remains (see page 125).

Every even year (2010, 2012) the architecture Biennale is held. This has a shorter run, from August to October, and has less of an impact on the city than the art festival but it can be just as adventurous, showcasing big names, such as Zaha Hadid, Norman Foster and Frank Gehry, as well as a host of lesser known architects from around the world.

## Biennale for beginners

It's not just for the arty set, it's for all of us. However, if you've never been before, it can be a bit of a daunting prospect.

Begin by doing some research on the Biennale's excellent website (labiennale.org) before you go. Check which artists are representing which countries and, if their pavilion isn't in the Giardini, find out its location. Find out about the exhibition in the Corderie, which is curated by a guest curator from one of the big or well-known international galleries and is usually global in outlook. And, get details of the show, again international but curated by an Italian, in the Italian pavilion (in the Giardini).

Check out the reviews in the newspapers. Although they are written by art world insiders, they can still give you a decent steer on what to see. You could also try to get your hands on one of the Biennale catalogues, if you really want to plan your time meticulously, although the pictures often don't do justice to the art work.

Book your tickets on the website, including an entrance time for the Corderie, although, unlike the basilica your time here isn't limited, so you won't be chucked out after 15 minutes.

Unless you have impressive powers of attention and stamina, allow two days to see both of the main sites: it takes at least four hours to get round the Giardini (more if you are lingering excitedly) and two or three to get round the Corderie. In high summer, visit the Giardini in the early or later part of the day, as it can get very hot padding from pavilion to pavilion. If you only have one day, see the Giardini in the morning and the Corderie in the afternoon.

The website has a map of the Giardini. The pavilions over the bridge, which include Greece, Brazil and Eqypt, are usually the last ones to be visited and so are always full of people sighing and dragging their feet in tiredness. Why not go and see them first?

Try to visit the off-site pavilions while you're exploring other areas of the city – red signs will help you find your way – but bear in mind that a lot of them are closed on Monday.

Make the most of the little cafés (including a lovely old bar at the garden entrance) dotted around the Giardini and the Corderie to recharge your batteries, and use the fabulous shops at both sites to stock up on exhibition catalogues and other arty things.

Turn up with an open mind and a comfy pair of shoes.

*Tijuanatanjierchandelier* by Jason Rhoades, Venice Biennale 2007.

# Cannaregio

On the northern fringes of the city, bordering Castello to the east, Cannaregio is perhaps the most varied of the *sestiere*. Synonymous with the Jewish ghetto created by the authorities in the 16th century, it is now a working-class area. Lista di Spagna and strada Nova are tourist traps, offering point-and-pick menus and cheap hotels but you can peel away from these streets into the ghetto and along the fondamenta della Misericordia and dei Morti for an utterly charming experience of old but very much living Venice. The churches and the art of the Madonna dell'Orto and the Gesuiti are worth a visit alone.

Below: Ponte De La Saponela, Cannaregio. Opposite page: Reading the papers on the Rio del Misericordia.

## Gesuiti

*Salizada dei Specchieri,*
*Cannaregio 4880, T041-528 6579.*
Daily 1000-1200 and 1400-1600.
Vaporetto: Fondamente Nuove.
Map Venice, F2, p83.

As you walk across the bridge over rio Santa Caterina towards the Gesuiti, your heart will soar as you catch the first glimpse of its jaw-dropping edifice bathed in the light the expanse of the *campo* affords.

A latecomer, as far as Venetian churches go, Santa Maria Assunta (to give its official name) wasn't built until 1714. The Republic's power struggle with the Vatican meant that the Jesuits were very unpopular in the city and were even expelled for a good number of years. When they were finally given permission to build their own church, it was on the basis that it would be on the outer reaches of the city, as far away from the opportunity to court influence and cause trouble as possible.

The Baroque façade by Domenico Rossi has four columns on each side of a large bronze door. Angels adorn the columns, the roof and the tabernacles inside. The simple barrel-vaulted nave is festooned with *trompe l'œil* paintings and carved green and white marble, which appears to be draped around the walls.

Note Titian's gruesome *Martyrdom of St Lawrence*, which shows the saint being roasted alive. It's a night scene: you can see the light glistening on the sweaty bodies and almost feel the heat of the fire.

## Tip…

Fondamenta Nuove is a long waterside street that stretches from the Ospedale Civile in Castello all the way up to canale della Misericordia. Regular maintenance means it is often closed but when it's open, it offers fabulous views of San Michele and a cooling breeze that's welcome on a summer's day. You can catch the vaporetto from here to San Michele, Murano, Burano and Torcello (see page 134) and there are gelaterie and bars offering refreshment.

## What the authors say

The *campo* in front of the Gesuiti was once used for games of football and is still a popular spot for youngsters to have a kick-about and for toddlers to chase pigeons. There is a bench directly in front of the church on which Nick, my travelling companion, and I always choose to sit, have a wee picnic and just take in the surrounding loveliness. The church has particularly fond memories for Nick, who was at university here and stayed in a student residence in the former monastery next door. He spent most of his time trying to creep out the back during the hours of the curfew imposed by Padre Dino, who looked after them. Early one morning, still intoxicated from a night out at Paradiso Perduto, Nick and some other young chaps were summoned by the Padre to help remove Tintoretto's richly hued painting of the *Assumption* from the church for restoration. It was hot work and a mammoth exercise getting the thing off the wall. Nick remembers getting rather panic-stricken when, up a ladder and holding the corner of this priceless artwork, he was overcome with a hangover sweat and thought he was about to be sick. An interesting debate can be had about when might be the best time to confess your sin: before you throw up on a Tintoretto or afterwards?

*Shona Main on Gesuiti*

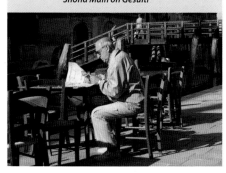

# Tintoretto (1518-1594)

Born Jacopo Comin Robusti in a humble abode in the Ghetto, Tintoretto was the son of a *tintor* (silk dyer), which led to his nickname, 'little dyer'. His father noticed the child playing with his dyes and took him along to Titian's studio to see if he could get an apprenticeship. Titian took him on but the apprenticeship lasted only a few days: it has been suggested that Tintoretto was too headstrong and painted too quickly for Titian, who himself had a slow, considered style. However, Tintoretto was not deterred by this experience and, according to popular belief, taught himself to paint instead. But how true is this? He must have completed an apprenticeship – Venetian law required it – but there is no record of the studio in which he served his time.

Tintoretto always showed professional respect towards Titian but despite becoming contemporaries they were never friends. A real loner, Tintoretto spent all his time drawing and making models from clay or wax, which he would use to create the scenes that he would later paint (a technique he learned from Titian). A fan of Raphael and Michelangelo, he had the same anatomical curiosity that led him into the dark recesses of Venice, where dead bodies could be opened up and examined. He worked tirelessly, assisting other artists and painting on a 'costs only' basis – the Madonna dell'Orto paintings are a legacy of this – and, some might say, prostituting himself artistically to try to find a patron. His first big commissions were from the Scuola Grande di San Marco. One of these, *Miracle of the Slave* (1548), can be seen in the Accademia and was his first real smash hit. From then on, the commissions kept coming, although Tintoretto didn't win himself any friends in the process, elbowing Salviati and Veronese out of the way to win the commission at the Scuola Grande di San Rocco (1564-1588) by offering his work for free.

Tintoretto's output was prolific and completed at an astonishing rate, so it is perhaps not surprising that there are some duds amongst the abundance of jewels: *The Nativity* (1581) in the Scuola di San Rocco, for example, is so diffuse in its construction that you don't know where to look. He sometimes copied the style of Titian, particularly in his use of colour, but, just as often, painted in an anti-Titian style and there is plenty in his body of work that demonstrates a unique technique. His ability to depict often violent movement and physicality, and his knack of unsettling the viewer are what make Tintoretto a master.

## Santa Maria dei Miracoli

*Campo dei Miracoli,*
*Cannaregio 1758, T041-275 0462.*
Mon-Sat 1000-1700, Sun 1300-1700.
€3 or Chorus Pass.
Vaporetto: Rialto. Map Canal Grande, G2, p87.

New churches were commonly bankrolled by the city but, such was the popular support for this church, built in 1489 by Pietro Lombardo and his sons, Antonio and Tullio, that private donations hugely surpassed what was needed, leading to a far more splendidly decorated construction than had originally been intended. There was even enough spare to build an adjoining nunnery for the order of St Clare. The reason for the locals' largesse was their belief in the powers of a painting of the Virgin and Child and their conviction that to preserve its miraculous abilities, the painting required a building worthy of Mary herself.

Below: Detail from Santa Maria dei Miracoli.
Opposite page: Tintoretto's house.

## Around the city

Inside, it's a slender space with an elevated chancel where the icon still hangs above the altar. The pastel shades of the marble make it look like a wedding cake, which perfectly suits the Venetians who consider this *the* place to get married.

### Madonna dell'Orto/San Cristoforo Martire

*Campo Madonna dell'Orto,*
*Cannaregio 3520, T041-275 0462.*
Mon-Sat 1000-1700, Sun 1300-1700,
€3 or Chorus Pass (see page 102).
Vaporetto: Madonna dell'Orto.
Map Venice, E1, p82.

On the northern edge of Cannaregio is one of Venice's great Gothic churches. Its solidity seems all the more impressive due to the square campo in front. The red-brick construction with marble decoration dates from the 14th and 15th centuries and was originally dedicated to St Christopher, the patron saint of travellers (he still stands above the portal). However, the discovery of a statue of the Virgin Mary in a nearby vegetable patch (*orto*) led to the reconstruction and renaming of the church. You can see this statue, buffed up somewhat, in the chapel.

This was Tintoretto's local church and the walls are filled with some of his most stirring works. He was in his late 20s and still learning his craft in the 1540s, when he started painting here, so he asked only to be paid for the cost of his materials. *The Last Judgement* (1563) would make even the most committed non-believer pause for thought: God's wrath sweeps away the sinners, who cling onto hope and desperately grab at the limbs of the dead as they fight against their fate. The speed of Tintoretto's painting allowed him to create very physical images. This is most apparent in the *Apparition of the Cross to St Peter* (1562) in which four angels hoist the cross above a startled Peter in his ecumenical robes. *The Martyrdom of St Paul* (c1570) shows the moment just before the Roman soldier, carrying out Nero's orders, swings the sword. Tintoretto captures the motion with such power that it feels as though you are just about to witness the

horrendous act itself, yet there is a calmness about St Paul as he beholds his fate. There are other great Tintorettos here but those three are unmissable. The artist himself now rests in peace in an austere spot to the right of the altar (see page 108). Nearby, fondamenta dei Mori, is where Tintoretto worked; it has a statue of a turbaned Moor outside.

### Sant'Alvise

*Campo Sant'Alvise,*
*Cannaregio 3282, T041-524 4664.*
Mon-Sat 1000-1700,
€3 or Chorus Pass (see page 102).
Vaporetto: Sant'Alvise. Map Venice, D1, p82.

Not far from the Madonna dell'Orto is this Gothic block (1388). It's nothing fancy on the outside but Giambattista Tiepolo's three supreme paintings – *The Flagellation, The Crowning with Thorns* and *Ascent into Calvary* (all c1740) – can be found in the chancel.

### Palazzo Labia

*Campo Santa Geremia 275, Cannaregio 30121,*
*T041-524 2812.*
Open by appointment only.
Vaporetto: Ferrovia. Map Venice, C2, p82.

West of the Ghetto, across the canale di Cannaregio, is this 16th-century palazzo. It was originally for Catalonian merchants who had bought their way into the Venetian nobility but is now owned by Berlusconi's RAI and operates as a congress centre. However, if you are a lover of Tiepolo it's worth the

Above: Tiepolo fresco. Opposite page: Palazzo Labia.

hassle of making an appointment in order to see his frescoes. The Salone del Tiepolo has a series of spectacular paintings depicting the love between Anthony and Cleopatra, and the Sala degli Specchi has some beautiful allegorical works relating to Spring and to the winds.

### Santa Maria di Nazareth degli Scalzi (Gli Scalzi)

*Fondamenta degli Scalzi, Cannaregio.*
Mon-Sat 0745-1145 and 1600-1845,
Sun 1600-1900.
Vaporetto: Ferrovia. Map Venice, C3, p82.

Built by Longhena and Giuseppe Sardi in 1656, this church is named after the Carmelitani Scalzi

(barefoot Carmelites), who, despite being shoeless, wanted the most extravagant Baroque creation possible. John Ruskin was very sniffy about the excesses used in the decoration of this church and, standing as it does next to the Fascist-style train station, it does look like an overdressed guest.

### Santa Maria Maddalena

*Campo de la Maddalena, Cannaregio 2116.*
Mon-Sat 1000-1200 & 1600-1800.
Vaporetto: San Marcuola. Map Venice, D2, p82.

Just off rio Terra della Maddalena, a continuation of strada Nuova, lies one of Venice's most mesmerizing churches. Originally an 13th-century oratory belonging to the Baffo family, it was rebuilt in 1778 by Tommaso Temazo as a Pantheon-esque structure that resembles an urn. Inside, Ionic columns line the walls and support the cupola. Look out for *The Last Supper* by Giandomenico Tiepolo (1727-1840), which is rather domestic compared to many depictions of the scene, and for the Masonic symbol, the all-seeing-eye, above the doorway.

## Ca' d'Oro

*Calle Ca' d'Oro, Cannaregio 3932, T041-523 8790.*
Mon 0815-1400, Tue-Sun 0815-1915, €5.
See p81 for details of cumulative tickets.
Vaporetto: Ca' d'Oro. Map Canal Grande, D1, p86.

Named the 'golden house' after the famous gildings on the façade (now sadly faded and washed away), this gothic palazzo was built in 1421 by a member of the Contarini family. It had a series of owners over the decades, all of whom added their own style. In 1894 the art collector Baron Giorgio Franchetti bought it and began to restore it to the dream-like palazzo it had once been. Following his death in 1922 he bequeathed it to the city, along with a fabulous collection of paintings, bronzes and marbles dating from the 15th to the 18th centuries.

On the second floor is an arresting terracotta maquette, Gian Lorenzo Bernini's *Allegory of the Nile* (c1645), depicting a muscular man pulling off his clothes. Amongst the religious paintings, look out for the huge, vivid golden altarpiece, *Passion of Christ Polyptych*, by Antonio Vivarini and assistant (c1470) and Andrea Mantegna's *St Sebastian* (1506), whose pain will make you wince. The relief by Domenica da Tolmezza, *St Roch Polyptych* (c1460), is so incredibly detailed, it's like a little dolls' house. The view from the balcony across the canal is pretty amazing, too.

# Il Ghetto

The western part of the island of Cannaregio was originally the site of the city's foundry – *geto* in Venetian dialect – but in the 16th century it became the place in which the city's Jewish population was herded and locked in at night: the original ghetto.

There had always been special rules applied to Jews in Venice, issued through decree by the Senate, relating to residence, taxes and the wearing of badges and caps so they could be identified. However, the creation of the "geto at San Hieronimo" by the Senate in 1516 went much further. It sought to prevent Jews from sharing houses with Christians, going about their business in the city and practising their religion, causing "grave offence to the Majesty of God and … the well-ordered republic". Effectively, the Senate evacuated non-Jews from the Ghetto and ordered all the Jews in the city to live there at a rent that was one third higher than the non-Jewish tenant had paid. Furthermore, they were required to pay the wages of the Christian guards who patrolled the border of the Ghetto by boat and those who locked and unlocked the gates of the ghetto come sunset and sunrise.

This ruling was a reaction to the large number of German Jews (known as Ebrei Tedeschi, even though many were Italian) that had come to Venice following the city's invasion of the Veneto in 1509. The city was willing to accommodate them, as they gave good service as money lenders, doctors and dealers of second-hand clothes, although some Jews– probably money lenders – were expelled between 1527 and 1533. The Ghetto's population was swelled by the arrival of Sephardic Jews, expelled from Spain and Portugal, and Levantine Jews, who were subjects of the Ottoman Empire. The gates of the Ghetto continued to be locked at night until Napoleon took control of the city in 1797 and the Austrians kept a tight control on the movement of Venetian Jews until Unification in 1866. Of course, a more terrible fate was to await Italian Jews when the Fascists took control of Italy in 1922.

Before the outbreak of the Second World War, 1500 Jews lived in the Ghetto. On 1 December 1943 members of the *carabinieri* and Fascist agents entered the Casa di Riposo Israelitica, a nursing home for elderly Jews, and arrested the residents, while other officers rounded up Jewish families. All were taken to one of the university buildings where they were held without food or proper facilities (some locals threw them food through the windows) until they were deported to extermination camps. The Nazis carried out more deportations in 1944. A total of 246 Venetian Jews were deported during the war, of whom only eight survived.

In 1980, the Lithuanian artist Arbit Blatas (1908-1999), whose mother died in the gas chamber of Bergen-Belsen and whose father survived Dachau, created the seven bas relief sculptures that hang on the far wall of the campo Ghetto Nuovo. They depict truly terrible scenes of Jews being rounded up, forced into trains, shot and their bodies piled into graves. Adjacent to the square is Blatas' final work, *The Last Train*, completed in 1993 and consecrated on the 50th anniversary of the deportation.

The character of the Ghetto is different from that of the rest of Venice. The palazzi and houses here are much taller with more stories, due to the need to utilize all available space. You can still find a Jewish baker (**Panificio Volpe**, calle Ghetto Vecchio, Cannaregio 1143, T041-715178), a school, kosher shops, a Jewish restaurant (**Gam Gam**, sottoportico del Ghetto Vecchio, Cannaregio 1122, T041-715284)

Opposite page: Well in the Ghetto.
Above: A menorah in the Ghetto.

and a Jewish bank here, as well as two operational synagogues (Scuola Grande Tedesca and the Scuola Canton) built into the attics of two houses. However, although 300,000 Jewish tourists visit the Ghetto every year, there are only three Jewish families and 33 Jewish residents living in Venice today.

The small Jewish museum has a few interesting liturgical artefacts and art from the 17th to the 19th centuries. However, it is the documents relating to the Venetian Jews' experiences during the Holocaust and the fascinating guided tours that make it a must-visit.

### Holocaust memorial & Museo Communità Ebraica

*Campo Ghetto Nuovo, Cannaregio 2902b, T041-715359.*
**Museum: Jun-Sep Sun-Fri 1000-1900, Oct-May Sun-Fri 1000-1800, closed on Jewish holidays.**
**Tours: May-Sep Sun-Fri 1030 and 1730, Oct-Apr Sun-Fri 1030 and 1630.**
**Vaporetto: Guglie. Map Venice, D2, p82.**

# Venice on foot

The author's favourite walk around the city

**T**his takes a day (I am a dawdler) but you'll avoid the crowds and spend just a few euros enjoying the very best of Venice. All you need is a map, some water, comfy shoes, some change to jangle in your pocket and the phrase *"Dove' è such-and-such, per favore?"* on the tip of your tongue.

Get up very early and head straight to **piazza San Marco** to see the **Torre dell'Orologio** and **Procuratie Vecchie** in the morning light without a tour group in sight. Pass the **Bridge of Sighs** and walk along riva degli Schiavoni to **Arsenale**. Look south across the water to see the morning sunlight on **San Giorgio Maggiore**: it's an uplifting sight.

You can have a quick coffee at **Bar Arsenal** next to the huge lions in campo dell'Arsenale, then head north towards **San Francesco della Vigna**, Palladio's first Venetian effort. After that, make straight for **SS Giovanni e Paolo**, a beautiful hangar of a church that houses my favourite painting, Giovanni Bellini's, *St Christopher*. Head towards **Chiesa di Santa Maria Formosa**, then, maybe, have another coffee at **Italo Didovich** in campo Santa Marina, nearby.

Stop off at **Chiesa Santa Maria dei Miracoli** en route to the **Gesuiti**. Before you go inside the latter, sit for a while on the bench right in front and gaze at the sheer beauty of its Baroque ornamentation. Then, head towards the rio del Noale and the rio Terra della Misericordia, making a slight detour to **Madonna dell'Orto**, Tintoretto's church.

Spend some time in the **Ghetto** before heading towards the train station and over the **ponte dei Scalzi** into Santa Croce. Follow the signs for the **Frari**. You're likely to be very hungry by now, so stop for a *pizza al taglio* (slice of pizza) at **Millefoglie di Tarcisco Gelato** in salizada San Rocco before going in.

Afterwards, try to comprehend the gorgeousness of what you have just seen over a spritz in **campo Santa Margherita**. Then head through the Campo and towards the **Ponte dei Pugni**. This 'Bridge of Fists' was a former boxing ring and was famous for its fights between the warring factions of the city, the Nicolotti and the Castellani. The bridge takes you over the Rio San Barnaba. **Campo San Barnaba** is just to your left so take a short detour but be sure to take the **Calle Lunga San Barnaba** (parallel to the canal). This takes you towards the church of San Sebastiano, which is smothered in Veronese's paintings. Take a walk along the **Zattere** in the late afternoon sunshine, stopping for some ice cream at **Gelateria Nico**.

If you still have some energy and it's not yet 1830, you could venture into the **Accademia** but, if not, head to **La Salute**. The church and the views over the Canal Grande are at their most beautiful as the light fades and the day ends. You'll be ravenous by now: dinner at **Osteria Vecio Forner**, at nearby Campo San Vio will end a singular day.

**Above: Heading towards the Gesuiti.
Opposite page: Between Campo Santa Margherita and the Zattere, the Ponte dei Pugni.**

# Santa Croce & San Polo

The meandering Canal Grande separates San Marco, Castello and Cannaregio from the *sestieri* of Santa Croce and San Polo. Santa Croce is an old residential area, although it does contain the University and the bus station, while San Polo buzzes with life. It has some great shopping thoroughfares, markets (the Pescaria and Erberie), restaurants and bars: try campo San Paolo for a laidback drink and campo San Giacomo for exuberance. San Polo is also home to the Scuola Grande di San Rocco and the Frari: two of the most quintessentially Venetian artistic encounters that the city has to offer.

Rialto at night.

## Pescaria & Erberie

*Fabricche Nuove, San Polo.*
Pescaria Tue-Sat 0700-1200.
Erberie Mon-Sat 0700-1200.
Vaporetto: Rialto Mercato.
Map Canal Grande, D1, p86.

Its strategic position on the cusp of both east and west and its strong political status meant that Venice was at the forefront of trade in the Middle Ages. Foreign traders swarmed the city as evidenced by the huge storerooms and lodgings provided for the Germans (Fondaco dei Tedeschi) and Turks (Fondaco dei Turchi). The city's markets moved to the Rialto in the 11th century and, although many deals were sealed in the palazzi along the Canal Grande, the markets were where traders congregated to buy and sell spices, such as pepper, saffron and ginger, and luxury products, such as sugar cane, essential oils, perfumes, gold and jewels

There are still plenty of traders in the Rialto markets today but now they are fishmongers and fruit and vegetable sellers. Housed under a neo-Gothic arcaded loggia (built by Domenico Rupolo and Cesare Laurenti in 1907), the **Pescaria** is an eye-opener with vast quantities of quietly scuttling *moeche* (soft shelled cabs), swordfish and baby octopus, all glistening with freshness. The **Erberie** (fruit and vegetable market) sits on campo della Pescaria, alongside the Canal Grande. You'll be stunned by the choice, then the quality, then the size and firmness of some of the vegetables on offer here. The campo de le Becarie runs along the side of the Pescaria and is where the butchers' shops are found.

Pescaria.

## Tip...

If you are buying fish at the Pescaria, look out for the label which states its origin (boat and stretch of sea). It's not unheard of for foreign fish to be passed off as local.

## Ponte di Rialto

*From riva del Vin, San Polo to salizada Pio X, San Marco.*
Vaporetto: Rialto. Map Canal Grande, E3, p86.

In 1181, a floating structure – the ponte de Moneta by Nicolò Barattieri – became the only bridge to span the Canal Grande. This collapsed and was replaced in 1255 by the strange wooden

construction that can be seen in Carpaccio's *The Miracle of the Reliquary of the True Cross* (1494) in the Accademia. This bridge suffered a fire in 1310 and a collapse in 1444 before falling apart conclusively in 1524. The authorities sought a few big names, including Palladio, Sansovino and Michelangelo, to build a stone replacement but finally settled on the design by Antonio da Ponte (born to build bridges), which was completed in 1591. The bridge is made of Istrian stone and spans 28 m, with arcades of shops on either side. The simplicity of its wide arches, 12 perfectly balanced Renaissance arcades and central gently pointing portal is what makes this bridge so pleasing to look at.

## Around the city

### Galleria d'Arte Moderna & Museo d'Arte Orientale

*Fondamenta di Ca' Pesaro,*
*Santa Croce 2076, T041-524 1173.*
Tue-Sun 0815-1400, €5.50, €3 concession.
Vaporetto: San Stae. Map Venice, E3, p82.

The building of Ca' Pesaro was inspired by
Sansovino, started by Longhena and finished
by Gasparo in 1710. Since 1902 the Baroque
rooms have housed the fabulous Museum of
Modern Art collection, purchased from the Biennale
exhibitions, including Vasily Kandinsky's *White zig
zags* (1922), Gustav Klimt's *Judith II* (1909), Umberto
Boccioni's *Portrait of the artist's sister reading* (1909)
and Giorgio De Chirico's *Portrait of Lionello de Lisi*
(1953). There is also a room containing work by
Henry Moore, Max Ernst, Hans Arp and Henri Matisse.

Upstairs is the Museum of Oriental Art, with its
idiosyncratic collection of mainly Japanese art,
arms, furniture and lady's paraphernalia from the
Edo period. If this floats your junk, it's a must-see. It
has the esoteric feel of someone's private
collection and certainly evokes the excitement a
Venetian lady must have felt on encountering such
other-worldly fripperies for the first time.

### Scuola Grande di San Rocco

*Campo San Rocco, San Polo 3052, T041-523 4864.*
Apr-Oct 0900-1730, Nov-Mar 1000-1700,
€7, €5 concession.
Vaporetto: San Tomà. Map Venice, C4, p82.

Bartolomeo Bon designed the ground floor of this
*scuola* for the confraternity of St Roch (see box
page 119) in 1515. Sante Lombardo continued his
work until 1527 when Antonio Scarpagnino took
over to complete the building. It is the artwork by
Tintoretto, however, that is the reason to visit.

Much has been written about the way Tintoretto
won this commission: he bribed the caretaker to let
him in and then painted his proposal directly onto
the walls. However, this was his life's work: the 50
dramatic paintings displayed within the three rooms
and along the walls of the majestic staircase took

Tintoretto 23 years to complete and their scale and
intensity is epic indeed. Highlights include *The
Crucifixion* (1565) in the gilt-ceilinged Sala Grande
Superiore (great hall) and the gruesome depiction
of mutilated babies and mothers in *The Slaughter of
the Innocents* (1587) in the hall downstairs.

As much as this is Tintoretto's showcase, the
effort of craning your neck to see his work means you
may end up taking more notice of the handiwork of
the eccentric 17th century sculptor Francesco Pianta
il Giovane, which is all at eye level. The first figures you
see around the Sala Grande Superiore are the busts
of maidens but as you progress clockwise around the
room the figures become weirder and altogether
more intriguing metaphors for emotions, deeds and
ideals: fathoming out each one is a riddle in itself.
There's a man with a horse's head, the muscular back
of a stone mason (his tools give him away), a cloaked
man and angels in chains. The scowling Tintoretto,
clutching his brushes, is easier to identify.

### Santa Maria Gloriosa dei Frari

*Campo dei Frari, San Polo 3004, T041-275 0462.*
Mon-Sat 0900-1800, Sun 1300-1800, €3.
Vaporetto: San Tomà. Map Canal Grande, A3, p86.

If you see only one church in Venice, this should be
it. Called 'i Frari' by the locals (a dialect version of
*frati* – brothers), it was built by the Franciscans. The
colossal bulk of this Gothic church is misleading: it's
even bigger on the inside and is packed with the
most extraordinary tombs, paintings and features.

There are suggestions that St Francis visited the
Venetian lagoon in transit to Egypt around 1220.
Certainly, around this time, Doge Jacopo Tiepolo
gifted the Franciscan community some land to
build a monastery. What stands here is actually the
third church built on this site (1441) which, on the
basis of its straightforward design and terracotta
bricks, adheres to the Franciscan's belief in keeping
things simple.

As you enter the vast nave, there are three
stunning monuments to your right. The first of these
is to Doge Giovanni Pesaro (1669) by Baldassare
Longhena, which shows four Moors in ripped

# The Scuole of Venice

Started in the 13th century, the *scuole* were confraternity guilds (religious and social working men's clubs) that funded hospitals, organized cultural events and helped those members and their families who had fallen on hard times. It was nigh on impossible to move up the Venetian social strata, so these confraternities created the supportive networks that helped families and businesses flourish. Membership was open to anyone who wasn't noble and who had lived in Venice and had paid taxes for a certain length of time. Six *Scuole Grandi* were formed from the 13th to the 16th centuries: the first was the Scuola Grande di San Marco (founded 1260; see page 100), then the Scuola Grande della Carità (1260, where the Accademia is now located; see page 121), the Scuola Grande di San Giovanni Evangelista (1261), the Scuola Grande della Misericordia (1308), the Scuola Grande di San Rocco (1480; see page 118) and the Scuola Grande di San Teodoro (founded 1530 or 1552). Napoleon closed them down (except for San Rocco, strangely) and looted many of the *scuole*'s artistic treasures.

and is more vivid and flowing than reproductions of it suggest. The frame is a corker, too. Giovanni Bellini's *Madonna and Child with Saints* (1488), Donatello's sculpture of John the Baptist (1438) and Bartolomeo Vivarini's *Triptych of St Mark Enthroned with Saints* (1474) are also all worth a look; note the gormless minstrels in the latter. In the sacristy is the *Altar of the Relics* (1711), which features a Baroque relief by Francesco Penso showing Mary collecting Christ's blood. A phial of the Holy Blood is encased within the altar itself and to the right is an intriguing glass cabinet that holds hands, fingers and unidentified bits of saintly bodies residing in a multitude of reliquaries.

There is a little museum containing old liturgical robes and the like but more interesting is the view out of the room's window on to the immense cloisters, the Chiostro della Trinità. Another cloister beyond that, Chiostro di Sant'Antonio, is closed to the public.

clothes and with whitened eyes lifting the entablature (with cushions for comfort) on which the Doge rests. Between the slaves are black skeletons and surrounding the prostrate Pesaro are a couple of beautiful maidens and some snarling dog-dragon beasts. Next to it is Titian's vast canvas, *Madonna of Ca' Pesaro* (1526), which incorporates members of the doge's family into a liturgical scene – a popular technique in the Renaissance. Along the wall is a puzzling pyramidal monument to Antonio Canova (1827), originally designed by the sculptor himself as a memorial to Titian but built by Luigi Zandomeneghi to hold Canova's heart; the sculptor's body was returned to his hometown of Possagno (see page 198). The pyramid is visited by statues of grieving maidens and children and a swooning angel but it is the mournful lion of Venice, with its head resting on its big, crossed paws that touches your heart. Across from here is the actual tomb of Titian, who died during the 1576 plague.

The elaborately carved Gothic choir stalls dominate the area between the nave and the altar. Titian's *Assumption* (1518) hangs above the high altar

Santa Maria Gloriosa dei Frari.

## Tip...

To get a real sense of the vast size and scale of 'i Frari', look out for aerial-view posters of Venice, which are sold in any number of tourist shops.

# Dorsoduro

Dorsoduro literally means 'hard back' and is the stretch of land that juts out from San Polo and across the Canal Grande from San Marco. This is where you'll find the University, Ca' Foscari, the world-famous collections at Ca' Rezzonico and the Accademia, the Collezione Peggy Guggenheim and the unforgettable landmarks of La Salute and the Dogana. On the south side of the *sestiere*, the open expanse along the Zattere is known as Venice's beach, while in the southwest of the district are three churches that shouldn't be missed. Dorsoduro is a well-heeled neighbourhood with a slightly bohemian, outward-looking feel and, though it may seem a little out of the way, San Marco is actually just a clump across the ponte dell'Accademia.

Santa Maria della Salute.

## Gallerie dell'Accademia

*Dorsoduro 1050, T041-522 2247.*
Mon 0815-1400, Tue-Sat 0815-1915 (last admission 1830), €6.50, free under 18s, students under 25 and over 65s including admission to Ca' d'Oro and Museo Orientale.
Vaporetto: Accademia. Map Venice, D6, p82.

Like its equivalents in Rome, Milan and Bologna, the Venice Accademia was created by the Senate in 1750 as a school teaching fine art and architecture. It was the first institution to develop art restoration in 1717 and formalized the teaching of it in the early 19th century. In 1807, it moved to its present site which is made up of three buildings: the Scuola della Carità (1260), the Convento dei Canonici Lateranensi (designed by Palladio in 1561) and the Chiesa di Santa Maria della Carità, the façade of which was built by Bartolomeo Bon in 1441.

If you arrive at the Accademia across the wooden ponte dell'Accademia you may be disappointed by your first impressions. Not only do the crowds choke the entrance but the building is usually swathed in builders' tarpaulin and, for a gallery spoken about in such revered tones, it seems quite small. But, if you commit to fighting your way through the queues and getting inside, not only will you realise that this is a veritable tardis but, whatever your knowledge of Renaissance art, you cannot fail to appreciate the magnificence that is all around you.

The gallery is laid out around a courtyard and visitors move in an anti-clockwise direction through a number of rooms. Although some of the paintings are moved from time to time, the best known and most interesting pictures are as follows:

**Sala 1** Paolo Veneziano's *The Coronation of the Virgin Polyptych* (1325) is a good starting point. This altarpiece is hugely complicated, colourful and elaborate, with the detail of the fabric and the glitzy use of gold adorning the majestic subject matter. Painting in Venice at this period was influenced by Byzantine art and wholly confined to liturgical subjects. It was intended

## Tip...

If you can avoid gallery fatigue, the Accademia is a magnificent place from beginning to end that truly succeeds in creating a beautiful, some may say spiritual, experience. Don't let this be brought to an abrupt end by using the toilets...

to nurture awe and create a respectful distance between the viewer and God. Note the *Coronation of the Virgin*, painted a century or so later by Michele Giambono, which shows a continued commitment to the liturgical format but also demonstrates a slightly freer style. There are some sparkling pieces by Vivarini here, too.

**Sala 2** Giovanni Bellini's *San Giobbe altarpiece* (1485) is a nice version of a popular scene showing the Virgin and the saints, including an arrow-strewn St Sebastian. The minstrels here are much more sheepish than Vivarini's in the Frari (see page 118).

**Sala 6** Things start to hot up a bit in sala 6 with the almost surreal *The Creation of Animals* (1552) by Tintoretto, his brutal *Cain and Abel* (1552) and some Veronese panels.

**Sala 7** This room is given over to Lorenzo Lotto's *Portrait of a Gentleman in his Studio* (1528). Lotto, unlike many of his Venetian contemporaries, got out of the city and spent a lot of his life travelling around Italy. Despite their 16th-century dress and hairstyles, his portraits of young men are timeless. Lotto could see through their reticence and painted the turbulence, arrogance and weight of expectation endured by young men in his time. It's the way they hold the viewer's eye that makes these portraits so subtle yet powerful.

**Sala 10** This huge room is generally regarded as the high point of the Accademia. Perhaps the scene stealer is Paolo Veronese's *Feast in the House of Levi* (1573), which got the painter into big trouble with the Inquisition. It was originally called *The Last Supper* and hung in Santi Giovanni e Paolo.

# Around the city

The Inquisition wanted Veronese to replace the little dog in the picture with a depiction of the Madonna. When he refused they hauled him in and questioned him about the inclusion of this as well as German guards, clowns, drunkards and dwarfs in such a holy scene. Veronese argued that while these characters appear in the same picture, they are not "within the place where the supper is being held". Technically he is correct, for these characters revel and hang about behind balustrades and columns. The Inquisition sent him on his way, demanding that he amend the picture but the only thing he altered was the title.

Tintoretto's *The Stealing of St Mark* (1562) seems more of a collage than an oil painting: the detail of the picture sits on an almost monochrome architectural background. It is very different from the theatrically chaotic style of *The Miracle of St Mark Freeing a Slave* (1548), which hangs to the side of it. This painting created some controversy: although the Venetians had 'abolished' slavery, the idea of St Mark freeing slaves caused outrage among Venice's ruling elite.

*Pietà* (1577), considered Titian's last painting although it was finished by Palma Giovane, has none of the rich, robust colours for which he was famous but, instead, has a roughness and a eerie quality to it. The translucent flesh of the dead Christ draped over Mary Magdalene will make your hair stand on end.

The art high you may experience in Sala 10 often leads to a subsequent crash in enthusiasm and energy which makes appreciating much else after the great room difficult. However, if you've got the stamina, there is much to enjoy in the remaining galleries:

**Sala 13** Giorgione's *Tempest* (1507) is hung in a smaller room, which adds to the feeling of enclosure created by the dark clouds that threaten the naked young woman breastfeeding her child. The moodiness of the environment and the vulnerability of the subject is unnerving. Alongside it, his other famous painting, *La Vecchia* (1505), is of a lined old woman who looks at the viewer almost accusingly and holds a document that warns *'Col Tempo'* (in time) as a reminder to all.

**Sala 16** Despite the potentially violent subject matter, Giambattista Tiepolo's *The Rape of Europa* (1725), painted some years after the Renaissance, has a gentle, indulgent feel with the only crime being an angel in the cloud peeing on his winged chum. *Diana and Acteon* (1732) is a depiction of the classical myth in which Diana, infuriated by Acteon's peeping-Tom antics, turns him into a stag which is then devoured by his own hounds. Here Acteon's horns suggest his fate is already sealed.

Above: *Feast at the House of Levi* by Paolo Veronese.
Opposite page: *Cain and Abel* by Tintoretto.

# Titian (1490-1576)

Born in Pieve di Cadore in the Veneto, Tiziano Vecelli came from a well-to-do family. He and his brother were sent to Venice to be apprenticed to the mosaicist Sebastian Zuccato and lodged with a family friend, Giovanni Bellini (1430-1516, son of Jacopo and brother of Gentile). He worked in Bellini's studio alongside Giorgione (c1477-1510) before making his own way as a painter.

After a short spell in Padua, Titian returned to Venice. Around this time his two great friends and mentors, Giorgione and Bellini died, leaving the 26-year-old Titian to complete many of the works that Bellini had left unfinished at his death. This position gave him influence and contact with the Venetian elite from which he won many prestigious commissions. Their deaths also allowed Titian to free himself from the styles of his masters and to create his own epic approach to composition, using bigger canvases, an abundance of colour and depicting lots of movement. Titian worked for patrons outside Venice (one of the reasons his work is so widely accessible and appreciated) and a number of retainers, which kept him and his family in an affluent position. Titian and, later, his son Orazio died in Venice during the outbreak of the plague in 1576. He is buried in the Frari (see page 118).

Titian is considered the father of the Venetian Renaissance. *The Assumption* in the Frari is considered his most successful work and, perhaps, best encapsulates what he brought to painting: heart-rending movement and fabulous colours. These colours weren't just for adornment but were employed to reveal the passion of the subject. Later, Titian moved away from religious art to paint portraits and scenes from classical mythology (including a number

*The Assumption* by Titian.

of Venuses). However, in old age he returned to religious scenes, finishing his career with the ghostly *Pietà* that can be seen in the Accademia (see page 122): despite the sketchy background and limited palette, it still stirs the emotions of the viewer.

**Sala 20**   The paintings in this room show the Venice of the past. Vittore Carpaccio's *Miracle of the Reliquary of the True Cross* (1494) depicts the Rialto bridge as it once was, while Gentile Bellini's *Miracle of the Cross at San Lorenzo* (1500) and *Procession in Piazza San Marco* (1496) show the city in all its glory, looking much the same as it does today.

**Sala 24**   In the final room hangs Titian's *Presentation of the Virgin* (1538), which was painted for the Scuola della Carità, part of which is now the Accademia. It shows the Virgin, childlike in blue and glowing with holy light, being presented to the Doge. What is interesting is the background: it's not Venice but a view of the Dolomites – perhaps a reminder of the artist's birthplace in Pieve di Cadore near Belluno.

## Collezione Peggy Guggenheim

*Palazzo Venier dei Leoni, Dorsoduro 701,*
*T041-520 6288.*
Apr-Oct daily 1000-2200, Nov-Mar Wed-Mon
1000-1800, €12, free under 10s, €7 students
under 26, €10 over 65s.
Vaporetto: Salute. Map Venice, E6, p82.

Built in the 1750s by Lorenzo Boschetti, the
unfinished Palazzo Venier dei Leoni is a striking
bungalow on the Canal Grande, which was
converted into a modern art gallery by Peggy
Guggenheim in 1951. After just a few moments
inside, you can feel yourself hurled forward into
modernity. However, this museum is far more than
a welcome novelty amongst all the old stuff. It is
the most important collection of cubist, surrealist
and abstract expressionist art in Italy and it is a
monument to the role that one collector can play
in shaping an entire artistic movement. All the

*Le Courier Cycliste (The Racing Cyclist)* by Jean Metzinger.

# Portrait of the art collector

Peggy Guggenheim (1898-1979) was the daughter
of Benjamin Guggenheim (who died on the *Titanic*)
and the niece of the multi-millionaire Solomon
R Guggenheim, whose foundation runs the
Guggenheim museums in Berlin, New York, Bilbao
and Las Vegas. An adventurer and a bohemian, she
was drawn to the artistic community although she
herself never painted. She moved to Paris when she
was 22 and began befriending and collecting the
work of avant garde artists. Although she is known
to have had a few passionate affairs with some
artists, Peggy was no groupie. Collecting wasn't
about acquisition to her: it was about funding the
creation of new work. She had a very sharp eye and a
keen business sense but, more than that, she utterly
believed in art and the role of the artist and was
totally committed to the new.

The first gallery she opened was in Cork Street
in London in 1938, where she showed Kandinsky,
Yves Tanguy, Constantin Brancusi, Hans Arp, Max
Ernst and Picasso. It lasted only a year and wasn't a
commercial success but created a buzz and opened
up the market for these and other artists. Plans
for another bigger museum of contemporary art
in London were scuppered when war broke out.
Instead, she began to amass the greater part of her
collection, buying works by Magritte, Man Ray, Dalí
and Klee. She stashed the pieces in a house in the
south of France and then fled to New York with Max
Ernst, who became her second husband. (She had
been married to the Dadaist Laurence Vail for a short
period, which produced two children, Sinbad and
Pegeen.) After the war she was reunited with her art
and her artist friends for the defining exhibition of
the age, *Art of the Century*, curated by herself. This
was a group show that combined her European
finds and the work of Americans, such as Willem de
Kooning, Jackson Pollock and Mark Rothko.

Her marriage to Ernst didn't last long – although
their friendship continued until his death – and
she moved to Venice in 1948 where she exhibited
some of her collection at the Biennale. She bought
Palazzo Venier dei Leoni and opened the gallery in
1951. Peggy remained an 'It' girl despite being well
into her 70s, threw the biggest and best parties and
was seen about town in her very own gondola and
outrageous sunglasses. Her legacy to 20th-century
art is as important as that of any of the great artists
she discovered.

Santa Maria della Salute.

recognized genres of modern art are represented: cubism (Jean Metzinger's *Le Coureur Cycliste,* 1914); futurism (Umberto Boccioni's *Dynamism of a Speeding Horse + Houses*, 1915); Dadaism (Hans Arp's *Overturned Blue Shoe with Two Heels Under a Black Vault*, 1925); surrealism (Salvador Dalí's *Birth of Liquid Desires*, 1932), and abstract expressionism (Jackson Pollock's *The Moon Woman*, 1942).

Although the palazzo has been given the 'white cube' treatment, there is still a sense that this is a domestic space. The galleries are on the ground floor and the basement, with an excellent café at the back and a shop on fondamenta Venier that is well worth a peruse.

### Galleria di Palazzo Cini

*Piscina Forner, Dorsoduro 864,*
*T041-521 0755, cini.it.*
Opening hours vary – phone for details.
Vaporetto: Accademia.
Map Venice, D6, p82.

A gallery showing Tuscan and Ferrarese art seems strangely out of place in Venice but refreshingly so. This gallery is based in Vittorio Cini's old palace and displays 14th- and 15th-century paintings by artists such as Fra Filippo Lippi, Sandro Botticelli and Piero di Cosimo. There is also some furniture, including a fabulous 14th century marriage chest from Siena, and interesting objects in silver and ivory.

### Santa Maria della Salute

*Campo della Salute, Dorsoduro 1b, T041-274 3928.*
Daily 0900-1200 and 1500-1730.
Vaporetto: Salute. Map Venice, E6, p82.

Sitting towards the end of the Canal Grande near the Dogana di Mare (customs house) and almost directly across from piazza San Marco is the church of St Mary of Good Health. It is known by locals as 'La Salute' and, unsurprisingly, holds a special place in the city's collective heart, since it was built in thanks at the end of the terrible plague of 1630 that took 80,000 Venetian lives (more than the current population).

Baldassare Longhena was only 26 when he won the commission to design this Baroque crown and it was completed 50 years later, just before he died. Longhena wanted to create a church that was utterly unique, yet admitted he was inspired by Palladio's Redentore (see page 133) and also by La Rotonda (see page 224). The foundations of the church had to be rock solid, so 100,000 pinewood logs were driven vertically into the ground to support it.

La Salute is so big inside it would struggle to be anything other than stark but this simplicity and spaciousness gives it an evocative solemnity. The two most spectacular artworks are Titian's *St Mark Enthroned with Saints Cosmas, Damian, Roch and Sebastian* (1512) and Tintoretto's *Wedding at Cana* (1551).

On the 21st of November the **Festa della Madonna della Salute** (see page 61) sees the great and the good of the city process from San Marco to La Salute across a specially created bridge to offer thanks for deliverance from the plague.

### Dogana di Mare

*Punta della Dogana di Mare, Dorsoduro.*
Vaporetto: Salute. Map Venice, E6, p82.

At the eastern tip of Dorsoduro, where it stretches out into the Bacino di San Marco, is the Dogana di Mare, a customs post built in the 1400s and replaced in the 17th century. The turret was built by Giuseppe Benoni in 1677 and the golden globe, the Palla d'Oro, was cast by Bernardo Falcone in the same year. The globe is secured by two bronze statues of Atlas, with Fortuna, the Goddess of good fortune, on top, balancing on one leg and waving a standard. The flat-arched, triangular building served as salt warehouses, the Magazzini al Sal, which were rebuilt in a neo-classical style in 1838. The building is now owned by François Pinault, an illustrious art collector, and is due to open as a contemporary art gallery in time for the Biennale in 2009. However, the tarpaulin wrappings may be on the Dogana for some time.

### Squero

*Rio di San Trovaso, Dorsoduro 1097.*

This boatyard is where Venice's gondolas have been crafted since the 17th century. The workshops are housed in picturesque Alpine-style huts and, although they are not open to the public, you can view the craftsmen at work (and smoking copious fags and chatting) from across the rio di San Trovaso.

## Gondola! Gondola!

A gondola is 11 m long and weighs 600 kg. Despite this weight, a single person with a single oar can easily handle it. Flat-based, it glides across the water, avoiding problems caused by variations in depth, and is slightly wider on the left side which allows it to be manoeuvred without a rudder. Eight different types of wood are used in the construction and each boat is made up of 280 pieces. The iron stabilizer at the head of the gondola has six prongs to symbolize the six *sestieri* of Venice. Following the sumptuary laws of 1562, all gondolas are painted black.

If you fancy a trip on one of Venice's iconic craft, look for men in striped jerseys and hats shouting *"gondola, gondola!"* near canals or call T041-528 5075. The gondoliers are part of a small fraternity who have plied their trade for over 500 years. A gondola ride doesn't come cheap – €80 for 40 minutes (€110 between 1900 and 0800), then €40 or €50 for every 20 minutes thereafter – so if there's a group of you, all the better. If you're a hard-nosed negotiator you might be able to get a better deal but don't count on it: gondoliers are a proud bunch.

## Around the city

### Ponte dei Pugni

*Rio de Santa Barbara, Dorsoduro.*
Vaporetto: Ca' Rezzonico. Map Venice C5, p82.

This bridge is one of a few where foot marks have been created in the corners. These were to aid the positioning of participants in the many organized punch ups between the hostile factions, the Nicolotti (from the area around San Nicolò dei Mendicoli in Dorsoduro) and the Castellani (from San Pietro di Castello on the other side of the city). The street fights between these gangs were ignored or perhaps even condoned by the authorities for years (two groups fighting each other being better than one group looking for a fight) but were finally banned following the 'war of the fists' in 1705, after they started to get totally out of hand.

### Ca' Rezzonico &
### Museo del Settecento Veneziano

*Fondamenta Rezzonico, Dorsoduro 3136,*
*T041-520 4036.*
Summer daily 1000-1700, winter Sat-Thu 0900-1600, €6.50, €4.50 concession.
Vaporetto: Ca' Rezzonico. Map Venice, D5, p82.

Baldassarre Longhena designed this Baroque palazzo in 1648 for the Bon family but it was finished by Georgio Massari 107 years later for its new owners, the Rezzonico family. As fortunes were lost and won, it continued to change hands and was divided and let out to well-to-do tenants. It is famous for being the house where Robert Browning lived out his last days before his death in 1889. It now houses the museum of 18th-century Venice, documenting the history of rich Venetians at the time, and is famous for its paintings and ornate furnishings.

On the first floor, the *trompe l'œil* architectural frescoes in the grand ballroom are by Pietro Visconti and are topped on the ceiling by a fresco of Apollo's chariot by Giovanni Battista Crosato, which seems to tumble out of its frame. The gilded chandeliers hang low but are stunning. The Sala dell'Allegoria Nuziale also has a heavenly chariot, this time by Giovanni

Ca'Rezzonico.

Battista Tiepolo. There's another Tiepolo – the *Allegory of Merit Between Nobility and Virtue* (1758) – in the throne room, which has lots of 3-D angels soaring through the air.

Ascending to the second floor, Giorgio Massari's staircase is crowned by two enormous Murano chandeliers. In the Portego dei Dipinti are two works by Antonio Canal, better known as Canaletto: *View of the Rio dei Mendicanti* (1725) and *The Grand Canal seen from Ca' Balbi toward the Rialto* (c1720). The only other Canaletto in the city is *Perspective* (1765) in the Accademia. At the end of the passageway are the Villa Ziniago rooms with Giandomenico Tiepolo's *New World* frescoes (1791), his comical paintings of *Pulcinella* (1797), the *Commedia dell'Arte* character, and a series of atmospheric monochromes (1759). In the Sala del Parlatorio, Francesco Guardi's *The Parlour of the Nuns of San Zaccaria* (1768) shows the dancing, feasting and general bad behaviour that was typical of the nunnery. His other piece, *Ridotto* (1748), shows the carnival. The Sala del Longhi is devoted to work by Pietro Longhi, the 18th-century realist painter who developed the 'conversation piece', a painting that showed engagement and shared activity: *The Lady and the Hairdresser* (1760) is a good example. Still on the second floor is the Sala dell'Alcove, which has an 18th-century wood-panelled recessed bed and a pastel drawing of the *Praying Madonna*, by Rosalba Carriera (1675-1752), one of the only female painters of this era. In the remaining rooms are some works by Venetian artists from the 15th to the 20th centuries, a puppet theatre and fittings from an old apothecary.

## San Sebastiano

*Fondamenta di San Sebastiano, Dorsoduro 1687, T041-275 0642.*
Mon-Sat 1000-1700, Sun 1300-1700,
€3 or Chorus Pass (see page 102).
Vaporetto: San Basilio. Map Venice, B6, p82.

San Sebastiano is strangely one of Venice's lesser known churches but it is one of the most joyful and remarkable. Veronese was allowed to run wild in this small neighbourhood church and the result? Every surface is festooned with colour, life and interest. In fact, his architectural effects are so beguiling that they seem to change the internal dimensions of the building itself: you don't know what is painting and what is relief. He started off in 1555 painting the panels in the sacristy depicting the martyrdom of the evangelists (look out for St Mark with, unusually, a black lion). It seems Veronese could find beauty and vivaciousness even in the untimely demise of a saint. For the next ten years he spent all his spare time here, painting the walls and ceilings of the nave with extravagantly clad figures, animals, fruits and foliage. He also painted the organ, which is so vividly decorated it becomes something else altogether. He and his son, Benedetto, are buried here.

## Chiesa dell'Angelo Raffaele

*Campo Angelo Raffaele, Dorsoduro 1721, T041-522 8548.*
Mon-Sat 0900-1200 & 1600-1800.
Vaporetto: San Basilio. Map Venice, B6, p82.

Made famous by Sally Vicker's novel, *Miss Garnet's Angel* (2000), this church feels like your grandmother's house: all antimacassars, swirling carpets, lacy tablecloths, pot plants and busy colour combinations. But it is so cherished and well looked after by local parishioners, who bustle about doing their chores, that you can't help but feel humbled by their devotion. A church has stood here since the eighth century but this building was not completed until the 17th. Its orientation is a bit confusing and the real focal point is not the altar but the organ. Here, Giovanni Antonio Guardi, with some help from his brother, Francesco, painted five scenes from the story of Tobias and his guardian angel Raphael, the protector of travellers and a healer. In addition to the paintings, there are sculptures of Tobias and Raphael above the organ (including a glistening gold fish) and over the entrance portal.

## San Nicolò dei Mendicoli

*Campo San Nicolò, Dorsoduro 1907, T041-475 0382.*
Mon-Sat 0900-1200 & 1600-1800.
Vaporetto: San Basilio. Map Venice, B6, p82.

*Mendicoli* were vagrants who lived in this poor part of town. Despite its lowly character, this church has a quiet dignity that you just don't feel in the city's larger, more opulent churches. It is a 13th-century Byzantine structure with a rare loggia at the front that was made famous in Nicolas Roeg's spooky *Don't Look Now* (1973), in which Donald Sutherland's character is involved in the renovation of the church. (Around the same time the Venice in Peril fund was doing extensive work to repair the damage done during the 1966 floods.) Inside it is even more unusual: the compact interior has been made smaller still by a carved, wooden internal structure that looks something like an elaborate pen. There is little by way of notable artworks here but lots of elaborate gilded wood columns and statues and a fantastic circular painting on the ceiling.

# The islands & the lagoon

The Venetian lagoon is a partially enclosed, shallow saltwater basin and is the largest wetland in the Mediterranean. It has a unique aqua culture that lagoon dwellers have harvested down the ages. It is fed by the rivers Sile and Brenta and by the tides of the Adriatic that stream though the inlets of the lagoon's land barrier at Lido, Malamocco and Chioggia. Rising sea levels and the increasing frequency of *acqua alta* (high tide), when water levels in the lagoon rise to over 1 m, have prompted the construction of the controversial MOSE (Modulo Sperimentale Elettromeccanico) barrier to isolate the lagoon from the Adriatic (see also page 57).

Venetians use the lagoon in the same way that most city-dwellers would use a park. This is where they go to escape the crowds, negotiating the *briccola* (wooden piles that stick out of the water) and using their knowledge of the sandbanks to reach little islands where they fish, dig clams and picnic.

Beyond the man-made city are 34 other islands: some are no more than marshy flats, some have deserted convents or forts, whilst others have trees, crops, vineyards and beaches. In the northern lagoon are San Michele, Murano, Burano, Torcello and Sant'Erasmo; to the south, San Giorgio Maggiore, San Servolo, San Lazzaro and the Lido. The vaporetti routes around the lagoon require a little time to negotiate but are remarkably efficient and reliable.

The main island between Dorsoduro and the Lido is **Giudecca**, a 2 km long stretch of land known as the '*Spinalonga*' (long spine). It is a largely residential island, famous for July's Festa del Redentore, centred around Il Redentore church, and for the illustrious Hotel Cipriani, considered the city's number one hotel for the rich and famous. In the channel of water between Giudecca and the Lido are a number of smaller islands, including **San Servolo** and **San Lazzaro degli Armeni** that, over the years, have served as monasteries, gardens, vineyards, hospitals, churches, leper colonies and quarantines for sailors, incomers and victims of the plague. The **Lido** is the strip of land that acts as the lagoon's barrier to the Adriatic sea. At its

southernmost tip is Malamocco, which served as Venice's first administrative centre from the eighth century (see page 30). Beyond that is the long, thin island of **Pellestrina**, which stretches down towards Chioggia on the mainland.

### Isola di San Giorgio Maggiore

Vaporetto: 82 from San Zaccaria to San Giorgio. Map Venice, G7, p83.

Separated from the main city by the Canale di San Marco, this island lies just to the east of Giudecca. There was a church here as early as the ninth century and the Benedictine monastery of San Giorgio was established in 982 but it wasn't until 1580, on the completion of Palladio's church with its gleaming white façade, that San Giorgio Maggiore became one of the symbolic images of 'La Serenissima'.

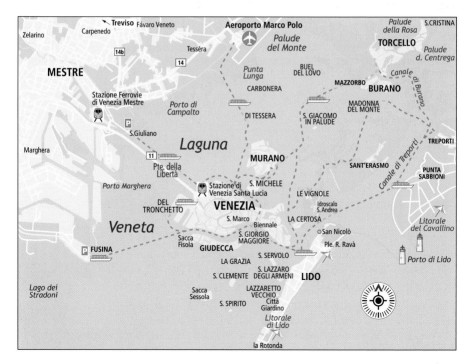

San Giorgio Maggiore.

The first stone of **Chiesa di San Giorgio Maggiore** (T041-522 7827, museum daily 0930-1200 and 1430-1800) was laid in 1566 but it wasn't completed until 14 years later, after Palladio's death, by Vincenzo Scamozzi and the city's *Proto* (chief architect), Simone Sorella. The frontage consists of two façades: a tall one on top of a wider one. The two entablatures and the four immense columns of the former create a feeling of depth and strength. However, it is only when you look at this building in profile, particularly from the Arsenale, that its vast scale becomes apparent. Inside, the high nave, with its two gently sloping aisles and perfectly proportioned columns, leads your eye heavenwards to the supremacy of the domed ceiling. This isn't an overly ornate church; its beauty resides instead in its architectural features, such as the exquisitely carved half-moon choir stall. On the right transept, Sebastiano Ricci's lavishly coloured *The Coronation of the Virgin* (1708) gives a bountiful,

**Tip...**

A lift (€3) takes you 60 m up to the top of the campanile where you can have your breath taken away by 360-degree views of the city and the lagoon.

Baroque interpretation to this traditional religious subject. On both sides of the nave are numerous epic works by Tintoretto. The piece that stands out is his version of the *Last Supper* (1594). Darker and more complex than most depictions of the scene, it features a swirling mass of angels within the light that shines from a lamp and from Jesus himself.

In 1951, the buildings and grounds of the monastery were bought by the **Fondazione Giorgio Cini** (T041-528 9900, cini.it, May-Sep daily 0930-1230 and 1430-1830, Oct-Apr daily 0930-1230 and 1430-1630, €12/10), which spent 19 years and millions of lire restoring them. The most stunning piece of restoration work are the cloisters by Palladio, whose cool white symmetry creates a perfect mirror image: even the four cypresses in the middle seem to be copying each other. Alongside the cloisters is the 17th-century library by Baldassare Longhena, with balconied bookcases that are bathed in light. They contain a rare book collection donated to the monastery by Cosimo de' Medici, the former ruler of Florence, who sought sanctuary in Venice when he was exiled from his own city in 1433. Don't miss the chance to walk along to the semi-circular **Teatro Verde**, an outdoor theatre that is popular in the summer (especially with guests of the Hotel Cipriani who can boat across the small channel between Giudecca and the island). There's another cloister, too, the Chiostro degli Allori by Andrea Buora (1526).

## Gesu Cristo Redentore

*Campo Redentore, Giudecca 194, T041-275 0462.*
Mon-Sat 1000-1700, Sun 1300-1700,
€3 or Chorus Pass
Vaporetto: 41 and 82 from San Zaccaria
to Redentore.

Designed by Palladio and completed in just five years, Il Redentore was Venice's first great monument thanking the Redeemer for deliverance from the plague, which had decimated the city's population in 1575 (see page 36). The dimensions of the columns, the dome and front steps were calculated with such precision to ensure a feeling of order and perfection. When the foundation stone was laid, Doge Sebastiano Venier processed across the water from San Marco to the church on a pontoon of eighty galleys. This ceremony is repeated annually on the third Saturday of July, accompanied by a magnificent firework display.

## Museo della Follia (Museum of Madness)

*San Servolo, T041-524 0119.*
Open for pre-booked guided tours only
Mon-Thu 0930-1530.
Vaporetto: 20 from San Zaccaria to San Servolo.

This complex was formerly a Benedictine monastery and nunnery but in 1725 the Venetian authorities designated it a hospital for the region's mentally ill. Initially, the inmates were male patients from well-off families but gradually poorer men were also admitted, most of whom were suffering from pellagra, a condition that affects the nervous system and is brought on by malnutrition, specifically a deficiency of vitamin B.

The tour takes you to a number of rooms filled with artefacts from the hospital's history, including straightjackets, shackles, electrotherapy machines and evidence of the numerous medical tests that were carried out on the patients' blood, tissue and brains. However, despite these disturbing pieces from the institution's past, there is a sense in which this hospital, as it developed, believed you could rehabilitate patients with mental health problems. 'Before-and-after' pictures of patients from the late 19th century show dishevelled men suffering from malnourishment, alcohol problems, *'lipemania con stupore'* and *'senza furore'*, transformed into clean, groomed, healthy-looking men who were then returned to the community. Less positive are the pictures of the women who came here from 1830 onwards and who do not seem to have been reassimilated so successfully.

The wooden pharmacy, with its big mortars and pestles, lion-decorated jars of herbs (all grown on the island) and old medicinal recipe books, is charming. However, the lasting memory will be of the autopsy room, dominated by the marble table and the case full of skulls and plasticated brains. When the hospital closed in 1978 and the last patient was transferred, the builders found huge quantities of preserved brains in plastic bags.

## Around the city

### Monastero Mekhitarista

*San Lazzaro degli Armeni, T041-526 0104.*
Open by appointment only, daily 1530-1700, €6.
Vaporetto: 20 from San Zaccaria to San Lazzaro.

San Lazzaro degli Armeni is a functioning monastery of the Armenian order of the Mekhitarist fathers. Formerly a leper colony, then a hospice for pilgrims, it had fallen into ruin by the end of the 17th century. Mekhitar, the monastery's founder, was born at Sebaste in Armenia in 1676. He entered an Armenian Catholic monastery as a young man and became a priest but, after joining the Roman Catholic church, created his own religious institute that sought to promote culture and learning. His order migrated to Venice in 1715 and the authorities let them build a monastery on San Lazzaro. Mekhitar died in 1749.

The tour of the monastery takes you through the cloister and into the Byzantine church, rich with blue mosaic work and golden arches. It also takes you to the library which houses some of the thousands of texts that the monks looked after or published in their on-site printing works. Lord Byron was a regular visitor to the monastery during his sojourn in Venice from 1816 to 1819, swimming from Palazzo Mocenigo on the Grand Canal to San Lazzaro in order to find solace and spiritual fulfilment. He studied Armenian in the library and repaid the monks' hospitality by translating many of their most important texts into English.

You will also visit rooms stacked with amazing gifts to the monastery from loyal donors: these include ceramics, jewellery, silver, a strange Chinese ivory contemplation ball and an Egyptian sarcophagus and mummy. The tour ends in the new cylindrical book vault, which protects the monastery's 40,000 books, some of which date back to the 14th century.

There were once 100 monks living and working here; now there are just 14. Seeing their favourite pickles and condiments lined up beside each place in the wood-panelled refectory is rather humbling. You're unlikely to see the monks while you are here, as they are not allowed to speak to anyone. However, there is a shop where you can buy souvenirs, books about the monastery and homemade rose petal jam (€8).

### Lido di Venezia

Vaporetto: 1, 51, 82 or LN from San Zaccaria or 61 from Zattere.

Famed for its beaches and film festival (see page 155), Lido is worth a day trip if you're in Venice for a week or more and is just a 15 minute vaporetto ride from the city. However, the **Spiaggia Comunale** (the beach on the Adriatic side) can be rather polluted and overcrowded in the middle of summer and the well-run private beaches charge around €60 for parasols, deck chairs and cabins. If you're after a bit more seclusion, take bus B southwest towards **Alberoni** and **Pellestrina**, where there are tranquil beaches, characterized by sand dunes, fishermen's nets and silence. You'll find quiet roads and tracks for cycling, and a golf course, too. There are no beach bars or ice cream sellers here, though, so you'll need to bring your own provisions.

The northern lagoon has a number of distinct little communities. **Murano** and **Burano**, famous for their artisan wares have populations of 7000 and 4000 respectively, but **Torcello**, once the nerve centre of the lagoon, is home to just 20 people and feels almost abandoned, despite its extraordinary cathedral. **Sant'Erasmo**, the garden of Venice, is a haven for those seeking escape

A Lido beach hut.

from the man-built city and provides cycle paths and golden shores for those who make the hour-long journey. And, of course, closest to the city is the cemetery at **San Michele**, a growing community of sorts but one that is silent.

## Cimitero di San Michele

*Isola di San Michele, T041-729811.*
Apr-Sep daily 0730-1800, Oct-Mar daily 0730-1600.
Vaporetto: 41 from Fondamente Nuove to
Cimitero. Map Venice, G/H1, p83.

In 1797 the Napoleonic authorities decreed that bodies would no longer be buried in Venice itself but would be interred at a new cemetery on San Michele. The great and the good of the city were transported to their final resting place on exquisite swagged gondolas and buried in elaborate marble tombs. Today, the deceased still get the gondola ride but, with space on the island at a premium, they are interred for just a few years before being exhumed and placed in a unit, stacked up like drawers in a filing cabinet. However, the cool cedars and fragrant bushes make the cemetery a pleasant, if slightly maudlin, place to visit. There are several elaborate gates studded around the red boundary walls but visitors enter from the west side. (Check out the map at the entrance before embarking on your search for the oldest graves.) To the left is a pleasant cloister and beyond that the lovely Renaissance church of **San Michele** in **Isola**, which was built by Mauro Codussi in 1469 and is looked after by Franciscan monks who shuffle about quietly. To the right is a curved pavilion, which houses some of the more grandiose mausoleums. These are the size of a beach hut and, if you look through the glass, you can see ornate stone tombs and decorated altars inside. Some have become dusty ruins, while others are still dressed with fresh flowers. The family graves have large numbers of occupants making it possible to trace back a whole family tree from just one grave. The northeast section of the cemetery is the resting place for non-Catholics, including the writer Ezra Pound, the impresario Sergei Diaghilev and the composer Igor Stravinsky.

Cimitero di San Michele.

**Tip...**

From July to September the cemetery is visited by horseflies and other flying *insetti* so cover your ankles and feet. It is also advisable to wear rubber-soled shoes to prevent yourself slipping on or marking the marble gravestones that are laid flat on the ground.

## Murano

Vaporetto: DM, 41 to Colonna.

Murano is the centre of the glass-blowing trade. This was based in the city until the 14th century when the authorities, terrified of the fire hazard from the furnaces, moved all glass production out to the island. Murano glass and mirrors were one of Venice's most desirable exports, so any glassmaker thought to have left the island or to have told secrets of the trade faced the state Inquisitors with the real threat of exile or even execution.

Some of the different types of glass created in Murano include *millefiori* (which has a number of colours spun through it), *aventurine* (glass with tiny strands of gold embedded in it) and *lattimo* (a 'milky', opaque glass). Murano today is awash with tat but it still has a number of foundries where real artisans struggle to keep the trade alive. It also has a glass museum, the **Museo del Vetro** (fondamenta Giustinian 8, Murano, T041-739586, Nov-Mar Thu-Tue 1000-1700, Apr-Oct Thu-Tue

## Around the city

1000-1800, €5.50), with a beautiful collection of glass and mirrors. If you are considering buying Murano glass, a trip to the museum is good way to start researching this artisan product.

### Burano

Vaporetto: LN to Burano.

Burano is a beguiling fishing village with brightly painted houses and a horde of lace shops. It's a pleasant place to stroll around, photographing the multi-coloured *calli* and eating ice cream; kids will enjoy running around the open spaces. Historically, the women of Burano stayed at home making lace while their husbands were out fishing. They developed their own distinctive style using the *punto in aria* (stitch in the air) method, where lace is created on its own using needles, not worked onto a woven fabric. If you are interested in lace and are considering buying some, make sure you can tell the real deal from the Chinese mass-produced imports. **Scuola di Merletti** (piazza Galuppi 187, Burano, T041-730034, Apr-Oct Wed-Mon 1000-1700, Oct-Mar Mon, Wed-Sun 1000-1600, €6/4) shows some complicated yet beautiful examples of Burano lacework through the ages from the 17th century to today.

### Torcello

Vaporetto: LN to Burano then T to Torcello.

After Venice's man-made riches, the beauty of desolate, overgrown Torcello will take you by surprise. From the seventh to the 13th centuries Torcello was the dominant city of the lagoon, with a population of 20,000 people and its own bishop. However, as the status of Venice increased and the waters around Torcello began to silt up, people moved away from the island, taking the stones of their houses with them to build new homes in Venice. All that remains today are two churches, a campanile, a couple of *locanda* and 20 inhabitants.

After alighting from the vaporetto, walk along the only path into a central square. The first building on your right is the well proportioned **Chiesa di Santa Fosca**, a 12th-century church with a gentle dome and arcaded porticos supported by Corinthian columns. It has a lovely pulpit suspended by columns above a mosaic floor and a beautiful iconostasis with peacocks supping from the fountain of youth.

To the right of the church sits the huge, haunting **Cattedrale di Santa Maria Assunta** (T041-270 2464, Apr-Oct daily 1030-1730, Nov-Mar daily 1030-1630, €5.50 or €8 including the campanile). The cathedral was founded in the seventh century, although what you see today consists largely of extensions dating from the ninth to the 11th centuries. Its vastness is almost chilling and is a welcome relief on a scorching hot day. The cathedral is renowned for its astounding Byzantine mosaics by an unknown artist who is believed to have studied in Salonica in the eighth or ninth

A family home in Murano.

Above: Burano at night.
Below: Mosaics at Cattedrale di Santa Maria Assunta.

century. Covering the entire inside façade of the nave, the *Last Judgement* has a narrative of Jesus' crucifixion at the top and five other levels depicting the progress of the dead through limbo and judgement, with resurrection for the righteous and the terrible furnace of hell for the sinners. Although the mosaics may be stylistically simple, they are undeniably potent and fearsome. The golden apse mosaics of the Madonna with baby Jesus were probably done by Turkish craftsmen and are revered as one of the best examples of Byzantine art. Climb the campanile for expansive views of the lagoon that confirm Torcello's isolation.

Next door are two small museums (if they are closed, ask someone near the lace stalls for the key): the **Palazzo del Consiglio** houses fragments of the mosaics taken from the cathedral during the rather ham-fisted renovation in the 19th century, as well as some Roman jewellery and small statues, and a collection of architectural stones, mosaics and wellheads propped up against the wall downstairs. The **Palazzo dell'Archivo**, meanwhile,

exhibits archaeological finds, such as Roman and Egyptian implements and figurines. Outside the museums is a squat little stone lump which may be an ancient judge's chair but is reputed to be Attila's Throne: the famous Hun was known to have raided this area during the Dark Ages.

# Bike ride round Sant'Erasmo

The beaches of Sant'Erasmo are where many Venetians flock in the summer months to escape the heat of the city and the tourists. This island is known as the garden of Venice as much of the city's fresh produce is grown here. This classic bike route is recommended by **Luca Giannini**, whose grandparents were originally from Venice. His family now live in Mestre and he's currently studying in Florence but he loves to cycle round the Venetian islands whenever he gets a chance.

**Length**  9 km/3 hrs (allow longer for a slower pace).

**When to do it**  The light is beautiful in the summer, especially during the morning and late afternoon but Sant'Erasmo is very exposed so you'd have to be a mad dog or an Englishman to cycle here in the midday sun; if you must, wear a hat. I like this ride in the winter months but it can be very cold so wear warm clothes.

**What to bring**  There is only one food shop on the island (on the last stretch of this ride) so bring your own water and provisions.

Sant'Erasmo is famous for its tender purple artichokes.

The verdant fields of Sant'Erasmo.

**Start** Take vaporetto 13 from Fondamente Nuove to San'Erasmo Capannone. You can hire a bike from the Lato Azzurro co-operative just where the vaporetto stops, although it is closed for one month from late December. Check the times of the boat back, then get on your bike and head south, following the coastal track that takes you anti-clockwise around the island. The first 4 km of the route are on smooth tarmac but thereafter it's a dirt track.

**En route** Your first and last views will be of the beautiful Venice skyline. You'll also see the **Torre Massimiliana** at the southern tip of Sant'Erasmo, where Emperor Maximilian sought sanctuary during the League of Cambrai in 1507. Just beyond it, the sandy beach on the eastern side of Sant'Erasmo is the place to stop to eat your *spuntino* (picnic). During public holidays and at weekends it can be busy with Venetians but during the week, especially in the morning, you may have

the sand to yourself. Some beautiful birds make their home here: curlews, sandpipers, ruffs and spotted redshanks wade around the sandbanks in the Seca del Bacàn between the island and the Lido harbour.

You may see people working in the fields as you cycle along the eastern shore. Not all of Sant'Erasmo is given over to agriculture but those areas that are cultivated can be very colourful with the purple of local artichokes and smell wonderful in the growing season. Don't be tempted to help yourself; this is someone's livelihood. As you head around the northern tip of Sant'Erasmo and along the western shore, you'll see the small cypress-shaded island of **San Francesco del Deserto**, which St Francis of Assisi visited around 1220. There are big sandbanks just offshore that glow gold in the late afternoon light.

# Sleeping

If you have arrived in Venice without a hotel reservation and need to find a bed for the night, contact the **Associazione Veneziana Albergatori** (T199-0173309, veneziasi.it, Easter-Oct daily 0800-2200, Nov-Easter daily 0800-2100). It has offices at Santa Lucia train station, piazzale Roma and Tronchetto car park.

### Self-catering
**Residence Corte Grimani**
*Corte Grimani, San Marco 4404, T041-241 0719, cortegrimani.com.*
Vaporetto: San Marco. Map Canal Grande, E5, p86.
There are 15 apartments in this central palazzo, all subtly decorated to a high standard. You also benefit from a reception desk with staff who can advise on every possible question about Venice: where to eat, where to shop, etc. Highly recommended for families, especially those with young children. €170-250 per night for a two-roomed apartment.

### Venice Apartments
*T335-568 4147, veniceapartments.org.*
A huge variety of very high quality accommodation, from sumptuous palazzi to chic-but-cheap studio flats, are on offer across all the *sestieri* of Venice. All are well kitted out with everything you need to create a Venetian home from home. The level of service, information and

attention you get is pretty hard to beat. €100-300 per night for a two-roomed apartment.

### San Marco

### Locanda Orseolo €€
*Corte Zorzi, San Marco 1083, T041- 204827, locandaorseolo.com.*
Vaporetto: San Marco.
Map Canal Grande, E5, p86.
Just five minutes from piazza San Marco is this spotless little B&B run by a team of highly motivated young Venetians who are unbeatable ambassadors for their city. The rooms are as neat as a pin and well furnished. The breakfast room is bright and cheery and the breakfasts are ample enough to sustain a doge. Many of the rooms overlook the Orseolo canal but even if yours is on the other side you can still here the gondoliers serenading their passengers with *"O Sole Mio"*.

### Novecento €€
*Calle del Dose, campo San Maurizio, San Marco 2683/84, T041-241 3765, novecento.biz.*
Vaporetto: San Marco/Santa Maria del Giglio.
Map Canal Grande, C7, p86.
The decor of this hotel plays on Venice's eastern links. Owned by the Romanelli family, who also run the nearby **Hotel Flora** €€ (calle XXII Marzo, San Marco 2283/A, T041-520 5844, hotelflora.it), this new venture builds on their well-earned

Above: Piazza San Marco.

reputation for hospitality. Popular with couples, the mix of modernism and orientalism is very well done. Some of the rooms are quite small but clever use of space along with artisan metal, glass and woodwork makes up for it.

## Castello

### Ca' dei Dogi €€
*Corte Santa Scolastica, Castello 4242, T041-413751, cadeidogi.it.*
Vaporetto: San Zaccaria.
Map Canal Grande, H5, p87.
A few steps away from the Bridge of Sighs lies this modern little hotel with only six rooms. The decor is upmarket, with clean lines and subtle lighting; some rooms even have Jacuzzis. There is also an apartment with a rooftop terrace to let on the top floor. Apart from the price, the big plus is the restaurant downstairs. Of course you'll want to go out and explore but for wiped-out travellers knowing there is somewhere excellent to eat inches away from your bed is a huge bonus.

### La Residenza €€
*Campo Bandiera e Moro, Castello 3608, T041-528 5315, venicelaresidenza.com.*
Vaporetto: San Zaccaria.
Map Venice, H5, p87.
Situated on a lovely *campo* just off Riva degli Schiavoni, La Residenza has visitors coming back year after year. Formerly

owned by the Grittis then the Badoers, its Gothic façade gives you some hint to how grand a home this once was. The 15 simple, no-nonsense bedrooms are a fine size but it's the grand breakfast room with its stuccoed walls and tinkling chandelier that tells of the palazzo's past.

## Cannaregio

### Ca' Pozzo €€
*Sottoportego Ca' Pozzo, Cannaregio 1279, T041-524 0504, capozzoinn.com.*
Vaporetto: Guglie.
Map Venice, D2, p82.
This boutique B&B is in the heart of the ghetto. Combining modern architecture and contemporary art, it will appeal to those who like the comfort of the new. There are 15 bedrooms; some are quite small but all are stylishly designed and fitted with mod cons. Breakfast is served in the chic internal courtyard.

### Ca' Vendramin di Santa Fosca €€
*Fondamenta de Ca' Vendramin, Cannaregio 2400, T041-275 0125, hotelcavendramin.it.*
Vaporetto: San Marcuola/ Ca' d'Oro. Map Venice, E2, p82.
Each of the 11 rooms in this small hotel on a quiet canal are beautifully furnished with original frescoes, antiques and parquet flooring (the classic rooms are on the small side). The gentle 'chink chink 'of china informs you that breakfast is served in the ultra-elegant breakfast room. The hotel bar is open until midnight (late for Venice!).

### Corte Gherardi €€
*Corte Gherardi, salizada San Canzian, Cannaregio, T041-523-7376, cortegherardi.com.*
Vaporetto: Rialto.
Map Canal Grande, G1, p87.
Near Santa Maria dei Miracoli, this gay-friendly B&B has three

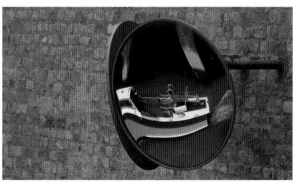
Helping you see round canal corners

chic rooms with great views and comes in at a nice price. You can order breakfast in bed or have it on the roof-top terrace. The owner Teresa speaks fluent English and is full of knowledge and passion for Venice; she will happily tell you where to go to eat and drink. The downside (for some) will be the number of stairs you have to climb.

### La Locanda di Orsaria €€
*Calle Priuli dei Cavalletti, Cannaregio 103, T041-715254, locandaorsaria.com.*
Vaporetto: Ferrovia.
Map Venice, C3, p82.
Right next to the train station, this B&B is in an ideal location for those who don't want heave their luggage across town. The rooms are basic but of good quality and are supplied with mosquito nets so, joy of joys, you can sleep with the windows open, although, be prepared to be woken by the Scalzi bells at 0730. The bathrooms are fresh and the breakfasts are generous.

San Polo & Santa Croce

### Antica Locanda Sturion €€
*Calle del Sturion, San Polo 679, T041- 523 6243, locandasturion.com.*
Vaporetto: San Silvestro.
Map Canal Grande, D3, p86.
Just a few *calle* down from Rialto, this inspirational little 'antique' hotel has featured in numerous paintings and literary works

Rio della Frescada, near San Toma.

about Venice. The 11 rooms are richly swagged and draped in the most Venetian of fabrics and the breakfast room looks out onto the Canal Grande. The stairs can be a bit daunting but the welcome you receive on arrival makes any other hardships worth bearing.

### Hotel Al Ponte Mocenigo €€
*Calle dei Preti, Santa Croce 2063, T041-5244797, alpontemocenigo.com.*
Vaporetto: San Stae.
Map Canal Grande, C1, p86.
Under the Italian system this is classed as a two-star hotel but, with its sophisticated 18th-century-inspired decor, marble bathrooms and Murano glass chandeliers, it feels far more glamorous than that. It has earned a reputation for excellent service and great value, so you'll need to book in advance to secure a room.

### La Villeggiatura €€
*Calle dei Botteri, San Polo 1569, T041-524 4673, lavilleggiatura.it.*
Vaporetto: Rialto Mercato.
Map Canal Grande, C2, p86.
Located at the top of a palazzo (no lift), the six well thought-out rooms in this B&B make the most of the attic space and are bright and immaculate. The B&B is staffed by friendly locals who have some great advice on the neighbourhood and lesser known sights. The breakfast room is light and airy and has a few books and magazines to read while you drink your cappuccino.

Dorsoduro

### Ca' Maria Adele €€€€
*Fondamenta di Salute, Dorsoduro 111, T041-520 3078, camariaadele.it.*
Vaporetto: Salute.
Map Canal Grande, E6, p83.
Ca' Maria Adele is owned by two lads from a Murano glass-blowing family, who wanted to do something different with their hotel. The theatrical and decadent bedrooms are swathed in damask, silk and ostrich feathers, while the public rooms – including a Moroccan inspired terrace – look like film sets and are littered with interesting objects that reference Venice's mercantile past. You'll get an effusive welcome too.

### Ca' Pisani €€€

*Rio Terrà Antonio Foscari, Dorsoduro 979, T041-240 1411, capisani.it.*
Vaporetto: Accademia.
Map Venice, D6, p83.

A frontrunner in the contemporary boutique hotel scene, Ca' Pisani is located right behind the Accademia. The architects and interior designers who overhauled this old building spared no cost, resulting in a

Above: Ca' Maria Adele.

# Get thee to a nunnery!

Venice once had more than 30 convents holding up to 2000 nuns. They were seen as convenient places for the nobility to deposit their youngest or unmarried daughters, particularly as entrance to a nunnery cost 200 ducats, whereas a dowry cost 25,000. The presence of so many inmates with little or no spiritual vocation meant that Venice's convents became infamous for all sorts of immoral behaviour, from feasting and dancing to prostitution. The church generally turned a blind eye to the debauchery until it had other reasons to be annoyed with Venice and then it would swiftly pass a Papal Bull ordering a large number of convents to be closed down. On Napoleon's arrival the nunneries were finally decommissioned and turned into barracks.

Venice now only has a few operational nunneries and monasteries, some of which provide cheap hostel accommodation for students, groups and single travellers. If you are a low-maintenance traveller, who doesn't like to carouse all night, and you are looking for a safe place to stay, a room in a convent or monastery may be ideal. However, bear in mind that these are religious institutions with strict rules, curfews and a religious context that you should respect.

### Casa Caburlotto €

*Fondamenta Rizzi, Santa Croce 316, T041-710877, caburlotto. casaperferie@virgilio.it.*
Vaporetto: Ferrovia.
Map Venice, B5, p83.

Just five minutes from the train station and only €52 per night (including a simple but generous breakfast), this convent offers a peaceful, uncomplicated stay in a variety of basic rooms (all with shower facilities) that will suit single travellers and families. No air conditioning; fans provided on request. There's a curfew at 2230.

### Centro Culturale Don Orione Artigianelli €

*Fondamenta Zattere ai Gesuati, Dorsoduro 909/A, T041-522 4077, donorione-venezia.it.*
Vaporetto: Zattere.
Map Venice, D7, p82.

This is a fairly large hostel, with upwards of 80 beds in single, double and multiple rooms, all with good, clean, private facilities. Public spaces include a gym, TV room and library, so it's good for single travellers who want to meet like-minded people. The curfew here is 0130.

### Istituto San Giuseppe €

*Ponte della Guerra, Castello 5402, T041-522 5352.*
Vaporetto: San Zaccaria.
Map Canal Grande, G4, p87.

Recently refurbished, this hostel offers clean, modern straightforward accommodation for around €43 per person per night. There is no air conditioning and you must be in by 2230. Breakfast is not provided but there are plenty of places to eat nearby.

A gondola glides past the Squero in Dorosduro.

thrilling profusion of comforts and gadgetry that'll have you oohing and aahing in delight. You can breakfast in your room or outside on the Rio Terrà, which is also the perfect location for an evening Spritz.

### La Calcina €€

*Fondamenta Zattere allo Spirito Sante, Dorsoduro 780, T041-520 6466, lacalcina.com.*
Vaporetto: Zattere.
Map Venice, D7, p82.
Situated in arty Dorsoduro and with a bright aspect right on the Zattere, La Calcina is perfect for those who want to be away from the bustle but close enough to the action. The 29 bedrooms (of varying sizes) and public spaces have a 19th-century atmosphere: you can just imagine John Ruskin

rustling his newspaper in the lobby. The restaurant sits on its own breezy deck and serves nicely prepared dishes and calorific *dolci*.

### Pensione Accademia €€

*Fondamenta Bollani, Dorsoduro 1058, T041-521 0188, pensioneaccademia.it.*
Vaporetto: Accademia.
Map Canal Grande, A7, p86.
You may recognise this place from the Katharine Hepburn film, *Summertime*. It's a good old-fashioned Italian *pensione*, full of charm and confidence in knowing what its guests want: friendliness, some outside space and a clean, plump pillow on which to lay your head. It has 27 bedrooms, two large gardens and lovely staff who bustle

about making you feel welcome. The owners also own an excellent canalside restaurant, **Raffaele**, in San Marco (€€, fondamenta Ostreghe, San Marco 2347, T041-523 2317).

### Fujiyama €

*Calle Lunga San Barnaba, Dorsoduro 2727A, T041-724 1042, bedandbreakfast-fujiyama.it.*
Vaporetto: Ca' Rezzonico.
Map Venice, C6, p82.
Upstairs from Venice's only real tea room (see page 154), this restful B&B has four rooms. The Shanghai is the biggest but all are well maintained. Breakfast is served in the shady courtyard – a perfect spot in which to take refuge from the midday sun. The surrounding neighbourhood has lots of shops, bars and restaurants and is within minutes of Ca' Rezzonico, the Accademia and the Peggy Guggenheim collection.

### The islands & the lagoon

### Hotel Cipriani & Palazzo Vendramin €€€€

*Giudecca 10, T041-520 7744, hotelcipriani.com, mid Mar-Oct.*
Vaporetto: Zittelle.
Map Venice, F7, p82.
If you're going to blow the budget in Venice, do it here. From the private launch that picks you up at San Marco to the celebrity-populated poolside bar to the little felt 'Cipriani' shoe bags, everything about this place

is full-on glamour. And it's friendly too: the staff lack any pretence and genuinely just want you to have the best time. Check the website for special offers. The annexe, Palazzo Vendramin, offers more privacy, choicer suites and views of piazza San Marco.

### Locanda Cipriani €€€
*Piazza Santa Fosca 29, Torcello, T041-730150, locandacipriani. com. Wed-Mon only.*
Vaporetto: LN (Laguna Nord) from Fondamente Nuove to Burano, then T to Torcello.
The Cipriani family keep this restaurant with rooms in restful Torcello as a bit of a hobby. You can dine on the terrace, in the garden, the portico or the Gritti room, each one a fitting setting for truly memorable food. What's more, you have the pleasure of being able to toddle upstairs to sleep off the meal of a lifetime. And what a marvellous place to wake up! The rooms are huge and very nicely furnished and breakfast is served in the leafy garden accompanied by the ringing of the cathedral bells.

### Ristorante Antica Dogana Locanda €€
*Via della Ricevitoria 1, Cavallino-Treporti, T041-530 2040, anticadogana.info.*
Vaporetto: LN or 13 from Fondamente Nuove to Treporti.
Cavallino-Treporti is located on the mainland peninsula of Cavallino, northeast of the Lido and about one hour away from the city by vaporetto. It's a marvellously rustic little place to eat and sleep. Maybe it's the sea air but the fish and crustaceans here seem exaggerated in size and flavour. The rooms are not as generous in size but are pleasantly furnished. One word of warning: if you're coming in high season slather yourself in mosquito repellent, as the insects have human appetites out here.

### Villa Casanova €€
*Via Orso Partecipazio 9, Lido, T041- 526 2857, casanovavenice.com.*
Vaporetto: Lido.
Maybe it's because of its location on the laid-back Lido or perhaps it's the adherence to feng shui: whatever the reason, a relaxed vibe will wash over you as soon as you step into this pink house with its leafy green terrace. The stone-walled bedrooms are deliciously cool in summer and the breakfasts are organic. Having the beach just a couple of hundred yards away adds to the sense of wellbeing.

### Il Lato Azzurro €
*Via Forti 13, Sant'Erasmo, T041-523 0642, latoazzurro.it.*
Vaporetto: 13 from Fondamente Nuove to Sant'Erasmo Capannone.
Sant'Erasmo is known as the market garden of Venice and is a world away from the crowded *calli* of the city. This restaurant with six rooms is perfect for outdoorsy types: you can jump on a free bike, cycle around the fields of asparagus and return for some hearty home cooking (€20 for three courses with wine). The bedrooms are plain but spotless. It's a 10 minute walk from the vaporetto stop but they'll pick you up if you call first.

House in Burano.

# Eating & drinking

## Bistrot de Venise €€€€

*Calle dei Fabbri, San Marco 4685,
T041-523 6651, bistrotdevenise.com.*
Daily 1200-0100
(closed 10-25 Dec).
Vaporetto: Rialto.
Map Canal Grande, E5, p86.
This bistro is the guardian of the
oldest, most traditional Venetian
dishes, some of which date back
to the 14th century, such as
*scampi in saor*: sweet and sour
prawns with onions, almonds,
Turkish grapes and spices. Not
only are you served a fine meal
but a historical one at that. The
programme of philosophy and
poetry evenings in the back
room means there is a decidedly
bookish and bohemian clientele.

## Trattoria da Fiore €€

*Calle delle Botteghe, San Marco
3461, T041-523 5310, dafiore.it.*
Restaurant: Wed-Mon
1200-1500 and 1900-2100.
Bar: Wed-Mon 1200-1500
and 1900-2230. Closed 2 weeks
in Aug and Jan.
Vaporetto: San Samuele.
Map Canal Grande, B6, p86.
Whether you just want to
*cicchettare* (snack) at Bar Fiore or
sit down for a full-on, slap-up
dinner in the intimate little
dining rooms, this restaurant
consistently serves well-
prepared vegetables from
Sant'Erasmo and fish from the
lagoon, including a tasty *zuppa
di pesce*. During the Festa del
Redentore the restaurant serves
bountiful plates of *bigoli in salsa*
(fat tubes of pasta with an
anchovy sauce).

## Alla Botte

*Calle della Bisa, San Marco 5482,
T041-520 9775.*
Mon-Wed and Fri-Sat
1000-1500 and 1730-2300,
Sun 1000-1500.
Vaporetto: Rialto.
Map Canal Grande, F3, p86.
Great *cicchetti* and reasonably
priced wine but be prepared to
be jostled by the crowds.

## Bacaro Jazz

*Salizada del Fontego dei
Tedeschi, San Marco 5546,
T041-528 5249.*
Thu-Tue 1600-0300.
Vaporetto: Rialto.
Map Canal Grande, F3, p86.
They say this bar is just for
tourists but you get a great
welcome and there is often
live music.

## Caffè Florian

*Piazza San Marco,
San Marco 56/59, T041-520 5641.*
Apr-Oct daily 1000-2400,
Nov-Mar daily 1000-2300.
Vaporetto: San Marco.
Map Canal Grande, F6, p86.
You'll not see any Venetians at
this famous café but why not
do as every other visitor from
Byron to Ruskin to Kylie has
done and drink coffee while
the orchestra plays?

Above: View from Caffè Florian. Opposite page: Lunchtime diners look on as Daniel Craig,
aka James Bond, prepares to film in Campo San Barnaba.

### Centrale

*Piscina Frezzaria, San Marco
1659b, T041-296 0664.*
Wed-Mon 1900-0200.
Vaporetto: San Marco.
Map Canal Grande, E6, p86.

It's billed as the bar where the
celebs hang out but you may
struggle to recognise anyone in
the photos. However, it's
definitely for the *superbella*!

### Torino@Notte

*Campiello San Luca, San Marco
4592, T041-522 3914.*
Tue-Sat 2000-0100.
Vaporetto: Rialto.
Map Canal Grande, D4, p86.

An unpretentious bar with a
mixed crowd and occasional
live music.

`Castello`

### Corte Sconta €€€

*Calle del Pestrin, Castello 3886,
T041-522 7024.*
Tue-Sat 1230-1400 and
1915-2200 (closed mid Jan-mid
Feb and mid July-mid Aug).
Vaporetto: Arsenale.
Map Venice, H5, p83.

It might seem out of the way for
a bit of fish but this restaurant
has a solid following of foodies.
There is a stark but nicely lit inner
dining room and a vine-laden
garden with canopies that is
perfect for summer nights. If you
are heartless enough, order the
live prawns which will be
barbecued in front of you.

### Al Mascaron €€

*Calle Lunga Santa Maria
Formosa, Castello 5225,
T041-522 5995.*
Mon-Sat 1200-1430 and
1900-2230 (closed Sun mid
Dec-mid Jan).
Vaporetto: San Zaccaria or Rialto.
Map Canal Grande, H3, p87.

It's all paper tablecloths and
fast-talking staff in this efficient
little restaurant just off campo
Santa Maria Formosa. The menu
features flavoursome fish dishes
made with surprisingly few
ingredients: try the tomato-
smeared *canoe*, a frightening
looking langoustine with
delicious tender flesh. Al
Mascaron's popularity amongst
Venetians and visitors-in-the-
know means you have to book.

## Tip...

Venetian chefs of repute
pick up their cars from the
Tronchetto car park and make
the 30-minute drive to the fish
market in Chioggia (pronounced
'kee-odd-ja'). Hardcore foodies
will recognise that, although
it's not as picturesque as the
Rialto market, Chioggia is the
real deal in terms of quality.
It's hard to reach without your
own transport but if you're
determined to get there, catch
vaporetto 11 from San Zaccaria
to Lido. Then catch a bus to
Alberoni where you'll get on a car
ferry to Pellestrina; from there,
catch the ACTV passenger ferry
to Chioggia. It's a bit of an effort
but worth it.

Listings

### Osteria Alle Testiere €€€
*Calle del Mondo Nuovo, Castello
5801, T041-522 7220.*
Mon-Sat 1st sitting 1900,
2nd sitting 2115.
Vaporetto: San Zaccaria
or Rialto.
Map Canal Grande, G4, p87.
This famous and much
celebrated Venetian restaurant
is very small (it seats around 20)
and hugely popular, which
means it has to have two sittings
to pack 'em all in. The cooking is
modern in style and the fish is so
fresh the waiters laugh that it is
still wriggling on the plate. The
raw shellfish platter is the best
you'll ever taste and the fried
*moeche* (soft shell crabs) melt
in the mouth.

### Pizzeria 84 €
*Salizada San Giustina,
Castello 2907Aa, T041-520 4198.*
Fri-Tue 1700-1930.
Vaporetto: Santa Giustina.
Map Venice, G4, p83.
Perfect for families when all the
little ones want is pizza. This
belt-and-braces pizzeria is
perhaps the most authentic in
Venice despite the fact that fire
restrictions prevent the use of
wood-burning ovens. It's
popular with Venetian families,
who queue up until a table is
free, and with students who
hang around outside waiting for
their takeaway.

### Cafés & bars
### Da Bonifacio
*Calle degli Albanesi, Castello
4237, T041-522 7507.*
Fri-Wed 0800-2100.
Vaporetto: San Zaccaria.
Map Canal Grande, H6, p87.
A cake shop that serves a mean
Spritz.

### Italo Didovich
*Campo Santa Marina, Castello
5909, T041-523 0017.*
Mon-Sat 0730-2000.
Vaporetto: Rialto.
Map Canal Grande, G3, p87.

*Five of the best*
## Spots to drink Spritz
**❶ Campo San Giacomo di
Rialto, San Polo** Right next to
the Rialto, this *campo* is a magnet
for the young and the beautiful.
Try **Naranzaria** (campo San
Giacomo di Rialto, San Polo 130,
T041-724 1035, Tue-Sun 1200-0200.
Vaporetto: Rialto Mercato), which
also serves Venetian sushi!

**❷ Campo Santa Margherita,
Dorsoduro** Throbbing with
Venetian vivacity, this is probably
the liveliest place in the city come
*la passeggiata.* Try **Il Caffè** (campo
Santa Margherita, Dorsoduro
2693, T014-528 7998, Mon-Sat
0700-0100. Vaporetto: San Tomà.)

**❸ Fondamenta degli Ormesini &
Fondamenta della Misericordia,
Cannaregio**
Beautiful when bathed in evening
light, this is a real Venetian
neighbourhood. Try **Al Mariner**

Fabulous bite-sized savoury
pastries for those who don't have
a sweet tooth.

### L'Olandese Volante
*Campo San Lio, Castello 5658.*
Mon-Thu 1100-0030, Fri-Sat
1100-0200, Sun 1700-0030.
Vaporetto: San Rialto.
Map Canal Grande, G3, p87.
Full of life. If the bar staff like you,
they'll give you extra bowls of
free crisps and popcorn with
your drinks.

(fondamenta dei Orimesini,
Cannaregio 2679, T041-720036,
daily 0800-2100. Vaporetto:
Madonna dell'Orto) a belt-and-
braces bar/osteria that's always
full of characters.

**❹ Via Garibaldi, Castello**
Beyond San Marco the pace is
slower and the Spritz seem longer.
Try **Caffè Garibaldi** (via Garibaldi,
Castello 1602, Mon-Sat 1600-2200.
Vaporetto: Arsenale), with its
genuinely nice staff.

**❺ Zattere, Dorsoduro**
Come here for the best of the
evening sun and a cooling breeze.
Try **El Chiochetto** (fondamenta
Zattere al Ponto Lungo, T348-396
8466, Apr-Oct daily 0730-0100,
Nov-Mar daily 0730-1700.
Vaporetto: Zattere).

### Rosa Salva

*Campo SS Giovanni e Paolo,*
*Castello 6799, T041-527 7949.*
Mon-Sat 0800-2030.
Vaporetto: Ospedale Civil.
Map Canal Grande, H2, p87.
The consistency of the froth
on your cappuccino and the
marmaladey *cornetti* are always
bang on in this Venetian
institution.

*Pesche biance* (white peaches).

### Cannaregio

### Boccadoro €€

*Campo Widmann, Cannaregio*
*5405, T041-521 1021.*
Tue-Sun 1200-1500 and
1900-2100.
Vaporetto: Ca' d'Oro or
Fondamente Nuove.
Map Canal Grande, G1, p87.
Some might call Luciano, the
owner and head chef of this chic
restaurant on a quiet *campo*, a
purist. His 'unplugged' approach
to the best seafood, bought in
Chioggia fish market each
morning, leads to dish after dish
of startlingly simple yet tasty
offerings. The *capelonghe* (razor
clams – weirdly translated as
'bivalves') are packed with
flavour despite the fact that he
hardly does anything to them:
that's skill.

## Tip...

If you have been treated badly
in a restaurant, hotel, café or
visitor attraction you can lodge a
complaint with the APT (Venice
tourist board). Call T041-529
8722/3, Monday to Friday, or
send an email to complaint.apt@
turismovenezia.it.

### Cafés & bars

### La Cantina

*Campo San Felice, Cannaregio*
*3689, T041-522-8258.*
Mon-Sat 1000-2200.
Vaporetto: Ca d'Oro.
Map Venice, E3, p82.
A lovely bar, just off the Strada
Novo, where you can sit outside
and affordably drink your way
through the wine list.

### Osteria al Ponte

*Calle Larga Gallina,*
*Cannaregio 6378.*
Mon-Sat 0800-2100.
Vaporetto: Ospedale Civile.
Map Canal Grande, H2, p87.
Just across from Santi Giovanni e
Paolo, this is a wonderful place to
sit with a Spritz.

### Puppa Roberto

*Calle del Spezier, Cannaregio*
*4800, T041-523 7947.*
Mon-Sat 0800-1900.
Vaporetto: Fondamente Nuove.
Map Venice, F4, p83.
Great gooey pastries on the way
to the Gesuiti.

### Osteria Da Fiore €€€€
*Calle del Scaleter, San Polo 2202, T041-721308.*
Tue-Sat 1200-1500 and 1900-2200, closed for 3 wks from Christmas and throughout Aug.
Vaporetto: San Stae.
Map Canal Grande, B2, p86.

Discerning Venetians come to Mara and Maurizio Martin's place when they want to celebrate, so be prepared to spend, spend, spend if you eat here: you'll pay at least €100 per head. The kitchen experiments with delicate flavours and demonstrates a sensual approach to food: between courses you will be served *amuse-bouches* that take you outside your comfort zone into a new world of flavour. Men will need a smart jacket for dining here but, don't worry: it's posh but not suffocatingly so.

If this is way out of your league, try **Il Refolo** (campo San Giacomo dell'Orio, T041-524 0016, Tue 1900-2300, Wed-Sun 1200-1500 and 1900-2300. Vaporetto: San Stae), a fabulous pizzeria in a buzzing *campo*, owned by the same couple.

# On the menu in Venice

*scampi crudi*  raw langoustines, halved and drizzled with olive oil.

*baccalà*  dried salted cod, often creamed (*mantecato*) and served on slices of polenta.

*bisato in tecia*  roasted eel with bay leaf and tomato sauce.

*brodetto*  fish soup/stew.

*bussolai buranelli*  butter biscuits that you dunk in sweet vin Santo.

*castraure*  artichoke buds from Sant'Erasmo; they're delicious dipped in olive oil and salt, *pinzimonio*, as the Venetians say.

*cicchetti*  Venetian tapas. This can be anything fishy in bite-sized portions.

*fegato*  calf's liver cooked in onions.

*frittura mista*  mixed small fried fish and vegetables.

*moeche frite*  small soft-shelled crabs dipped in egg and fried.

*moscardini*  baby octopus (only a few days old) stewed and served with polenta.

*risi e bisi*  a creamy pea risotto fit for a Doge.

*sarde in saor*  fried sardines with onions, marinated in a sweet vinegary sauce with raisins and pine nuts.

*spaghetti al nero di seppia*  spaghetti cooked in black squid ink.

*spaghetti alle vongole*  spaghetti with clams.

**Alla Madonna €€**
*Calle de la Madonna, San Polo
594, T041-522 3824,
ristoranteallamadonna.com.*
Thu-Tue 1200-1500 and
1900-2200. Parties of 8 or more
should make a reservation.
Vaporetto: Rialto Mercato.
Map Canal Grande, E3, p86.
This place is popular with
families and returning visitors to
Venice, so you may have to
queue for some time to get a
table (come early). However,
once you are seated, you can feel
triumphant in the knowledge
that you are about to eat one of
the best meals of your life. There
is nothing fancy about it: just
seafood done fabulously well.
The salty, inky blackness of the
*vermicelli al nero* and the
light-touch *fritto misto* (mixed
fried fish) are both worth raving
about.

**Osteria Al Vecio Fritolin €€**
*Calle della Regina, Santa Croce
2262, T041-522 2881,
veciofritolin.it.*
Tue-Sun 1200-1430 and
1900-2230.
Vaporetto: San Stae.
Map Canal Grande, C1, p86.
Near Ca' Pesaro, this restaurant
lacks pretence but serves up
splendid versions of classic
Venetian fare, fried on the spot.
It's run by the be-spectacled
Irina, who makes visitors very
welcome. The menu changes
regularly but don't miss the
sweet fried scallops or stuffed

*Five of the best*
# Gelaterie

**❶ Algiubagio**
*Fondamente Nuove, Cannaregio
5039, T041-523-6084.*
Wed-Mon 0630-2330.
Vaporetto: Fondamente Nuove.
It's a restaurant too but, due to
its location, the gelato is the
biggest seller.

**❷ La Boutique del Gelato**
*Salizada San Lio, Castello 5727,
T041-522 3283.*
Tue-Sun 0700-2200.
Vaporetto: Rialto.
This tiny ice cream boutique is
worth tracking down between
Rialto and Santa Maria Formosa.

**❸ Millefoglie di Tarcisco Gelato**
*Salizada San Rocco, San Polo 3033,
T041-524 4667.*
Daily 0730-2400.
Vaporetto: San Tomà.
When you see Venetian dads
on their way home from work

stopping here to buy huge
tubs of the stuff for their
children, you know it must
be good. Also sells huge slices
of pizzas.

**❹ Nico**
*Fondamenta Zattere ai Gesuati 922,
Dorsoduro 922, T041-522 5293.*
Fri-Wed 0645-2200.
Vaporetto: Zattere.
A favourite of those who want
to stroll along Venice's 'beach'.

**❺ Paolin**
*Campo Santo Stefano, San Marco
3464, T041-522-5576.*
Wed-Mon 0630-2300.
Vaporetto: Santa Maria del Giglio.
What, only 12 flavours? You'll want
to try every one of them.

Croccante.

zucchini flowers if you get the chance. It's always busy with young professionals and couples (who are obviously regulars), so take whatever seat you can, either inside or on the terrace. If there's no space, you can have your fried fish wrapped in paper to take away.

### Osteria La Zucca €€
*Calle del Tentor, Santa Croce 1762, T041-524 1570.*
Mon-Sat 1200-1500 and 1900-2200.
Vaporetto: San Stae.
Map Canal Grande, B1, p86.
La Zucca is run by a couple of very amusing ladies and is a winner for vegetarian visitors to Venice, who can sometimes struggle to find a decent meal. Try *radicchio di Treviso* and *carciofo violetto di Sant'Erasmo* (the tenderest buds of the purple artichoke) for proof of their winning ways with veg. There are two tables outside, as well as a dining room with pumpkin-inspired decor.

### Ruga Rialto €€
*Ruga Rialto, San Polo 692, T041-521 1243.*
Wed-Mon 1000-2400.
Vaporetto: San Silvestro.
Map Canal Grande, D3, p86.
One of the best places to try a stand-up *ombra* and *cicchetti* (small glass of wine and fishy bites). Choose from fried things like calamari, *gamberi* and *folpeti* (squid, prawns and baby octopus), as well as creamed *baccalà* and bread spread with anchovy paste. There are also sliced meats and grilled veg. The dining room at the back offers a large set lunch, with coffee, biscotti and a carafe of red wine for just €20.

### La Patatina €
*Calle Saoneri, San Polo 2741/A, T041-523 7238, lapatatina.it.*
Mon-Sat 1100-1500 and 1800-2200.
Vaporetto: San Tomà.
Map Canal Grande, B3, p86.
If you're short of time and in need of some sustenance, this very popular osteria is never too busy to be friendly. Help yourself to a huge array of *cicchetti* and vegetables, with lots of *fritti* and *patatine* (chips).

Cafés & bars
### Ai Nomboli
*Calle dei Nomboli, San Polo 2717, T041-523 0995.*
Mon-Sat 0730-2000.
Vaporetto: San Tomà.
Map Canal Grande, A4, p86.
There's nothing fancy about this bar in the busy thoroughfare between Rialto and the Frari but the coffee is really good.

### Al Pesador
*Campo San Giacomo di Rialto, San Polo 126, T041-523-9492.*
Tue-Sun 1200-0200.
Vaporetto: Rialto Mercato.
Map Canal Grande, E2, p86.
An atmospheric *cicchetteria* that's popular with a younger crowd.

### Al Prosecco
*Campo San Giacomo dell'Orio, Santa Croce 1503, T041-524 0222.*
Daily 0800-2200.
Vaporetto: San Stae.
Map Canal Grande, 86, p86.
In a beautiful *campo*, this simple little wine bar serves salame, cheese and other nibbles.

### Ancora
*Campo San Giacomo di Rialto, San Polo 120, T041-520 7066.*
Daily 1200-2400.
Vaporetto: Rialto Mercato.
Map Canal Grande, E2, p86.
A modern bar overlooking the Canal Grande which sells cocktails, Spritz and snacks, including oysters.

### Caffè dei Frari

*Fondamenta dei Frari, San Polo
2564, T041-524 1877.*
Mon-Sat 0800-2100.
Vaporetto: San Tomà.
Map Canal Grande, A3, p86.

Around about aperitivo time this
place is hopping. There's a lovely
mezzanine.

### Easy Bar

*Campo Santa Maria Mater
Domini, Santa Croce 2119,
T041-524 0321.*
Fri-Wed 0800-0200.
Vaporetto: San Stae.
Map Canal Grande, C1, p86.

Shows Serie A and international
football on a big screen.

**Dorsoduro**

### Ristorante Ai Gondolieri €€€€

*Ponte del Formager,
Fondamenta Zorsi Bragadin,
Dorsoduro 366, T041-528 6396,
aigondolieri.com.*
Wed-Mon 1200-1500 and
1900-2200.
Vaporetto: Accademia.
Map Venice, E6, p82.

This restaurant is full of
well-heeled Venetians who need
a meat fix. The menu packs an
iron-rich punch, featuring horse,
duck, pork and beef fattened on
Veneto's plains: fillet of beef in
Barolo wine with a potato tart is
one of the classic dishes. The
same management runs the
Guggenheim's Museum Café
(just across the canal).

# Planning a picnic?

The **Erberia** at Rialto is the best
place to buy fruit and veg but for
other staples the supermarkets
offer great choice and value for
money. In general, Venetian bread
is drier, paler and not quite as
exciting as bread from the rest
of Italy, however, there are some
bakers, such as **Panificio Volpe**
in Cannaregio, that bake exciting
breads with figs, fennel and
nuts in them. The local delis and
supermarkets sell all the classic
cured meats and cheeses, including
*formaggio imbriago* from Treviso.
For details, see Shopping, page 161.

You can be fined for picnicking
in some parts of Venice but you
should be fine in the following so
long as you tidy up behind you:

**Campo Gesuiti**, Cannaregio
(Vaporetto: Fondamente Nuove)
There is a bench perfectly
situated right in front of this
beautiful church.

**Giardino Papadopoli**,
Santa Croce (Vaporetto: Piazzale
Roma) The trees create lovely cool
spots in the heat of summer.

**Parco Savorgnan**, Cannaregio
(Vaporetto: Guglie) A beautiful
park near the ghetto.

**Viale Garibaldi**, Castello
(Vaporetto: Arsenale)
A leafy spot near the
Biennale's Giardini Pubblici.

Every neighbourhood has a *frutti-vendoli*.

# Tip...

Whatever you do, don't try to
picnic on piazza San Marco. If
you do, numerous officials from
the Office of Urban Decorum will
suddenly appear and try to fine
you €50.

### Osteria Vecio Forner €€€

*Campo San Vio, Dorsoduro 671B,*
*T041-528 0424.*
Mon-Sat 1100-1500 and
1900-2100.
Vaporetto: Accademia.
Map Venice, D6, p82.
Located between the Accademia
and the Guggenheim, this
understated osteria has changed
hands twice over the last few
years but, so far, it has always
been run by people who have an
enthusiasm for food. The current
menu is a bit pricier than before
but continues to offer classic fare
and some more unusual dishes,
such as sweet *tagliatti piseli*,
which resembles pasta with
mushy peas.

### Osteria ai Carmini €€

*Campo Santa Margherita,*
*Dorsoduro 2894a, T041-523 1115.*
Mon-Sat 0930-0100.
Vaporetto: San Toma.
Map Venice, C5, p82.
In one of the most happening
*campos* in Venice, this osteria is
proof that you can eat well on a
shoestring. Popular with the
boffs from the University, it
serves ample portions of simple
dishes like spaghetti with *seppia
nero* (black ink) or *vongole*
(clams). For those on the go,
there's *calamari fritti*, served in a
paper cone.

### Cafés & bars

### Caffè Blue

*Calle dei Preti, Dorsoduro 3778,*
*T041-710227.*
Mon-Fri 0800-0200,
Sat 1900-0200.
Vaporetto: San Tomà.
Map Venice, C5, p82.
If you're desperate for a pint of
Guinness or a cup of tea, this
place will more than happily
oblige.

### Fujiyama Tea Room

*Calle Lunga San Barnaba,*
*Dorsoduro 2727a, T041-724 1042.*
Daily 1400-2000.
Vaporetto: Ca' Rezzonico.
Map Venice, C6, p82.
One of the few places in Venice
(bar the posh hotels) where you'll
get a decent cup of tea. It's also
wonderfully tranquil.

### Suzie Caffè

*Campo San Basegio, Dorsoduro*
*1527, T0141-522 7502.*
Mon-Thu 0700-1900, Fri and
occasional Sat in summer
0700-0100.
Vaporetto: San Basilio.
Map Venice, C6, p82.
In a campo just a stone's throw
from the Zattere, this café plays
ska and reggae on Fridays.

### Tonolo

*Calle San Pantalon, Dorsoduro*
*3764, T041-523 7209.*
Tue-Sat 0745-2230,
Sun 0745-1300.
Vaporetto: San Tomà.
Map Venice, C5, p82.

One of the best run bars in the
city: it's fascinating to watch the
staff cope with the sudden
surges of locals looking for Spritz
or *caffè corretto*.

## The islands & the lagoon

For restaurants with rooms,
see also page 145.

### Cafés & bars

### Skyline

*Hilton Molino Stucky,*
*Giudecca 810, T041-723311.*
Daily 1000-0100.
Vaporetto: Palanca.
Come on up to the ninth floor of
the Hilton for breathtaking views
along the Giudecca canal as far
as piazza San Marco. It's beautiful
by day and very romantic at
night, with the lights of Venice
twinkling on the water. Warning:
the dizzy height makes drinks
seem more potent.

**A pigeon's-eye view of piazza San Marco.**

# Entertainment

### Giorgione Movie d'Essai
*Rio Terra dei Franceschi,*
*Cannaregio 4612, T041-522 6298.*
€7/5.
Vaporetto: Fondamente Nuove.
Low on blockbusters but high
on quality. There are three
screenings each day held in two
cinemas (late afternoon, evening
and late evening).

### Multisala Astra
*Via Corfu 9, Lido, T041-526 5736.*
€7/5.
Vaporetto: Lido.
There are some Hollywood
hits on the two screens but,
otherwise, it's mainly European
and arthouse films.

### Palazzo del Cinema
*Lungomare G Marconi, Lido,*
*T041-272 6501.*
€7/5.
Vaporetto: Lido
With five screens, this grand
multiplex caters for all types
of cinema-goer.

## Clubs
Despite its student population
and steady supply of pleasure
seekers, Venice has little in the
way of nightclubs.

## Mostra Internazionale d'Arte Cinematografica di Venezia

The Venice Film Festival (labiennale.org) was founded in 1932 and
takes place in late August/early September. It's based around the Lido,
with showings in the Sala Grande of the Palazzo del Cinema and other
purpose-built venues. The buzz of helicopters and paparazzi drowns
out the gentle flip-flop of beachgoers and, suddenly, the whole place
is awash with industry professionals and cinema enthusiasts. It's not
confined to the Lido however: the great and the good also commandeer
some of the city's best restaurants, hotels and palazzi for receptions,
photo calls and launches.

The public can watch films on maxi screens and in a movie village
in front of the venues. There's also a pagoda in front of the Hotel des
Bains that offers a bar, food and entertainment well into the night for the
duration of the festival. Those staying in the city centre but wanting to
party are helped by the vaporetti which run regularly until 0200.

The main prize, the Leone d'Oro (Golden Lion), is awarded to the best
film shown at the festival. Previous winners include *Brokeback Mountain*
(2005), *Vera Drake* (2004) and *The Magdalene Sisters* (2002). In addition,
there's the Coppa Volpi for best actor or actress, a jury's prize for the
runner-up to the Leone d'Oro, the Controcorrente for new talent and
Golden Osellas for directors, cinematographers, screenwriters and others.

### 947 Club
*Campo Santi Filippo e Giacomo,*
*Castello 4337, T340-477 3693,*
*club947@hotmail.it.*
Wed-Mon 2300-0400, €10.
Vaporetto: San Zaccaria.
Just behind the Danieli Hotel, it's
glamorous yet unpretentious
and fun.

### Pachuka
*Spiaggia San Nicolò, Lido,*
*T041-242 0020.*
Jun-Sep 0900-0400, Oct-May
Wed-Mon 0900-0400, €10.
Vaporetto: Lido.
A shuttle bus runs back and forth
between the vaporetto stop and

this popular bar/pizzeria/club,
which serves up pop, Euro house
and a bit of, er, soft rock.

### Paradiso Perduto
*Fondamenta della Misericordia,*
*Cannaregio 2640, T041-720581.*
Tue-Sat 1800-0200.
Vaporetto: San Marcuola.
Not the club it once was but this
restaurant and bar is still popular
with students and visiting
alternative types. It has DJs on
most nights and hots up later on
when the lights are turned down
and the music is turned up.

## Tip...

On Sundays at 1600 there are free organ concerts at **La Salute** (see page 126). Hearing the vast nave filled with music is an experience you won't forget.

# Festival Internazionale di Danza Contemporanea

The dance festival (Palazzo Giustinian Lolin, San Marco 2893, T041-521 8898, labiennale.org) is held in even years in June and has established itself as one of the most cutting-edge dance events in the world. The festival is directed by a celebrated choreographer around a theme (beauty in 2008) and, in addition to arresting dance performances, includes a series of lectures. Venues include the Teatro Malibran (next to Chiesa San Giovanni Grisostomo, not far from Rialto) and several Biennale buildings in the Arsenale: Teatro Piccolo, the open-air Teatro alle Tese and Teatro alle Vergini.

At other times, La Fenice and Teatro Malibran host visiting ballet companies. To see if there are any other dance events happening in Venice during your stay, visit the city's website comune. venezia.it; the 'culture' page lists all current and upcoming cultural events.

### Piccolo Mondo
*Calle Corfu, Dorsoduro 1056/A, T041-520 0371.*
Tue-Sun 2300-0400, €10.
Vaporetto: Accademia.
This club is tiny and plays pop and '80s music.

### Gay & lesbian
Venice is certainly not anti gay but there is a lack of an openly gay scene here. Carnevale is becoming popular with the gay community but if you're looking for clubs, pubs and nights that cater for the gay and lesbian community, head for Padua (see page 185).

### Music
There isn't much of a pop and rock scene in Venice, due to the lack of suitable venues and complaints about noise, but you'll find plenty of classical concerts and jazz gigs.

### Al Nono Risorto
*Sottoportego de Siora Bettina (near campo San Cassiano), Santa Croce 2338, T041-524 1169.*
Thu-Tue 1100-2400.
Vaporetto: San Stae.
This cheap eatery doubles up as a jazz venue. Phone or pop in for more info.

### Fondazione Querini Stampalia
*Campo Santa Maria Formosa, Castello 5752, T041-271 1411, querinistampalia.it.*
Vaporetto: San Zaccaria.
This wonderfully restored and enhanced Venetian residence is now a cultural institution and always has a programme of classical music concerts on the go. Concert tickets are included in the admission price to the museum (€8).

### Interpreti Veneziani
*Chiesa di San Vidal, San Marco 2862b, T041-277 0561, interpretiveneziani.com.*
€24/19.
Vaporetto: Accademia.
San Vidal is a perfect setting for this orchestra which focuses on the work of Venetian composers, such as Domenico Dragonetti and Tommaso Albinoni, as well as works by Haydn, Vivaldi and Mendelssohn.

### Jazz Club 900
*Campiello del Sansoni, San Polo 900, T041-522 6565, jazz900.com.*
Tue-Sun 1200-1500 and 1900-2400.
Vaporetto: San Silvestro.
There's live jazz every Wednesday, when serious aficionados come to eat and wobble their heads in time to the music. It's a small place, so reservations are essential.

### Orchestra Collegium Ducale

*Palazzo delle Prigioni, riva degli Schiavoni, San Marco 1.*
*Chiesa di Santa Maria Formosa, campo Santa Maria Formosa, Castello 5267, T041-984252, collegiumducale.com.*
€25/20.
Vaporetto: San Zaccària.
Playing the same tunes night after night has not robbed this group of passion. It performs three programmes across two venues: Baroque (think Vivaldi and Albinoni), classical (Mozart and Bach) and jazz (Miles Davis and George Gershwin), all starting at 2100.

### Palazzo Barbarigo-Minotto

*Fondamenta Duodo o Barbarigo, San Marco 2504, T340-971 7272, musicapalazzo.com.*
€48.
Vaporetto: Santa Maria del
A recreation of the *salotto musicale* (music salon), these little operatic or classical concerts featuring Verdi and Rossini feel all the more intimate for the domestic (albeit rather grand) setting.

### Venice Jazz Club
*Fondamenta del Squero,*
*Dorsoduro 3102, T041-523 2056,*
*venicejazzclub.com.*
Mon, Wed, Fri, Sat 1800-0200,
€15.
Vaporetto: Ca' Rezzonico.
Lots of famous names play at this
dimly lit old favourite but don't
feel cheated if the resident VJC
Quartet are on the bill when you
visit: they are smooth.

### Theatre, opera & dance
### Teatro Carlo Goldoni
*Calle Goldoni, San Marco 4650,*
*T041-240 2011,*
*teatrostabileveneto.it.*
€7-30.
Vaporetto: Rialto.
A wide range of theatrical
productions – from Shakespeare
to Voltaire to Chekhov – as well as
concerts are held at this theatre,
which is named after the great
Venetian playwright, Carlo
Goldoni (1707-1798). Goldoni splits
opinion in Italy: you either love
him because he dumped the
formulaic *commedia dell'arte*
approach to theatrical storytelling
or hate him because his plays are
done to death and considered
too 'popular' by some critics. He
was at the vanguard of the
development of the *opera buffa*
(comic opera), which eschewed
tales of kings and princesses in
favour of funny stories about
those from the wrong side of the
canal. His plays are written in the
Venetian vernacular and are still
performed here.

La Fenice.

You can visit his gothic
palazzo, **Casa di Goldoni** (calle dei
Nomboli, San Polo 2794, T041-275
9325, museiciviciveneziani.it,
Mon-Sat 1000-1900, €2.50/1.50.
Vaporetto: San Tomà.)

### Teatro La Fenice
*Campo San Fantin, San Marco*
*1965, T041-2424, teatrolafenice.it.*
€20-600.
Vaporetto: Santa Maria del
Giglio.
This is where the finest
productions and touring
companies perform opera,
classical concerts and ballets. If
you really want to do La Fenice in
style, book a gondola to take you
there. See also page 96.

### Teatro Malibran
*Corte del Milion, Cannaregio*
*5873, T041-2424, teatrolafenice.it.*
€17-100.
Vaporetto: Rialto.
Teatro San Giovanni Grisostomo
was built in 1677 on what is
believed to be the site of Marco
Polo's old house. It was renamed
Teatro Malibran in 1837 in
honour of the famous Spanish
mezzosoprano, Maria Malibran.
The local authorities took it over
in 1992, thus ensuring the city
could still host operas while
La Fenice was being rebuilt.
Although it's not quite as
sumptuous as La Fenice, it
offers a similar range of opera,
ballet and theatre and still has
an element of extravagance
about it.

# Shopping

### Art & antiques

**Antichità Santomanco della Toffola**
*Ramo Secondo Corte Contarina, San Marco 1567, T041-523 6643.*
Tue-Sat 0930-1300 and 1600-1930.
Vaporetto: San Marco.
Second-hand curiosities and jewellery from as far away as Russia.

**Gallo Alberto**
*Salizada San Samuele, San Marco 3083, T041-523 8120.*
Mon-Sat 0930-1230 and 1500-1930.
Vaporetto: San Samuele.
Massive and smaller fish-eye mirrors with all types of frame.

**Langolo del Passato**
*Campiello degli Squillini, Dorsoduro 3276, T041-528 7896.*
Mon-Sat 1000-1300 and 1600-1900.
Vaporetto: Ca'Rezzonico.
Antique furniture and ceramics as well as second-hand and new glass.

### Books

**Cluva**
*Campo dei Tolentini, Santa Croce 191, T041-522 6910.*
Mon-Sat 0900-1300 and 1500-1930.
Vaporetto: Piazzale Roma.
A huge range of books on architecture.

**Filippi Editore Venezia**
*Calle del Paradiso, Castello 5762, T041-523 6916.*
Mon-Sat 0930-1300 and 1600-1930.
Vaporetto: San Zaccaria.
A family-run shop with a comprehensive collection of books about Venice.

**Libreria della Toletta**
*Sacca della Toletta, Dorsoduro 1214, T041-523 2034.*
Mon-Sat 0930-1300 and 1600-1930.
Vaporetto: Accademia.
An academic bookshop that has a number of English-language titles.

**Mondadori**
*Salizada San Moisè, San Marco 1346, T041-522 5068.*
Tue-Sat 0930-1930.
Vaporetto: San Marco.
Bookshop with a café, the Bacaro Lounge.

### Clothing, shoes & accessories

Those looking to splash the cash in designer shops should head towards the Mercerie, Frezzeria, calle Goldoni, calle Vallaresso and calle Larga XXII Marzo, all of which lead off piazza San Marco. Here are all the best known Italian designers, as well as some boutiques selling British, US and French labels.

Second hand shops are popping up all over Venice.

**Fanny**
*Calle dei Saoneri, San Polo 27,*
*T041-522 8266.*
Mon-Sat 0930-1300 and
1600-1900.
Vaporetto: San Tomà.
Fabulous leather gloves and
gauntlets in every colour and
at amazing prices.

**Giovanna Zanella**
*Calle Carminati, Castello 5641,*
*T041-523 5500.*
Tue-Sat 0930-1230 and
1530-1900.
Vaporetto: San Zaccaria.
These aren't shoes: they are
handmade works of art you
wear on your feet.

**Mazon le Borse**
*Campiello San Tomà, San Polo*
*2807, T041-520 3421.*
Mon-Sat 1000-1230 and
1600-1930.
Vaporetto: San Tomà.
Handmade belts and wallets
made from leathers of all colours
and finishes.

**Micromega**
*Campo Santa Maria del Giglio,*
*San Marco 2436, T041-296 0765,*
*micromegaottica.com.*
Mon-Sat 0930-1300 and
1530-1900. Vaporetto: Santa
Maria del Giglio.
Outrageously gorgeous
spectacles: not too dear, either.

**As You Like**
*Campiello Riccardo Selvatico,*
*Cannaregio 5671, T041-520 9232,*
*asyoulikevintage.com.*
Mon 1600-1900, Tue-Sat
1000-1300 and 1600-1900.
Vaporetto: Ca' d'Oro.
One of Venice's only vintage
clothing shops; there are some
great pieces to be found here.

**Calzature Andrea Baldan**
*Salizada San Rocco, San Polo*
*3047, T041-528 7501.*
Mon 1600-1930, Tue-Sat
0930-1300 and 1600-1930.
Vaporetto: San Tomà.
An old-style shoe shop selling
high-quality classic and
contemporary shoes.

### Ottica Urbani
*Bocca de Piazza, San Marco 1280,*
*T041-522 4140, otticaurbani.com.*
Mon-Sat 0900-1300 and
1600-1930.
Vaporetto: San Marco.
Where to buy the Le Corbusier
glasses that Italian intellectuals
wear.

### Shanti Daan
*Calle del Fabbro, Dorsoduro*
*3284, T041-241 1916.*
Mon-Sat 0900-1300 and
1600-1900.
Vaporetto: Ca' Rezzonico.
Ethnic trinkets, incense and
kaftans. The cat in the window
is not for sale.

### Venetia Studium
*Calle Larga XXII Marzo, San*
*Marco 2425, T041-523 6953,*
*venetiastudium.com.*
Tue-Sat 0930-1930, Sun
1200-1900. Vaporetto: San
Marco.
Gorgeous Fortuny scarves in
every possible hue.

### Zazu
*Calle dei Saoneri, San Polo 2750,*
*T041-715426.*
Tue-Sat 1000-1300 and
1600-1930.
Vaporetto: San Tomà.
Fabulous unusual designs in
tactile fabrics. There is a favourite
outfit in here for every woman.

### Department stores
### Coin
*Salizada San Giovanni*
*Gristoforo, Cannaregio 5787,*
*T041-520 3581.*
Mon-Sat 0930-1930,
Sun 1100-1930.
Vaporetto: Rialto.
A comprehensive shop selling
anything you might need.

### Standa
*Ponte San Felice, Cannaregio*
*3659, T041-523 8046.*
Mon-Sat 0930-1930,
Sun 1100-1930.
Vaporetto: Ca' d'Oro.
Clothing, perfume, homewares
and food.

### Food & drink
For general food shopping, try
the supermarkets: **Biga**
**Supermercato** (rio terrà Frari,
San Polo 2605b, daily 0900-2000.
Vaporetto: San Tomà); **Billa**
(strada Nova Cannaregio 3660,
Mon-Sat 0830-2000, Sun
0900-0800. Vaporetto: Ca' d'Oro);
**Billa** (fondamenta Zattere Ponte
Lungo, Dorsoduro 1491,
Mon-Sat 0830- 2000, Sun
0900-0800. Vaporetto: Zattere);

**Suve Supermercato** (salizada
San Lio, Castello 5811. Vaporetto:
San Zaccaria).

### Aliani
*Ruga Vecchia San Giovanni, San*
*Polo 654, T041-522 4913.*
Mon-Sat 0800-1300 and
1530-1930.
Vaporetto: San Silvestro.
A great selection of *formaggi,*
*salumi* and antipasti for picnics
in the city, as well as things to
take home.

### Casa del Parmigiano
*Erberia Rialto, San Polo 2153,*
*T041-520 6525,*
*casadelparmigiano.it.*
Mon-Sat 0830-1300 and
1600-1930.
Vaporetto: Rialto.
A legendary *formaggeria.*

Top: Gloves by Fanny.
Above: Pescaria.

### Dolceamaro
*Campo San Canciano,*
*Cannaregio 6051, T041-523 8708.*
Mon-Sat 0930-1300 and
1530-1930.
Vaporetto: Ca' d'Oro.
Irresistible chocolates in all
percentages, shapes and
flavours.

### Il Laboratorio
*Calle dei Caffettier,*
*San Marco 6672.*
Mon-Sat 0830-1300 and
1600-1930.
Vaporetto: San Marco.
Carry-out lasagne, *cicchetti*
and pizza.

### La Serenissima
*Calle Fiubera, San Marco 832,*
*T041-523 2346.*
Mon-Sat 0900-1300 and
1600-1900.
Vaporetto: San Marco.
This 'green' grocer sells organic
fruit, veg, meat and cheese.

### Mauro el Forner de Canton
*Strada Nova, Cannaregio 3845,*
*T041-523 0991.*
Mon-Sat 0830-1300 and
1600-1900.
Vaporetto: Ca' d'Oro.
Fabulous bread, especially
the fennel and fig varieties.

### Panificio Volpe
*Calle Ghetto Vecchio,*
*Cannaregio 1143, T041-715178.*
Mon-Fri 0800-1300 and
1600-1930, Sat 0800-1300.
Vaporetto: Guglie.
Well known Jewish baker. Fans of
fennel should try the fennel
shortbread.

**Souvenirs**
### Arcobaleno
*Ponte Campo Santissimi*
*Apostoli, Cannaregio 5623,*
*T041-520 3989.*
Mon-Sat 1000-1300 and
1600-1930.
Vaporetto: Ca' d'Oro.
Jewellery with a novel use of
colour.

### Biblos
*Calle Larga XXII Marzo, San*
*Marco 2087, T041-521 0714.*
Mon-Sat 0930-1230 and
1530-1930. Vaporetto: San
Marco.
Gorgeous marbled paper,
writing materials and bound
books.

### Ca' Macana
*Calle delle Botteghe, Dorsoduro*
*1169, T041-522 9749.*
Mon-Sat 0930-1300 and
1600-1930, Sun 1100-1930.
Vaporetto: Sant'Angelo.
Makers of marvellous Venetian
masks. The animals and
bejewelled creations are almost
too good to wear.

Venetian masks.

### Lellabella
*Calle della Mandola, San Marco*
*3718, T041-522 5152.*
Mon-Sat 0930-1300 and
1600-1930.
Vaporetto: Rialto.
Perhaps the most colourful and
imaginative wool shop in the world.

### Marina e Susanna Sent
*Campo San Vio, Dorsoduro 669,*
*T041-520 8136,*
*marinaesusannasent.com.*
Mon-Sat 0930-1300 and
1600-1930.
Vaporetto: Accademia.
Murano glass for and by funky
young women. Also at ponte
San Moisè, San Marco 2090,
T041-520 4041.

### Diego Rosettin
*Calle del Capeler, Dorsoduro*
*3220, T041-522 4195.*
Mon-Sat 0930-1300 and
1600-1900. Vaporetto: Ca'
Rezzonico.
This family has been pouring
molten bronze into moulds for
100 years. They also polish up
old stuff.

### Gianni Basso Stampatore
*Calle del Fumo, Cannaregio*
*5306, T041-523 4681.*
Mon-Fri 0930-1300 and
1630-1930, Sat 0930-1300.
Vaporetto: Fondamente Nuove.
Reliable old artisan printer.
This is where Nigella Lawson
and Hugh Grant get their
business cards made.

### I Vetri a Lume di Amadi
*Calle dei Saoneri, San Polo 2747,*
*T041-523 2747.*
Mon-Sat 0930-1300 and
1600-1930.
Vaporetto: San Tomà.
Little glass insects, vegetables,
flowers and animals.

### La Scialuppa
*Calle Seconda Saoneri, San Polo*
*2681, T041-719372.*
Mon-Sat 1000-1300 and
1600-1900.
Vaporetto: San Tomà.
Ready-made models, kits and
intricate plans of Venetian boats,
curated by boat-lover, Gilberto
Penzo.

### Signor Blum
*Campo Santa Barnaba,*
*Dorsoduro 2840, T041-522 6367,*
*www.signorblum.com.*
Mon-Sat 0930-1300 and
1600-1930.
Vaporetto: Ca' Rezzonico.
Amazing wooden toys that
will last forever.

### Totem
*Campo Carità, Dorsoduro 878b,*
*T041-522 3641.*
Tue-Sat 1000-1300 and
1600-1900.
Vaporetto: Ca' Rezzonico.
African and 'tribal' jewellery
made from a variety of materials.

# Activities & tours

### Art & crafts
**Bottega del Tintoretto**
*Fondamenta dei Mori,*
*Cannaregio 3400, T041-722081*
*tintorettovenezia.it.*
Vaporetto: Madonna dell'Orto.
Watercolour, oil painting and
print-making classes round the
corner from where the master
himself worked. A five-day
course starts at €500.

### Ca' Macana
*Calle delle Botteghe, off campo*
*San Barnaba, Dorsoduro 1169,*
*T041-522 9749,*
*camacanacourses.com.*
Vaporetto: Ca' Rezzonico.
Classes on carnival mask making
and decoration for around €40
for two-and-a-half hours.

### Scuola Internazionale
### di Grafica
*Calle del Cristo, Cannaregio 1798,*
*T041-721950, scuolagrafica.it.*
Vaporetto: San Marcuola.
If you see little groups of people
painting a canal scene, it is likely
that they are with the Scuola. It
offers a comprehensive range of
courses in painting for all levels.

### Boating
**Canottieri Bucintoro**
*Fondamenta Zattere allo Spirito*
*Santo, Dorsodoro 15, T041-520*
*5630, bucintoro.org.*
Vaporetto: Zattere.
The Reale Società Canottieri
Bucintoro welcomes
accomplished rowers and
beginners to have a go at *voga*
*veneta* (Venetian rowing),
*canotaggio* (regular rowing) or
sailing. It costs €40 for an hour.

**Canottieri Giudecca**
*Fondamenta del Ponte Lungo,*
*Giudecca 259, T041-528 7409,*
*canottierigiudecca.com.*
Vaporetto: Palanca.
Learn to be a gondolier.
Two-hour lessons on the
lagoon cost about €240.

### Cycling
**Lido on Bike**
*Gran Viale 21, Lido di Venezia,*
*T041-526 8018, lidoonbike.it.*
Apr-Oct daily 0830-1930.
Vaporetto: Lido.
Cycle along the quieter canals
and the proms of the Lido, or
even down to Alberoni and

Pellestrina, via the ferry. €3 per hour or €9 for a day.

## Golf

**Circolo Golf Venezia**
*Alberoni, Lido di Venezia,*
*T041-731333, circologolfvenezia.it.*
Vaporetto: Lido, then Bus A or B.
The Venice Golf Club in Alberoni has an 18-hole course and is open all year round. €60 for a round.

## Food & wine

**Millevini**
*Ramo del Fontego dei Tedeschi,*
*San Marco 5362, T041-520 6090,*
*millevini.com.*
Vaporetto: Rialto.
Wine appreciation sessions that focus on the wines and grappas of Veneto. €50 including wine and *cicchetti*.

**RiViviNatura**
*Calle Vitturi, San Marco 2923,*
*T041-296 0726, rivivinatura.it.*
Learn to cook traditional Venetian dishes like *sarde in saor* and the cakes eaten during Carnevale. A three-hour lesson including food and wine costs €60. There are also tours around the wetlands of the lagoon in a *bragozzo*: €150-200 for up to four people.

**Venice & Veneto Gourmet**
*San Polo 2308, T041-275 0687,*
*venicevenetogourmet.com.*
Visit a Venetian palazzo or a villa on the Lido for a four-hour class on cooking local dishes. There's also a 'Crazy for Fish' class starting at the Rialto market, followed by a demonstration on preparation by the President of the Rialto Fishmongers. Classes cost from €135 per person.

Hourly train services to Milan (3 hrs), Verona (1½-2 hrs), Padua (40 mins), Treviso (30 mins) and Vicenza (1 hr). Frequent buses to Marco Polo Airport (25 mins) and Treviso Airport (40 mins) from piazzale Roma. Regular boats to Marco Polo Airport (1hr 20 mins) from piazza San Marco.

## Restoring Venice

Walk around Venice and you'll notice that much of the city is under tarpaulin wrappers. The cycle of restoration and maintenance is unrelenting. Since the days of the Grand Tour visitors to Venice have been aware of the significant challenges faced by Venetians in holding back the years and the water. The floods of 1966 focused the minds of Venice lovers everywhere, galvanizing members of the British artistic, architectural and historical communities, under the leadership of the former British ambassador to Italy, Sir Ashley Clarke, to found the **Italian Art & Archives Rescue Fund** to fundraise for urgent works in Venice and Florence, which had also suffered terribly in the floods. In 1971 it became the **Venice in Peril Fund** (Unit 4, Hurlingham Studios, Ranelagh Gardens, London SW6 3PA, T020-7736 6891, veniceinperil. org). Its past work includes the restoration of Madonna dell'Orto and San Nicolò dei Mendicoli and it is currently fundraising for work to save the 19th-century Armstrong Mitchell Hydraulic Crane at the Arsenale (a groundbreaking piece of British engineering in its day). Set up at around the same time, **Save Venice** (San Marco 2888a, T041-528 5247, savevenice. org) was founded by three Americans: John and Betty McAndrew and Sydney J Freedberg. This organization holds lectures in the USA and produces a fascinating newsletter for all lovers of the city. It has raised money for numerous projects, including the repair and cleaning of Tiepolo's frescoes of Pulcinella in Ca' Rezzonico and the complete restoration of Santa Maria dei Miracoli. They are currently funding the restoration of San Sebastiano, Veronese's former parish church.

# Contents

**Padua & around**

Statues in the Prato della Valle.

# Introduction

## What to see in…

...one day

Go to the **Cappella degli Scrovegni** and the **Museo Eremitani**. Visit the **University**, the two piazzas and have a Spritz in **Caffè Pedrocchi**. Then catch a tram direct to **Il Santo**.

...a weekend or more

Spend a morning browsing the stalls in **piazza Erbe**, being sure not to miss the **Palazzo delle Ragione**, and add the **Duomo**, **Orto Botanico** and the **Museo del Precinema** to your one-day itinerary. Venture into the **Euganean Hills** and take a boat trip along the **Brenta Canal**. The latter is a pleasantly leisurely way to travel between Padua and Venice.

Christians will associate Padua (Padova) with St Anthony, who lived and preached here and to whom a massive basilica was dedicated, bringing swarms of pilgrims every year. Alongside its saintly appeal, this city has long been an attraction for those seeking artistic and intellectual stimulation. Allegedly founded in 1183 BC by a Trojan, the former Roman settlement of Patavian fell into the hands of Huns, Goths, then Greeks before the Lombards almost destroyed it in 1614. In the 11th century it declared its independence and elected a member of the Este family as *podestà* (mayor). A university town since 1222, Padua was a centre of humanist thought, attracting Dante, Petrarch and Galileo and a host of international scholars who went on to change the way the world was understood. It is also home to one of Europe's most significant artistic treasures: Giotto's frescoes fill the Cappella degli Scrovegni with a richly hued, realist narrative that inspired the Venetian Renaissance. Padua's café culture, once a fertile ground for revolutionary activity, still buzzes and, along with the legacy left by many great minds and artists, is a key element of the city's enduring appeal.

Giotto's frescoes in the Cappella degli Scrovegni.

The sights are clustered in three areas – around piazza Eremitani, in the *centro storico* and south around Prato della Valle – and are all within walking distance of each other, which makes sightseeing easy.

## Cappella degli Scrovegni

*Piazza Eremitani, just off Corso Garibaldi, T049-201 0020, cappelladegliscrovegni.it.* Daily 0900-1900, €12/8 or €1 booking fee for those with a PadovaCard. Booking is compulsory.

For those who are struggling to muster any enthusiasm for seeing yet *another* fresco, just take our word for it: the Scrovegni frescoes are the ultimate and the story behind them encapsulates the mindset of the 13th and 14th centuries.

Enrico Scrovegni was a wealthy banker and merchant who wanted to build a chapel to adjoin his home (demolished in the 19th century). Scrovegni was a troubled soul. He had inherited a highly successful business from his father, Reginaldo, lending money to individuals and businesses at extortionate rates. However, both the church and his contemporaries believed usury to be a sin, ensuring a fast-track into hell. And, as you can see from Giotto's frescoes, the idea of hell was truly horrifying to the medieval mind. (Dante condemned Reginaldo Scrovegni to the inner ring of the seventh circle of his Inferno, where he sat on burning sand with fiery sparks raining down on him from the sky; read Canto XVII for more grisly detail.)

Before seeing the frescoes you must spend 10 minutes in the decontamination chamber and watch the short video describing what you will see. You only have 15 minutes to see the frescoes so it's good to make the best use of your time before the buzzer goes.

You enter the nave of the church from the north side. To your left is the altar and, above you, is the azure blue ceiling with golden stars and medallions of Jesus and the four prophets: John, Ezekiel, Jeremiah and Micah. The frescoes on the south

## Tip...

You can make huge savings by buying a **PadovaCard** (www.padovacard.it), which admits you to Cappella degli Scrovegni (you will still have to book your slot and pay a €1 booking fee), Musei Eremitani, Caffè Pedrocchi and the Museo di Risorgimento, Palazzo delle Ragione, Basilica del Santo, Orto Botanico, Petrarch's house and more. It includes one adult and one child under 14 and also allows you free travel on all buses and trams. The card is available from the tourist office and the above sights: €15 for 48 hrs, €20 for 72 hrs.

# Essentials

**❶ Getting around** Trampadova (T049-824 1111, trampadova.it) runs a single tram line from the train and bus station every 10 mins (€1 single, €3 for a day ticket), right past Eremitani, through the *centro storico* and on to Il Santo, meaning all the major sights are on its one and only route. City buses are run by ACAP (T049-20111). Bus 10 will take you from the station to piazza Cavour. There are also **CitySightseeing** buses (T049-870 4933, citysightseeing.it, hourly, €13/6), which run from Easter to September. Use **Sita** buses (T049-820 6811, sitabus.it) for regional destinations.

**❷ Bus station** ACAP, piazzale Stazione, T049-20111. Buses to Venice depart from piazzale Boschetti.

**❸ Train station** Padova Centrale, piazzale Stazione, T892021, trenitalia.it.

**❹ ATM** There are a number of ATMs around the piazzas dei Signori and delle Erbe and on via Monte di Pietà and via San Canziano.

**❺ Hospital** Complesso Clinico Ospedaliero, via Giustiniani 1, T049-821 1111.

**❻ Pharmacy** Farmacia Andretta, piazza Garibaldi 5, T049-876 6657, Mon-Sat 0900-1230 and 1600-1900; **Farmacia All'Angelo**, piazza Erbe 54, T049-875 8486, Mon-Sat 0900-1300 and 1600-1900.

**❼ Post office** corso Garibaldi 25, T0830-1430, Mon-Sat 0900-1900.

**❽ Tourist information** Padova Centrale Stazione FS, piazzale Stazione, T049-875 2077, www.turismopadova.it, Mon-Sat 0915-1900, Sun 0900-1200; **Galleria Pedrocchi**, T049-876 7927, Mon-Sat 0900-1330 and 1500-1900; piazza del Santo, T049-875 3087, Mar-Oct only Mon-Sat 0900-1330 and 1500-1900.

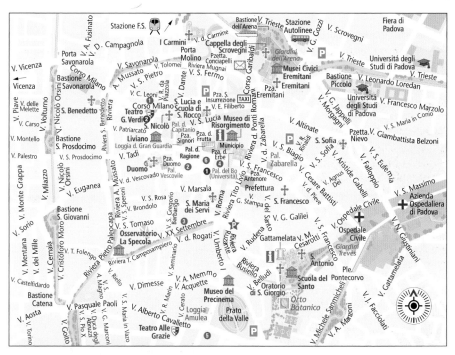

## Listings

**❶ Sleeping**

1 Majestic Toscanelli *via dell'Arco 2*
2 Verdi *via Dondi dall'Orologio 7*

**❶ Eating & drinking**

1 Antico Brolo *corso Milano 22*
2 Caffè della Piazzetta *Via San Martino e Solferino 49*
3 Caffeteria Roma *via XX Settembre 53*
4 Osteria l'Anfora *via dei sonsin 12*
5 Pizzeria Orsucci *corso Vittorio Emanuele II 18*
6 Vescovi *piazza delle Erbe*

Piazza Erbe.

and north walls are on three levels, with a lower register below. Those on the top level of the south wall tell the story of the Virgin's parents, Joachim and Anna (including the lovely *Meeting of Joachim and Anna at the Golden Gate*). Mary's life is depicted on the top level of the north wall (look for *Mary is Presented at the Temple of Jerusalem*, which inspired Titian), ending with the *Annunciation*, the *Visitation* and *God the Father Sends Archangel Gabriel*. The second level on the south wall starts with Christ's birth and the *Massacre of the Innocents*, before moving into his adult life. *The Expulsion of the Merchants from the Temple* on the north wall moves the intensity of the frescoes up a gear. Look out for *Judas Betrays Jesus for Thirty Pieces of Silver* on the south wall, which depicts Judas as a golden version of Satan, who stands at his back. On the third level you see the last few days of Christ's life. *The Betrayal of Christ*, with Judas' kiss, is full of violence and *Jesus before Pilate* is also very powerful. Around the fourth register are the Virtues and the Vices: *Fortitudo* (fortitude), *Stultitia* (folly), *Inconstantia* (inconstancy) and *Ira* (wrath) are rather amusing, but *Invidia* (envy) and *Desperado* (despair) are more troubling images. Finally, the *Last Judgement* takes up the whole of the west wall, where the entrance once was. The regimented rows of angels and golden order of heaven are in stark contrast to the dark, fiery, chaos of hell.

Painting was very flat and stylized in the early 1300s. Giotto's understanding of perspective, his use of architectural settings, his employment of colours beyond the usual liturgical palette and his desire for realism were all remarkable for the age. As Ruskin said in his book, *Giotto and his works in Padua*, the artist was "a daring naturalist, in defiance of tradition, idealism and formalism".

### Musei Eremitani

*Piazza Eremitani 8, T049-820 4551.*
Feb-Oct Tue-Sun 0900-1900,
Nov-Jan Tue-Sun 0900-1800, €10, €8 concessions (under 18, students up to age 29 and over 65s).

The museum hosts a fine archaeological collection of Egyptian, Roman, Etruscan and Paleochristian artefacts and antiquities, including statues of beefy Romans and tombstones from the Volumni family that date back to AD 1. The Museo di Bottacin is a vast coin collection including Venetian grossos and ducats as well as Roman medallions and some rather impressive seals. The Emo Capodilista collection of art stretches from the 1300s through the Venetian Renaissance and into the 1700s, with works by Giotto, Giorgione, Titian, Tiepolo, as well as Giovanni Bellini's *Portrait of a Young Senator* (1485) and Tintoretto's *Crucifixion* (1565).

### Chiesa degli Eremitani

*Piazza Eremitani 8, T049-875 6410.*
Mar-Oct Mon-Sat 0815-1845, Sun 1000-1200 and 1630-1900, Nov-Feb Mon-Sat 0815-1830, Sun 1000-1300 and 1645-1900.

This church was built in 1276 and dedicated to San Giacomo and San Filippo (St James and St Philip). Despite its massive interior, it has heaps of charm. The series of frescoes are the work of local artist, Andrea Mantegna (1431-1506). His masterpiece, the *Martyrdom of St James* (1450s) was all but destroyed by American bombs in the Second World War. It has been reconstructed using the little that could be saved. You can, however, still see his *Martyrdom of St Christopher*, which was rescued before the bombs hit.

Musei Eremitani.

**Caffè Pedrocchi.**

### Caffè Pedrocchi & Museo del Risorgimento

*Via VII Febbraio 15, caffepedrocchi.it.*
*Café T049-878 1231, Museum T049-820 5007.*
Cafe: Tue-Sun 0800-2400. Museum: Sep-Jul
Tue-Sun 0930-1230 and 1530-1800, €4/2.50.

There has been a café on this site since 1772.
The original humbler version was owned by
Francesco Pedrocchi. His son, Antonio,
commissioned the Venetian, Joseph Jappelli,
to build a neoclassical beauty on the triangular
site that it now dominates. The ground floor was
completed in 1831 and the upper floors and salons
in 1842. Pedrocchi had a little bit more about him
than a nice frothy coffee: he worked with a number
of Italian artists to create a monument to the great
civilizations of the world. The Sala Egizia (inspired
by the Paduan egyptologist Giovanni Battista
Belzoni) is most famous but the curved Sala
Romana and the ceiling of the Sala Etrusca are just
as amazing. There is also a huge ballroom, known
as the Sala Rossini. Upstairs, the Corinthian loggia
overlooks the piazza.

Today, these upper rooms house a museum
tracing the 19th-century struggle for Italian
unification. The museum itself, having to compete
with the decor, is low-key but the displays do give
some sense of the local determination to oust the
Austrians following the fall of Venice to Napoleon
in 1797. At this time, Caffè Pedrocchi became
famous as the place where the intellectual wing

of the Risorgimento (unification movement)
came to meet, debate and plan. After the
unification of Italy and the death of Antonio
Pedrocchi's adopted son, the café was passed onto
the Paduan authorities in 1891. Bombed to bits in
World War II, it was completely rebuilt by Angelo
Pisani in its original style but was closed during
the 1980s and '90s, due to council wrangling.
It reopened in December 1998 and today is, once
more, at the heart of the city. Downstairs there are
a number of salons where you can sit and while
away the time or, of course, you could plan some
kind of uprising while tucking into a *panino* on the
tables overlooking the piazza.

### Università

*Via VII Febbraio 2, T049-820 9711, unipd.it.*
Tours Mar-Nov Tue and Thu 0900, 1000, 1100, 1500,
1600, 1700, Wed and Sat 0900, 1000, 1100, €5/2.

You know you are in an Italian varsity town when
you here the graduands song 'Dottore, dottore...'
fill the streets. Italy's second oldest university
dates back to 1222 and its motto is *Universa
universis patavina libertas* (Paduan freedom is
universal for everyone). The university is housed in
the Palazzo Bo. (There are numerous explanations

## Il Risorgimento

In 1797 the Venetian Republic fell and Padua was
ceded to the Austrian Empire. Paduan intellectuals
and its working men shared an intense dislike of
their new rulers. On 8 February 1848 the students
and locals rose up in revolt, turning the University
and the Caffè Pedrocchi into a battleground. Four of
the student leaders were executed by the Austrians
for their part in the rebellion. It wasn't until 1866
that the Austrians were kicked out of the north of
country and the whole of Italy was united. Padua's
street fighting years were not over, however.
The *Resistenza* (Italian partisans who sought to
undermine Mussolini and his Nazi puppeteers)
had a solid kernel of support here: one of the
main leaders was Concetto Marchesi, the
Vice Chancellor of Padua University.

# Famous alumni

Padua's university was at the peak of its power in the 15th and 16th centuries, when everyone who was anyone wanted to study medicine and/or law here.

**Thomas Linacre** founder of the Royal College of Surgeons (1492)

**Pietro Bombo** 'founder' of the Italian language (c1495)

**Nicolaus Copernicus** astronomer (1501)

**Sir John Caius** Queen Elizabeth I's doctor (1539)

**Gabriele Falloppio** discovered fallopian tubes (c1551)

**Sir Francis Walsingham** Queen Elizabeth I's spymaster (studied law c1553)

**Dr William Harvey** discovered the circulatory system (1602)

**Galileo Galilei** astronomer (taught mathematics c1610)

**Elena Cornaro Piscopia** a Venetian noblewoman who was the first ever female Doctor of Philosophy (1678)

**Moses Chaim Hayyim** famous kabbalist (studied medicine c1724)

**Carlo Goldoni** Venetian playwright (studied law c1735)

**Giacomo Girolamo Casanova** writer and womaniser (studied law 1742)

**Ippolito Nievo** writer and one of Garibaldi's right-hand men (1854)

**Francesco Rossetti** (taught physics c1866)

The Università is home to the world's oldest anatomical theatre.

for this strange name, including that it stood on the site of the old Ox Inn, that it was handed over to pay for a butcher's bill or that there used to be butcher's near here.) Andrea Maroni is name-checked as the architect but others claim Palladio built the courtyard, which was completed around 1552. You enter through the vaulted Atrio degli Eroi (atrium of heroes), where an accumulation of crests and plaques encrust the walls in commemoration of those students who died in the various wars that scar the history of the region. Crests (or *scholae*) also decorate Ippolito Nievo hall, indicating the privileged backgrounds of the university's former students. Look out for Sala dei 40 (Hall of the 40), which has a gallery of 40 great foreign students who studied at Padua. It also houses Galileo Galilei's wooden desk and the world's oldest anatomical theatre (1594). This is made of wood in an elliptical design and could accommodate 300 (squashed) students over six tiers.

The university has nine small museums in total. If you have some spare time the **Museo di Macchine Enrico Bernardi** (viale Venezia 1, T049-827 6775) will appeal to lovers of vehicles, whilst the **Museo di Antropologia** at the Orto Botanico (T049-827 2118) will tickle the fancy of those who love weird, mutated creatures. There are more details on the university website.

### Osservatorio La Specola

*V.lo dell'Osservatorio 5, T049-829 3469.*
Guided tours Oct-Apr Sat and Sun 1600,
May-Sep Sat and Sun 1800.
Tickets from San Michele Oratorio (50 m away),
Tue-Fri 1000-1300, Sat and Sun 1500-1600, €8.
Bus 12, 18.

It's a faff getting the tickets but if you're a star gazer, it's a must. The observatory of the university was built in the 18th century inside a 14th-century tower. The guided tour leads you past telescopes, globes and quadrants to the top of the tower from where there are some cracking views of the city.

Detail from the astronomical clock at Palazzo del Capitano.

## Palazzo delle Ragione

*Piazza Erbe, T049-820 5006.*
Tue-Sun 0930-1230 and 1430-1800, €8,
€5 concession.

At 80 m long, 27 m wide and 27 m high, Padua's massive former law court in the Palace of Reason dominates piazza Erbe and the central market area of the city. The ground floor (known as the Sottosalone) is divided into halls of permanent stalls and shops selling regional and artisan products (see page 186). The upper salon is a single uninterrupted space and is colourfully enriched by 333 frescoes by Nicolò Miretto and Stefano da Ferrara (1445) depicting gods, fruits, vegetables, planets, stars and signs of the zodiac. These frescoes took 15 years to complete after the originals by Giotto were destroyed by fire in 1420.

A wooden copy of the horse from Donatello's *Gattamelata* (the bronze version, with rider, sits outside Il Santo; see page 176) stands at one end of the salon and, despite being pretty big itself, manages to look quite dainty in this vast hulking space. The salon is used for temporary exhibitions.

## Piazza dei Signori

Just a few steps away from piazza Erbe is the more enclosed piazza dei Signori. The **Palazzo del Capitano** (1605) has a triumphal arch and tower by Falconetto (1532) that houses one of Italy's oldest astronomical clocks, dating from 1344. Across the courtyard is the **Liviano** (part of the arts faculty of the university), whose entrance hall is decorated with a fresco showing Petrarch reading his books.

# The saint of all things lost: St Anthony (1195-1231)

Fernando Martins de Bulhões was born in Lisbon in 1195 to a wealthy family but he rejected his riches and joined the local order of Augustinians, where he studied theology. He crossed the floor to the Franciscan order after learning about the Franciscan martyrs whose bodies were buried in his monastery; St Bernard, St Peter, St Otho, St Accursius and St Adjutus had been beheaded and mutilated by the Moors after preaching Christianity in Morocco in 1220.

At the age of 25 he began his own missionary work in Morocco but illness caused him to abort the trip and he travelled instead to Sicily and then to Forli, near Bologna. Here, the church authorities heard about the moving power of his preaching and dispatched him across Europe to teach at the universities of Montpellier and Toulouse before assigning him to northern Italy as the Pope's envoy and sermon writer. At the age of 35 Anthony was living and preaching in Padua but was struggling with ill health. He exhausted himself giving day-long sermons at Prato della Valle, where up to 30,000 people would hear him preach. His popularity meant he needed a bodyguard to keep the crowds at bay. After a particularly gruelling series of sermons to mark Lent, Anthony went to a retreat outside Padua, where he died, aged just 36.

Anthony is considered the patron saint of all things lost and stolen. Should you have the grave misfortune to lose something, like a sock perhaps, just cry: "Anthony, Anthony, turn around, something's lost and must be found," to ask for the Saint's assistance.

## Duomo

*Piazza Duomo, T049-656914.*
Apr-Oct Mon-Sat 1000-1900,
Nov-Mar Mon-Sat 1000-1800, €4.

The main part of the cathedral dates back to the 11th century but was totally rebuilt in 1552 using designs by Michelangelo. The façade was never finished, which explains why the plain, flat front looks so terribly austere next to the smaller but more stylish baptistery. In the main church there are some interesting works by Francesco Bassano and Giorgio Schiavone but it is in the fresco-laden baptistery that the eyes have something to feast on. The cycle of frescoes was painted by the Florentine Giusto de' Menabuoi in 1378. Invariably, visitors compare them to Giotto's work in the Scrovegni chapel and, admittedly, these compositions lack a bit of drama. However, when you raise your eyes to the huge interior dome you can see that de' Menabuoi was capable of so much more than merely following in Giotto's footsteps. The dome is swathed in concentric rings of halo-illuminated angels and saints, all looking down on you, urging you to be holy, with a rather portly Christ at his most beseeching in the centre.

## Basilica del Santo (Il Santo)

*Piazzo del Santo, T049-878 9722.*
Mar-Oct Mon-Sat 0630-1945,
Nov-Feb Mon-Sat 0630-1900.

Up to five million pilgrims come to Padua and the basilica every year to pray to St Anthony. Unusually, he was a saint that died, not of any ghastly impaling, flaying, roasting or beheading, but from a simple case of dropsy. A year later, he was canonized and, not long after, the city began work on this splendid, sturdy structure to house his bones. Begun in 1232, the unusual fusion of Byzantine domes, simple Gothic brickwork and Romanesque features is certainly eye-catching.

The Florentine Renaissance sculptor Donatello (aka Donato di Niccolò di Betto Bardi; c1386-1466) came to Padua in 1443 and spent 10 years plying

Above: The Orto Botanico. Opposite page: The façadeless Duomo.

his trade and developing his technique of *schiacciato* (bas-relief). Some good examples, celebrating St Anthony, his miracles and his death, are found inside the basilica on the high altar: look out for the *Miracle of the Ass* and *Entombment*, which exudes a moving gentleness despite being in a sorry state of repair. Apart from the high altar, Donatello's bronze Crucifix is perhaps his most famous piece of work. Look out, too, for his *Madonna and Child* in the choir: no, the two chunky legs at either side don't belong to the virgin, they're part of a chair! There are also some marble reliefs by Sansovino and Lombardo.

The Cappella del Tesoro holds the relics of St Anthony. Rather gruesomely, his tongue and another unidentifiable part of his anatomy (his larynx?) are on display behind glass in two golden reliquaries.

## Gattamelata

*Piazza del Santo.*

In 1443 Donatello was called to Padua by the family of the late Erasmo da Narni and asked to create a monument to the *condottiero* (mercenary leader) who had assisted the Venetian Republic in their scuffles with the Milanese in 1434. Known as 'Honey Cat' (a rather unwarlike nickname), this

magnificent free-standing equestrian statue in bronze is 3.7 m high and sits atop a marble plinth with the inscription: "Narnia me genuit Gattamelata fui" (I was born in Narni, I was Gattamelata).

## Orto Botanico

*Via Orto Botanico 15,*
*200 m south of Il Santo, T049-827 2120.*
Apr-Oct Mon-Sat 0900-1300 and 1500-1800,
Nov-Apr Mon-Sat 0900-1300, €4.

Founded in 1545, this is considered to be the oldest university garden in the world. Its purpose was the cultivation of medicinal plants for the medics at the university. The first keeper was Luigi Squalermo whose collection policy helped increase the garden, secure its reputation and place Padua at the forefront of the study of botany.

The garden is circular and perfectly proportioned but not over-manicured and is surrounded by a wall and four big gates. It has a large collection of species that were once new to Italy (such as lilacs and potatoes) and also protects rare or endangered indigenous species. As you enter, there are pungent magnolia trees and shady cypresses. To the right is the arboretum, where black walnut and various oaks create a leafy shelter. At the edge of the inner circle, facing east are the azaleas and camellias, while, at the very centre, is a pond with water lilies. This is surrounded by the gingko quarter, a tamerix quarter, albizia quarter and a magnolia quarter, behind which are some rare species from the Euganean hills. On the Il Santo side of the garden is an orchid house and orangeries, where succulents, carnivorous plants and orchids are kept. Goethe's palm (which he mentions in his book *Voyages in Italy*) is contained in an octagonal treehouse that protects it from the harsh Paduan winters.

### Prato della Valle

*South end of via Umberto I.*

One of Padua's most wonderful sights is the Prato della Valle, supposedly the biggest piazza in Italy at 90,000 sq m. Previously the site of a Roman theatre and also used by St Anthony to preach his sermons, it is now a most striking park. Its design – so perfectly complemented by the palazzi that hug it – takes the form of an elliptical canal encircling the fountain-adorned Isola Memmia, which is reached by four bridges. The bridges and the edges of the canal are lined with 78 statues of some of Padua's most famous students and citizens, including Dante, Petrarch, Giotto and Andrea Memmo. It was Memmo who had the vision for the park and who drained the swamp that was once here. He lived nearby at Palazzo Angeli, where the Museo del Precinema is now housed.

### Museo del Precinema

*Palazzo Angeli 1a, Prato della Valle, T049-876 3838, minicizotti.it.* Mid Jun-mid Sep Mon-Sat 1000-2200, mid Sep-mid Jun Mon-Sat 1000-1600, closed 2 wks Aug, €3, €2 concessions.

This museum is an absolute delight, full of interesting and charming objects collected by Minici Zotti relating to the history and pre-history of cinema. There are thaumatropes and phenakistoscopes, early flick books, magic lanterns,

optical instruments and original hand-painted slides going back to the 18th and 19th centuries. The Javan, Chinese and Turkish shadow puppet theatres and some intricately cut-out silhouettes are so simple but inventive, they make IMAX look gaudy.

## Around Padua

### Canale del Brenta

As their control of the seas and lucrative trade routes waned, the Venetians looked inland to see how the next fortune could be made. The Republic's expansion into terra firma led to the 36-km River Brenta being canalized in the 16th

The Prato della Valle.

century, optimizing its potential as a transportation route between Padua and Venice. A number of Venetian nobles built villas along the Brenta, where they sought to cultivate profits from the land and to retreat from the city in the hot summer months. There are 30 of these villas in total, located in and between the canalside towns of Strà, Dolo, Mira and Malcontenta. Most can be glimpsed from the canal and some of the grander ones have been maintained and allow public access.

A number of companies provide a range of boat tours along the Brenta Canal, embarking early in the morning from beside the train station in Padua (see page 187). Prices and itineraries vary but expect to pay around €50 for a half-day trip and up to €100 for a whole day. The Strà to Mira stretch is the most interesting; bear this in mind if you'd like to book a boat trip but don't have a whole day or €100 to spare.

Arguably the grandest villa on the canal, the late-Baroque **Villa Pisani** (via Alvise Pisani 7, T049-502270, Apr-Sep Tue-Sun 0830-1900, Oct-Mar Tue-Sun 0900-1600, €5/2.50) in Strà was built for Doge Alvise Pisani and looks like an English stately home. Giovanni Tiepolo celebrated the Pisani family's power and fame in a stunning fresco on the hall ceiling, completed in 1760. Frescoes by his son, Gian Domenico, can be found in the banqueting hall. Napoleon briefly owned the villa after the fall of Venice, and Hitler and Mussolini met here in 1934.

Further east, in Mira, is **Villa Widmann-Foscari** (via la Nazionale 420, T041-424973, Apr and Oct Tue-Sun 1000-1700, May-Sep Tue-Sun 1000-1800, Nov-Mar Sat-Sun 1000-1700, €5), which was built by the Persian Sceriman family in the early 18th century but later bought by the Widmanns who added many rococo flourishes. Its ballroom and gardens are lavish indeed. Also in Mira, behind a trimmed-within-an-inch-of-its-life box hedge, is **Barchessa Valmarana** (via Valmarana 11, T041-426 6387, villavalmarana.net, Mar-Oct Tue-Sun 1000-1800, €10). The pursuit of modernity led this handsome villa to be partially demolished and its frescoes to be painted over in the early part of the 20th century. However, it has since been restored to a new glory

# Francesco Petrarca (1304–1374)

Known as the father of humanism, Petrarch was a scholar, a poet and a great friend of Boccaccio (the saucy storyteller of the early Renaissance). Born in Arezzo, he was the son of Pietro Petracco, a public notary who, exiled from Florence along with Dante, was employed by the papal court in Avignon. Petrarch followed in his dad's footsteps and studied law at Montpellier and Bologna but he was more interested in literary pursuits, viewing the legal profession with distaste: in a letter to his brother Gherardo he wrote, "I couldn't face making a merchandise of my mind".

His first work, *Africa*, about the Roman emperor Publius Cornelius Scipio Africanus, earned Petrarch, now 35, the honour of being Rome's poet laureate. He went on to write prolifically, exploring theories of human thought, learning and love outside the confines dictated by the church. He unearthed works by Homer and Cicero, developed the sonnet as a model of lyrical poetry and is credited with creating the genre of travel writing (although debate rages about whether he actually visited the places he wrote about!). When not travelling, he lived with his daughter in Venice and, later, in Arquà Petrarca where he died (see page 181). Ever the caring friend, in his will he left a small amount of money to Boccaccio "to buy a dressing gown".

In 2003 anatomists from the University of Padua decided to exhume his remains and test them. It turned out the skull amongst the bones was not his. They have since made a plea for the return of his skull.

and the frolicsome frescoes by Michelangelo Schiavoni, aka 'il Chiozzotto' (1712-72), a pupil of Tiepolo, can now be enjoyed again.

At the eastern end of the canal, close to the lagoon, is **Villa Foscari Rossi** (known as La Malcontenta; via dei Turisti 9, Malcontenta, T041-520 3966, May-Oct Tue and Sat 0900-1200, €7). Vincenzo Scamozzi used Palladio's drawings to build this villa for the Foscaris, one of Venice's most noble families. Its suburban location meant it could easily be reached by boat from the centre of Venice. A neoclassical refurb has changed the exterior but its imposing design, raised high on a podium above the canal bank, is still something to behold.

# Take to the hills

**S**outh of Padua, the Euganean Hills are an ideal escape from the city and offer the chance to work off all that pasta. The 120,000 hectares and 81 hills of the Parco Regionale offer a vast array of terrain, from wide open fields and cherry tree-lined paths to Mediterranean scrub and chestnut groves. The protected environment shelters rare shrubs and flowers, such as the tree heath and the sage-leaved cistus. Sparrowhawks swoop above and, when you stop to eat your sandwiches, you might be visited by a lovely libellula dragonfly.

Within the park (Parco Regionale dei Colli Euganei) are 15 towns and villages including Este, the walled former stronghold of this historical family, and the spa towns of Montegrotto and Abano Terme, famous for its mineral-rich hot mud and waters. The hills enchanted the Romantic writers Shelley and Lord Byron, as well as Francesco Petrarca, the medieval humanist, who lived out the last years of his life at Arquà.

Wine producers in the area have clubbed together to form the **Strada dei Vini DOC dei Colli Euganei** (Viale Stazione 60, Montegrotto Terme, T049-891 2451, stradadelvinocollieuganei.it) and offer various tours of wineries and other places of interest on foot, by bike or by car or minibus.

## Hiking

The park is criss-crossed by a range of designated walking trails to suit all levels of fitness and available time. **ANCI** (Hotel Terme Igea Suisse, via Busonera 19, Abano Terme, T049-866 9131) offers Nordic walking tours of the park, using poles to propel you along.

If you prefer to go hiking independently, make sure you are wearing suitable footwear and a showerproof jacket, and that you have a decent map and compass and enough water to keep you going (especially in the summer). It's also a good idea to leave details of your intended route and expected time of return with your hotel or B&B. For further information contact the park headquarters (via Rana Ca' Mori 8, Este, T0429-612010, parcocollieuganei.it).

## Atestino trail

**Start and end** Arquà Petrarca (a 1-hr bus journey from Padua).
**Length** 21.5 km or 1 day.
**Level** Relatively easy unless you attempt to reach the summits, which will involve some steep gradients.

This trail circles the peaks of Monte Orbieso (330 m), Monte Fasolo (289 m) and Monte Rusta (396 m); if you're fit enough, you may choose to tackle the summits. The route will delight lovers of flora: chestnut trees shade the path along which rare orchids grow and, in spring, the bloom of almond trees surpasses that of the cherry blossom.

## Monte Ricco & Monte Castello trail

**Start and end**  Monselice railway station
(a 25-min train journey from Padua).
**Length**  5 km or 2-3 hrs.
**Level**  not very demanding; more of a ramble
than a hike.

Recommended for spring and autumn, this walk
offers panoramas that bring peace to your soul,
including a lovely view of Arquà Petrarca.

## Horse riding & cycling

If walking is not for you, the **Centro Equestre
Montagnon** (via Mezzavia 49, Montegrotto
Terme, T049-793289, €25 for 2 hrs/€50 for half day,
reservations essential), close to the train station
(a 15-min train journey from Padua), offers guided
horseback tours of the hills. Alternatively, there are
a number of bike routes on the park website and
bikes available for hire in Montegrotto Terme from
**Noleggio Biciclette Brombin** (via Roma 10,
T049-793491) and **Noleggio Biciclette Battisti**
(via Catajo 1, T049-793099).

## Casa di Petrarca

*Via Valleselle 4, Arquà Petrarca, T042-971 8294.*
Mar-Oct Tue-Sun 0900-1200 & 1500-1830.
Bus 806 from piazzale Boschetti in Padua;
by car, take N16 and turn off at Monselice,
then follow signs

Once just Arquà, this small medieval town added
the name of its most famous pensioner in 1868.
Petrarch spent the last few years of his life here and
his former home is open to the public. You can see
the poet's desk, his bookcase and his mummified
cat. Petrarch himself rests in peace in a
sarcophagus in the garden.

# Tip…

Fancy some fangotherapy or a splash of
hydrokinetics? The bubbling mud and thermal
waters of the area have eased and invigorated
since Roman times. Visit Padua's tourism
website for more information about the
Terme Euganee (turismopadova.it).

# Sleeping

Padua

## Hotel Majestic Toscanelli €€
*Via dell'Arco 2,
T049-663244, toscanelli.com.*
This affable little hotel is well placed just a few steps away from piazza Erbe, one of the three beating hearts of Padua's nightlife. The breakfast room downstairs is like a comfy old American bar and the 32 bedrooms are neatly furnished and supply the means to make a much-needed cup of tea.

## Hotel Verdi €
*Via Dondi Dall'Orologio 7,
T049-8364163,
albergoverdipadova.it.*

Not far from piazza dei Signori, this small hotel has good-sized rooms that are modern and clean, with solid windows that keep the city bustle at bay. There's a sitting room and a sunny breakfast room and, although the breakfast is pretty unexciting, it's good value.

## Gioia B&B €
*Via Pietro Liberi 8A,
T049-606302, bbgioia.com.*
Located near the train station, this B&B has huge rooms, marble floors, contemporary furniture and lots of light. The owners are hugely enthusiastic about their little business but still suitably laid back. Its location means that you won't have to heave your luggage across town if you arrive by train but it is a bit of a walk to get to the action.

Around Padua

## Villa Rizzi-Albarea €€€
*Via Albarea 53, Pianiga,
T041-510 0933, villa-albarea.
com.*
The gardens, the pool and the fabulous service are the stand-out features of this getaway, set amongst lush countryside 23 km from Padua. A former monastery, it is now owned by Dr Pierluigi Rizzi and his wife Aida (a countess, don't

you know), who have carefully restored the building and the works within it and take huge pleasure in looking after you. There are nine rooms and a generous breakfast is served on the terrace. Regular cultural and artistic events are held here.

## Villa Ducale €€
*Riviera Martiri della Libertà 75,
Dolo, T041-560 8020.*
Just 10 km from Padua, this 19th-century villa offers a grand experience at a very reasonable price. Its 11 rooms (even the smaller ones) are all decorated with a bit of munificence, including twinkling Murano glass chandeliers, sturdy iron bedsteads and classy marble bathrooms. Le Colonne restaurant looks out onto the gorgeous statue-lined gardens, which lead you down to the Brenta Canal itself.

Above and right: Hotel Verdi.

# Eating & drinking

Padua

### Antico Brolo €€€
*Corso Milano 22,*
*T049-664555, anticobrolo.it.*
Mon 1900-2200, Tue-Sat
1200-1500 and 1900-2200.
Across the road from the Teatro
de Padua, this swish restaurant is
popular with families and has a
delightful inner salon and a
beautiful candlelit garden. The
food – such as fried calamari with
puréed cauliflower (try it before
you knock it) – is all carefully
presented but you can still expect
a generous helping. There's a
great value set menu for €25.

### Osteria l'Anfora €
*Via Dei Soncin 12, T049-656629.*
Mon 1900-2200, Tue-Sat
1200-1500 and 1900-2200.
This is a fail-safe choice for those
who don't want to splash out,
offering good, reliable fare, such
as *tortelloni al zucca* (stuffed with
sweet pumpkin purée), and a
very affordable selection of

wines by the glass. Perhaps
just as good as the food is
the people-watching: varsity
professors come here to unwind
from the pressures of knowing so
much. There is sometimes live
jazz, too.

### Pizzeria Orsucci €
*18 Corso Vittorio Emanuele II,*
*T049-875 9313.*
Fri-Wed 1800-2300.
This tiny little pizzeria outside
the historic centre has only eight
seats but, if you are visiting Prato
della Valle, it's definitely worth
checking it out. The pizzas are
made in round flat trays, which
give the bases a crisp, almost
fried crunch.

### Cafés & bars
**Caffè Pedrocchi** (see page 173)
is Padua's most celebrated café
but there are plenty of other
places to while away the hours
drinking and chatting. Every
evening piazza Erbe and piazza
dei Signori are both full of locals
enjoying a wind-down Spritz.

### Azienda d'Affari
*Via Dante 16,*
*T392-928 0055 (mobile).*
Mon-Sat 0800-2400,
Sun 0800-1800.
Smart little wine bar with DJs
on Friday and Saturday nights.

### Bar Café El Pilar
*Piazza dei Signori 8,*
*T049- 657565.*
Mon-Sat 0800-2100.
This is the place to come for
early evening aperitivi.

### Bar Munerato
*Piazza Erbe 45.*
Mon-Sat 1100-2300.
Big glasses of Spritz served
by friendly staff.

### Caffè Baessato
*Largo Europa 14,*
*T049-873958.*
Tue-Sun 0700-2400.
A traditional bar on three
levels, with *stuzzichini* (bite-size
appetizers) served on the first
floor. A great place to come for
aperitivi.

## Pick of Padua's picnic spots

Raid the Sottosalone covered
market in the Palazzo della
Ragione (see page 186) for
regional goodies, including
Montagnana ham, then head
to one of the following al fresco
eating spots:

**Corso del Popolo**  Lots of
greenery and very close to
the Cappella degli Scrovegni.

**Piazza Garibaldi**  Modern
benches amongst stylish
concrete.

**Prato della Valle**  The city's
finest and biggest park.

Spritz – they drink it all over the Veneto.

### Caffè della Piazzetta
*Via San Martino e Solferino 49,*
*T049-657057.*
Mon-Fri 0730-2000,
Sat 0730-2100.
Located in the old ghetto, it has
tables on the lovely *piazzetta*
outside. If you fancy a bite, try
the excellent *piadine* (flat bread
sandwiches) and temple-
achingly sweet *dolci*.

### Caffeteria Roma
*Via XX Settembre 53,*
*T038-326 4947 (mobile).*
Mon-Sat 0800-2200.
A great place to kick-start
your morning with custard filled
*cornetti*. It's abuzz with a young

crowd all day long.

### Enoteca da Severino
*Via del Santo 44,*
*T049-650697.*
Tue-Sun 0900-2300.
Great wines and fabulous food
with a mix of interesting and
mature customers.

### Grom
*Via Roma 101, T049-659266.*
Mon-Thu 1200-2400,
Fri 1200-0100, Sat 1100-0100,
Sun 1100-2400.
Life-changing gourmet
organic gelato: try the cinnamon
(*cannella*) or pear (*pera*) sorbet.

### Patagonia
*Piazza dei Signori 27,*
*T049-875 1045.*
Tue-Sun 1100-2400.
Perfectly located for late-night
licks, this gelateria has some
classic fruity flavours to choose

from.

### Vescovi
*Piazza Erbe, T049-876 0669.*
Mon-Sat 0700-1930.
A café since 1927, this old
palazzo serves great coffee and
old-fashioned sweet snacks.

Around Padua

### Margherita €€€
*Via Nazionale 312, Mira,*
*T041-426 5800,*
*dalcorsohotellerie.it.*
This restaurant with rooms is
located in a leafy, shady spot
bang on the Brenta Canal, 28 km
from Padua. Built by the Venetian
Contarini family, it is still
ridiculously grand but has a
simple chic charm, created by
the current owners, the Dal
Corsos. The menu is all very fishy:
highlights include a fabulous
Veraci clam soup and *spaghetti
aragosta* (with lobster). If you stay
overnight (€€€) expect huge
beds in rather regal bedrooms
and a big breakfast.

Villa Margherita.

# Entertainment

### Cinema
**Cinema Multiastra**
*Via Tiziana Aspetti 21,*
*T049 604 078.*
€5.50.
Right next to the train station, this cinema has three screens showing a good mix of Italian, independent and mainstream films.

### Clubs
**Fishmarket Showbar**
*Via Frà Paolo Sarpi 37,*
*T335-643 9002 (mobile).*
Tue, Wed, Fri and Sat 2200-0400, €10.
Live music and DJ sets in the old fish market, now adorned with installation art and a rather leftfield crowd.

### Gay & lesbian
**Fresh'n'fruit @ Pachuca**
*Via Bernina 18,*
*T347-002 9389, freshnfruit.com.*
Wed, Fri and Sat 2200-0300, €15.
Thumping house and Euro pop until the early hours. There's a happy hour from 2200 till 2400.

### Music
Each year in November the
**Padua Jazz Festival**
(padovajazz.com) hosts an impressive international line up in venues across the city. Gigs range from intimate piano bar affairs to concerts in Teatro Comunale Verdi (see below).

**Victoria**
*Via Savonarola 149,*
*T049-872 1530.*
Tue-Sun 1900-0200.
The Victoria pub sells pizza and features live jazz concerts on Thursday nights.

### Theatre
**Teatro Comunale Verdi**
*Via Livello 32, T049-877 7011,*
*teatrostabileveneto.it.*
€10-30.
Built in 1751, this circular arcaded theatre glows peach in the evening light. Plays by Pasolini, Shakespeare, Goldoni and wild cards like Michael Frayn prove hugely popular, as do regular concerts and ballets.

# Shopping

An upwardly mobile town with a large student population means lots of books and clothes shops. The main shopping areas are the streets that lead off of piazza Erbe and piazza della Frutta; you can find most things from shoes to medicines to homewares. High-street shops are to be found around piazza Garibaldi and piazza Cavour, whilst via Zabarella and via Altinate have a number of boutiques and

Sottosalone.

## Tip...

Don't handle the goods: the stallholders get annoyed when people disturb their carefully stacked wares. If you're buying, indicate to the stallholder whether you'd like *questo* (this one) or *quello* (that one).

independent shops. Clothes and kitchen things are also sold from stalls in bustling piazza della Frutta daily except Sunday.

### Art & antiques
**Mercato dell' Antiquariato**
*Prato della Valle.*
3rd Sun each month
0700-sunset.
If you can get there early enough, you can pick up some gobsmackingly good finds: exquisite old books with botanical drawings, brass knockers in the shape of foxes and Baroque picture frames.

### Books
**Feltrinelli International**
*Via San Francesco 14,*
*T049-875 0792.*
Mon-Fri 0900-1930,
Sat 0900-2000, Sun 1000-1300 and 1530-1930.
Some gorgeous coffee table tomes and a satisfying assortment of books in English.

**Libreria Draghi**
*Via Santa Lucia 11,*
*T049-876 0306, libreriadraghi.it.*
Mon-Fri 0930-1930,
Sat 0930-1230.
Fascinating cultural bookshop with some great international finds and a programme of events and exhibitions.

**Musei Civici degli Eremitani**
*Piazza Eremitani 8,*
*T049-8204 5450.*
Feb-Oct Tue-Sun 0900-1900,
Nov-Jan Tue-Sun 0900-1800.
The gift shop at the museum has an extensive selection of books about art and history.

### Clothing
The Saturday market (0800-1800) in Prato della Valle sells clothes, shoes and leather accessories; you'll find some tat but also some real bargains.

**Galeazzo Padova**
*Via Altinate 63, T049-875 3352.*
Mon 1500-2000,
Tue-Sat 0930-2000.
Beautifully tailored clothes for men and women, Italian homewares and a hip café-restaurant all conscientiously rolled into one.

### Department stores
**Coin**
*Via Rinaldi Rinaldo 12,*
*T049-650277.*
Mon-Sat 0930-2000.
Upmarket but reasonably priced.

**Upim**
*Piazza Garibaldi 8,*
*T049-876 5612.*
Daily 0900-1930.
A handy store with everything from insoles to sunhats.

Sottosalone.

### Food & drink
A fruit-and-vegetable market is held on piazza Erbe every morning, except Sunday. The shiny aubergines, the coy blush of the white peaches and the gleam of clean asparagus are a joy to behold. However, Paduans are purist in their approach to seasonality: ask for *asparigi bianchi* (white asparagus) after the 13 June and you'll be snorted at derisively.

**Sottosalone**
*Palazzo della Ragione, piazza Erbe.*
Mon-Sat 0900-1300 and 1500-1900.
The Sottosalone (1218) on the ground floor of Palazzo della Ragione is one of the oldest covered markets in Europe and has more than 50 shops selling cheese, salame, oils, wine and other regional produce. (Some of the most interesting are listed under 'Five of the best shops in Sottosalone', see page 187.) There are also a few bars populated by the shopkeepers who regularly nip out for a *caffè corretto* to keep their spirits up. **Bar Dae Tose** at No 30 is a great workman's hang-out, full of photos of local football teams.

# Activities & tours

## Five of the best

# Shops in Sottosalone

**❶ Al desco di Collesei Nicola** (Sottosalone 13, T049-654960). This butcher will vacuum pack any of its typical local cured meats, such as Montagnana ham and tombolo cotechino (a local sausage) so that you can take them home.

**❷ Anrico Forno Vecchiato dal 1887** (piazza della Frutta 26, T049-875 1873, anticofornovecchiato.it). A traditional baker's shop selling dolce di Sant'Antonio (domed cakes), zaleti (hard but sweet biscotti) and a plenty of chocolate.

**❸ Antica Drogheria** (piazza della Frutta 46, T049-875 0263). This apothecary was founded in 1841 and sells rare spices and candied fruits.

**❹ Casa del Parmigiano "da Roberto"** (Sottosalone 51, T049-876 3014, daroberto.com). With over 300 different cheeses and salamis to choose from, you might be here for some time.

**❺ Pastificio Artusi** (Sottosalone 26, T049-875 6770). Sells all kind of pasta made in their own factory: the bigoli and tortellini are great buys.

### Boat trips
The following all offer trips along the Brenta Canal: **Battelli del Brenta** (Antoniana Viaggi, via Porciglia 34, T049-876 0233, antoniana.it/battellidelbrenta); **Consorzio Battellieri di Padua e Riviera del Brenta** (Galleria Pedrocchi, T049-876 6860, padovanavigazione.it); **Delta Tour Compagnia di navigazione** (via Toscana 2, T049-870 0232, deltatour.it); **Il Burchiello** (via Orlandi 3, T049-820 6910, ilburchiello.it); **Navigare con Noi** (via Pontedera 71, T049- 880 9219/348-521 5987, navigareconnoi.it).

### Cycling
**Noleggio Biciclette Ditta Degani**
*Stazione FS, T348-701 6374.*
€15-20 per day.
Handily located near the train station, this bike hire shop gives holders of the PadovaCard a 20% discount.

### Guided tours
**Guide Turistiche Padova**
*Piazza Virgilio Bardella 3, T049-820 9711, guidepadova.it.*
There are a whole variety of tours of the city, the Euganean Hills and the Brenta Canal on offer but the scientific itineraries, including the University, the Botanical Garden and the Observatory, are the real attraction for those who want to know all the factoids about Italy's oldest university town.

# Transport

Hourly train services to Milan (2 hrs 20 mins), Venice (40 mins), Verona (40 mins), Vicenza (20 mins), Monselice (25 mins) and Montegrotto Terme (15 mins). Frequent buses to Venice (1 hr) and Arquà Petrarca (1 hr 15 mins) from piazzale Boschetti.

# Contents

A lion reflects...

Treviso & the north

# Introduction

**B**eyond the main cities of Venice, Padua, Vicenza and Verona, lie the cultivated plains, vine-covered hills and snow-crowned mountains of the northern Veneto. The freshness of the air and the sweep of the vistas here inspired artists like Palladio, Canova and, more recently, Carlo Scarpa. After the Second World War, the region transformed itself from the second poorest in Italy to one of the richest. Today, the dynamism and industriousness of the people of the Veneto is evident all around: fertile fields and vineyards yield bumper crops year after year and the countryside is dotted with factories and small businesses.

Just 25 km inland from Venice, Treviso is a moated medieval city that enjoys the fruits of its labours, with a great quality of living and an appetite for fine food and wine. North of Treviso, 'La Strada del Prosecco' between Conegliano and Valdobbiadene, is where the best regional wine and prosecco are produced. In the hills further west, Asolo continues to attract artists and bohemians with its slow pace and gorgeous surroundings. Visiting the towns and villages in this area, you may feel as if you are a million miles from Venice but in fact the city is only an hour away. Go a little further and you're into the marvellous mountain terrain of the mighty Dolomites, where Cortina d'Ampezzo is the glitterati's winter playground.

**Treviso** is best visited in the late afternoon when shops and sights are open. A meander through its arcades, along its canal and beside its fortifications will build up your appetite for dinner in one of the city's *osterie* or *trattorie*. **Maser**, **Possagno** and **Asolo** (maybe even **Tomba Brion**) could also be visited on a day trip from any of the main cities of the Veneto.

**…a weekend or more**

Stay overnight in **Asolo** to enjoy properly its unique atmosphere. The **Dolomites** are a little further out of the way so, if you want more than just a gasp at their beauty, plan a couple of days in **Cortina** and the surrounding mountains – or more if the powder's good.

Villa Contarini, near Asolo.

Those expecting a poor relation of Venice will be surprised. Called the *'città d'aqua'*, this moated medieval city is one of the richest in Italy but has an unpretentious vibe and a real foodie culture that makes for an easygoing stay. Formerly a Lombard duchy, Treviso became a free commune before, like the rest of the region, becoming part of the Venetian Republic in 1389. The city was badly bombed during both World Wars; the most devastating attack came on Good Friday, 1944, when half the town was destroyed in minutes. The walled city had three gates (Altinia, Santi Quaranta and San Tommaso), until the beginning of the 20th century when five more were built, and is crossed by 15th-century canals that create a very pleasant setting for idle sightseeing.

# Essentials

◉ **Bus station** ACTT (for buses around Treviso), piazzale Duca d'Aosta 26, T0422-3271; **La Marca** (for buses around the region), Lungosile Mattei, T0444-577311; **ACTV** (for buses to Venice), Lungosile Mattei, T041-2424, actv.it.

◎ **Train station** Treviso Centrale, piazzale Duca d'Aosta, T89-2021, trenitalia.it.

❷ **ATMs** There are banks on viale Cairoli Fratelli and piazza Vittoria.

⊕ **Hospital** Ca' Foncello, piazzale Ospedale 11, T0422-322111.

✚ **Pharmacy** Farmacia Fanoli, piazza Duomo 29, T0422-541246. Mon-Sat 0900-1230 and 1500-1930.

↻ **Post office** piazza della Vittoria 1, T0422-653211, Mon-Sat 0830-1830.

❶ **Tourist information offices** APT, piazzetta di Pietà 8, T0422-547632, trevisotourism.com, Mon 0900-1230, Tue-Fri 0900-1230 and 1400-1800, Sat-Sun 0900-1230 and 1500-1800.

# Tip...

From May to December the tourist board offers free two-hour tours of the city every Saturday. Meet at Palazzo dei Trecento at 1000.

## Piazza del Duomo

Mon-Fri 0730-1200 and 1530-1900,
Sat-Sun 0730-1300 and 1530-2000.

Treviso's 12th-century cathedral has been rebuilt and refashioned over the years, most notably in the 19th century when its grandiose neoclassical façade was added, giving it an almost governmental guise. In the Cappella Malchiostro, to the right of the apse, are two rousing paintings: Il Pordenone's *Adoration of the Magi* (c1520), commissioned by Brocardo Malchiostro, just about outcolours and outclasses Titian's *Annunciation* (1522).

## Piazza dei Signori

The main thoroughfare, Calmaggiore, runs from the Duomo to piazza dei Signori, which is dominated by the **Palazzo dei Trecento**, once the seat of government and now used for council meetings, conferences and the odd photographic exhibition. The square's main attraction, however, is **La Fontana delle Tette** (yes, the Fountain of the Tits), erected in 1559. On the appointment of a new governor red and white wine would flow from the statue's left and right breasts for three days but this was no miracle: a government employee used to fill them up. When Napoleon took control of the Venetian Republic in 1797, the wine stopped flowing but locals still gather around la Fontana in high spirits on the third weekend of October to celebrate Ombralonga, a food and wine festival.

## Museo Civico di Santa Caterina

*Via di Santa Caterina, T0422-544864.*
Tue-Sun 0900-1230 and 1430-1800, €3,
€1 under 16s and students.

Santa Caterina dei Servi is a former convent whose cloisters house a stirring sequence of frescoes by Tomaso da Modena (1325-79) on the martyrdom of St Ursula. They were rescued in the 19th century from a church that closed down. There is also a collection of Renaissance paintings

Canal in Treviso.

by the likes of Titian, Tintoretto, Guardi and Lorenzo Lotto, including his thought-provoking *Portrait of a Dominican* (c1542), plus some ancient artefacts, archaeological fragments and statues.

### Chiesa di San Nicolò & Sala del Capitolo

*Church: via San Nicolò, T0422-548626.*
*Chapterhouse: piazzetta Benedetto XI 2, T0422-3247.*
Church: Mon-Sat 0700-1200 and 1530-1900.
Chapterhouse: Mon-Fri 0800-1600.

The unwieldy 14th-century Benedictine church of St Nicholas dominates the western skyline. Not to be missed is its chapterhouse (Sala del Capitolo), which has 40 psychological portraits of monks illuminating manuscripts by Tomaso da Modena (1352). The portraits show the monks carrying out practical, everyday tasks: cutting paper with scissors, reading with spectacles (this is claimed to be the first ever visual representation of these)

or blowing on the nib of a pen. Individually, they aren't that remarkable but taken together they are an amusing and absorbing look at a monk's life.

### Villa Emo

*Fanzolo, 24 km west of Treviso,*
*T0423-701244, villaemo.org.*
Apr-Oct Mon-Sat 1500-1830, Sun and public hols 1000-1230 and 1500-1830, Nov-Mar Mon-Fri 1400-1600, Sat-Sun and public hols 1400-1630, closed Dec, €5, €3 children and students, €4 over 65s.
Take the N53 to Castelfranco and then the exit for Fanzolo or take the train to Castelfranco and change for Fanzolo.

Leonardo Emo, a leading figure in the government of the Venetian Republic, commissioned this building in 1558. Using economical materials, such as bricks and plaster, Palladio designed a classical

# What the locals say

If you like wine, there is nothing more exciting than finding out how and where it is made. Prosecco is one of my favourite wines. Its grapes are grown in a hilly region north of Treviso, between the DOC regions of Valdobbiadene and Conegliano. The countryside is breathtaking with vineyards everywhere along the slopes. In your search for good wines, you will find delightful villages with great traditions and an enchanting atmosphere.

My favourite prosecco is a Cartizze, which comes from a small zone within Valdobbiadene where there is a particular soil and microclimate; Bisol (bisol.it) makes one of the best. I always think of how much work is needed to produce such a great wine.

Everything has to be done by hand with only minimal help from machines. If you visit during the two-week grape harvest in September, you can try the unique experience of tasting the wine alongside the grapes, and appreciating how natural its flavour is.

Nearby flows the river Piave. The stony ground provided by the ancient riverbed is ideal for growing grapes, especially red varieties. The Venetian Republic used to source its wine from this area, not least because they could reach the vineyards by boat. My favourite local red wine is the Cabernet Piave by Castello di Roncade (castellodironcade.com), a winery 20 minutes east of Treviso.

*Pier Luigi Bertotti is a sound engineer from Treviso.*

*St Agnes* by Tommaso da Modena, Chiesa di San Nicolò, Treviso.

**Look out for the sheaves of maize, a crop that had only just been brought to the Veneto from the New World and which symbolized innovative production techniques and the prosperity they brought to the region.**

villa of beauty and utility. The colonnaded buildings at either side of the central residence are *barchesse*, which Palladio attached to the main building to be used as cellars, barns and stables. On the first floor Battista Zelotti (1526-1578) illustrated episodes from classical mythology and Roman history, which were all the rage amongst the new landowning aristocracy. Look out for the sheaves of maize, a crop that had only just been brought to the Veneto from the New World and which symbolized innovative production techniques and the prosperity they brought to the region.

Head north of Treviso and west of the river Piave, through fields of maize and row upon row of vines, to reach the rippling Colli Asolani. These hills form a backdrop to the town of Maser and Villa Barbaro but it is in Asolo that you'll really appreciate the glorious scenery. Browning wasn't the only artist to wax lyrical over this enchanting hilltop town. Giosuè Carducci, the national poet of Italy following unification, called it "a city of a hundred horizons" thanks to its fabulous views. The verb *'asolare'* – to pass the time without purpose – was coined by the 15th-century Italian linguist, Pietro Bembo who served as a courtier here to his cousin Caterina Cornaro, the exiled Queen of Cyprus. She was one of the town's three famous female residents, the others being the actress and great beauty Eleonora Duse (1858-1924), whose lover was the fascist Gabriele D'Annunzio, and the British explorer and travel writer Freya Stark (1893-1993). Artists and celebrities still come here to relax, wander through the arcaded streets, sup the local wines, peruse the swanky shops and indulge in the town's restaurants.

## Piazza Giuseppe Garibaldi

Via Roberto Browning is the town's main drag and is laden with shops and 16th-century villas. It leads to piazza Giuseppe Garibaldi or piazza Maggiore, as the locals call it, around which you'll find the municipal buildings, the cathedral and a fountain that is fed by the remains of a Roman aqueduct. The relatively modern **cathedral** (Mon-Sat 0900-1200 and 1500-1900, no visits during mass), with its sparkling external mosaics, was itself built over the town's Roman baths in 1747. (For more Roman remains check out the still functioning aqueduct, known as 'La Bott', near piazza Brugnoli.) In the left aisle of the cathedral hang an extremely colourful *Assumption* by Lorenzo Lotto (1506), with a rather matriarchal Mary, another by Jacopo da Ponte Bassano (1549), and a copy of Titian's *Martyrdom of St Lawrence* (the original is in the Gesuiti in Venice; see page 107).

## Essentials

☺ **Bus station** Ca' Vescovo, Asolo, T0422-577311, for buses to Treviso.

💲 **ATMs** via Browning, Asolo.

✚ **Pharmacy** Farmacia Bonotto Massimo, piazza Giuseppe Garibaldi 79, Asolo, T0423-55136, Mon-Sat 0900-1230 and 1500-1900.

➲ **Post office** viale Tiziano 27, Asolo, T0423-52291, Mon-Sat 0800-1800.

❶ **Tourist information offices** piazza Giuseppe Garibaldi, Asolo, T0423-529046, asolo.it, Mon-Wed 0930-1230, Thu-Sun 0930-1230 and 1500-1800.

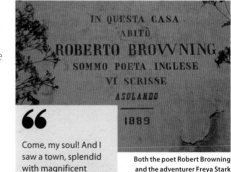

> **66**
> Come, my soul! And I saw a town, splendid with magnificent architecture perfect in every aspect **99**
>
> *Asolando, Robert Browning*

Both the poet Robert Browning and the adventurer Freya Stark lived in Asolo and are well rememebered by the Asolani.

# The Queen of Asolo

Caterina Cornaro (1452-1510) was the daughter of a Venetian noble family. At just 14 she married James II of Cyprus, thus securing trading rights and a political alliance for the Venetian Republic with this strategic Mediterranean island. James' sudden death left the pregnant Caterina to rule as Regent and, when her infant son also died in suspicious circumstances, she became Queen. However, the Republic was unhappy about leaving such a key ally in the hands of a woman and in 1489 she was forced to abdicate. In recompense, Venice gave her the title of Sovereign Lady of the county of Asolo, which included the castle and sizeable estate. The town thrived under Caterina's rule and became a cultural and artistic hub, with the likes of Pietro Bembo holding court. She lived here until she returned to Venice to die in 1510.

### Museo Civico

*Palazzo della Ragione, via Regina Cornaro 74, T0423-952313.*
Sat-Sun 1000-1200 and 1500-1900,
€4, €3 under 15s, students and over 65s.

This small museum contains a collection of archaeological and palaeontological artefacts and a few pleasing sculptures by Canova. There's also some fascinating memorabilia relating to Caterina Cornaro (including her spherical perfume burner, or is it a hand warmer?), Eleonora Duse (some of her dresses and her tea set) and, most interestingly, the explorer Freya Stark. Little heard of in Britain, this English Dame was much loved by the Asolani, who cherish the documents that relate to her travels around the Middle East, visiting places that no European, never mind a lone woman, had ever been.

### Castello della Regina

*Via Sottocastello.*

Now the home of the Teatro Duse (performances are regularly held here) there is little to help you conjure up what the castle may have looked like when Queen Caterina lived and ruled from here. However, the outside water fountain in the shape of a lion is worth a look, and a walk around the fringes and battlements affords some splendid views over the terracotta-tiled rooftops. On the western side, you'll also see 16th-century **Villa Contarini**, built by the Venetian Contarini family. The villa is joined by an underground passage to another on the other side of the hill. It was once owned by the monks from San Lazzaro degli Armeni in Venice.

Above left: Fresco on via Canova. Below left: Young Asolani playing in the streets. Below right: One of the main piazzi, dedicated to the fascist daredevil and sometime dramatist, Gabriele D'Annunzio. Opposite page: View from the Castello towards La Rocca.

## La Rocca

*Piazza Brugnoli, T0423-524637.*
Apr-Jun and Sep-Oct Sun and public hols
1000-1900, Jul-Aug Mon-Sat 1000-1200 and
1500-1900, Sun and public hols 1000-1700,
Nov-Mar Sun and public hols 1000-1700.

The town's medieval fortress dates from the 12th and
13th centuries but little remains except an irregular,
empty shell. There's quite an arduous walk up Monte
Ricco to reach it but the views are awesome.

## Via Canova

On via Canova you'll find the villa of the American
actress Eleonora Duse and her lover, Gabriele
D'Annunzio. Continue along via Canova to reach
**Chiesa de Santa Caterina d'Alessandria,** a tiny
14th-century church with a gentle, soothing
atmosphere. It is decorated with subtle frescoes in
pastel tones and a regular supply of wild flowers
picked by local women. Just along the road,
**Chiesa de Sant'Anna** has a beautiful little hillside
cemetery overlooking Mount Grappa where both
Freya Stark and Elenora Duse rest in peace.

## Tomba Brion

*San Vito di Altivole, 7 km south of Asolo,*
*T0423-564200.*
Apr-Oct daily 0800-2000,
Nov-Mar daily 0800-1700.

Architecture fans shouldn't miss out on a visit
to Tomba Brion in nearby San Vito di Altivole.
The Brions were wealthy industrialists, who
commissioned Carlo Scarpa, the modernist
Venetian architect, to create a family tomb in 1969.
Built mainly in concrete, the site is designed to look
like a ruin and is characterized by geometric
abstractions and carefully placed structures made
from various metals, marble and water. In 1978,
aged 72 but at the height of his powers, Scarpa
fell down a flight of steps in Sendai, Japan, and
died of his injuries. He was buried here standing
up, between the main building and the grounds.
This is one of the only entire schemes, including
both buildings and grounds, that he designed and
is considered by architects to be his greatest and
most ingenious work.

## Possagno

*10 km north of Asolo.*

This one-street town is the birthplace of Antonio Canova, one the great sculptors of the 19th century. At the foot of Col Draga, the neoclassical **Tempio** (Apr-Sep daily 0900-1200 and 1500-1800, Oct-Mar daily 0900-1200 and 1400-1700) nods to Rome's Pantheon (central construction), Athens' Parthenon (the Doric colonnade) and the apsal chapel (like the early basilicas) and represents the three great phases of civilization: the Greek, the Roman and the Christian. Designed and funded by Canova and built by the people of Possagno, who volunteered their time as well as various materials, the first stone was laid by Canova himself in 1819 but he died before it was completed in 1830. The town is immensely proud of it and of Canova. Indeed, the iridescent quality of the local stone, lumachella, means that the building itself seems to glow with pride. Inside is a vast circular space, simply decorated and with marble-effect painted walls.

Also in Passagno is the **Gipsoteca Museo Canoviano** (T0423-544323, museocanova.it. Tue-Sat 0900-1230 and 1500-1800, Sun 0900-1230 and 1500-1900, €7, €4 under 16s and students under 26.). Even if you're only half interested in Canova, this splendid, soothing museum is well worth an hour of your time. It contains many drawings, clay models and plaster casts used in the creation of his beautiful sculptures; a number of the finished versions can be seen in the Museo Correr in Venice (see page 96). Canova's brother-in-law, Monsignor Sartori, commissioned Francesco Lazzari to build a basilica to house Canova's art. The original building was completed in 1836 but was badly bombed during the First World War, as documented in the permanent display of *l'arte ferita* (wounded art), which has some peculiarly upsetting images of shattered casts and of soldiers salvaging dismembered sculptures. In 1957 Carlo Scarpa designed a new wing, whose minimalist aesthetic lit by natural light works so well with the delicate realisation of naked flesh in stone that Canova

Canova's Tempio in Possagno.

## Marble maestro

Antonio Canova (1757-1822) was orphaned at three and brought up by his grandparents. His grandfather was a stonemason, who encouraged Antonio to draw and learn about architecture. It is said that his prodigious talent was first observed at a dinner party held by his grandfather's patron, Giovanni Falieri, at which the seven-year-old Canova fashioned a lion out of a block of butter. Falieri became his friend, mentor and patron and secured him an apprenticeship with Giuseppe Bernardi. He was only 18 when he delivered his first commission, *Orpheus and Eurydice*, to critical acclaim. Canova moved to Rome in 1780, where he studied the antiquities of the city and developed his technique. His papal commissions and aristocratic fan base meant he was rarely out of work. He travelled throughout Italy and to Paris and London, where the Duke of Bedford commissioned the second version of his most famous work, *The Three Graces* or *Tre Grazie* (now shared between the Victoria & Albert Museum in London and the National Gallery of Scotland). You can see the plaster cast in the Gipsoteca but the original version, in veined marble, is in the Hermitage, St Petersburg. Canova died at the age of 65. His heart was interred in the mausoleum he had designed as a temple to Titian in the Frari in Venice but the rest of his body was returned to Possagno to be buried in the Tempio.

mastered. Look out for plaster statues of the savage *Hercules and Lica*, the enduringly enchanting *The Three Graces* and a touchingly playful *Venus Placing a Garland on the Head of Adonis*. And, as for his grieving lions, they'd bring a tear to a marble eye.

## Villa Barbaro

*Via Cornuda 7, Maser, T0423-923004, villadimaser.it.* Mar-Oct Mon-Sat 1000-1800, Sun 1100-1800, Nov-Feb Sat, Sun and public hols 1430-1700, €5.

East of Asolo and some 33 km northwest of Treviso is one of the treasures of the Veneto. Villa Barbaro is perhaps Palladio's most gracious building and its frescoes are among Paolo Veronese's finest work (although it has been suggested that Palladio thought they detracted from the purity of his design). It was built from 1550 to 1560 for Daniele Barbaro, the Patriarch of Aquileia, and his brother, Marcantonio, Ambassador of the Venetian Republic. It changed owners a number of times before falling into the hands of warring sisters who failed to keep it maintained and let it fall into ruin. In 1850 Sante Giacomelli, an industrialist, bought it and began a hugely complicated and expensive renovation. He sold it in 1934 to the Volpi di Misurata family who continued the work and live in the villa today.

Looking out onto the plains, with a backdrop of trees and hills, the villa sits in perfect harmony with its surroundings. The gardens are elegantly composed, with lawns and box hedges as well as statues and stuccos by Alessandro Vittoria,

Sansovino's pupil. True to Palladio's upholding of the principles of proportion and symmetry, the design of the building is equally melodious.

The main living quarters are at the centre with the public rooms at the front in what resembles a Roman portico with four ionic columns. On either side are symmetrical arcaded agricultural buildings, known as *barchesse*, each of which ends with a pavilion that serves as a dovecot. There is no front door: access is from inside the arcade, up a staircase to a considerable but perfectly divided piano nobile. (At this point you are asked to put on and scuff about in a pair of felted slippers to prevent you from scratching the highly polished floor.)

Both the public rooms and the private living quarters have been decorated with striking *trompe l'œils* paintings by Veronese. By painting architectural features, such as columns, balconies and friezes, and using perspective he has created a three-dimensional effect that complements Palladio's vision of precision and order, and by

> ## Tip...
>
> If you visit Villa Barbaro on a Tuesday, make an appointment to see **Il Tempietto** (via Cornuda 7, T0423-565002, Tue by appointment only). Intended to be the villa's chapel, it ended up becoming the town's parish church. Bijou but nonetheless magnificent, it follows the design principles of Rome's Pantheon and, alongside Vicenza's Teatro Olimpico, was one of Palladio's last gasps.

Detail from the nymphaeum at Villa Barbaro.

Statue in the grounds of Villa Barabro.

adding 'windows' and 'views' he completes the balance of the rooms. Barbaro's humanist and intellectual brief was a far cry from the religious paintings of the time and gave Veronese an artistic freedom that he obviously relished. His trademark palette of silvery, pastel tones make you believe you are looking at coloured marble.

The main rooms are the **Hall of Olympus**, where the four elements – Vulcan (Fire), Cybele (Earth), Neptune (Water), and Juno (Air) – are joined by depictions of abundance (a common theme throughout the villa), fertility, the wheel of fortune and love. Giustiniana, Barbaro's wife, Marcantonio, his youngest son, their nanny and pets are all given cameo appearances. Veronese was obviously taken with the family's spaniel, as it appears again in the **Room of the Little Dog**, while Fortune takes on Ambition and Envy in the background. The villa's staff get a starring role in the **Crociera Room**, sneaking a peek through half-closed doors. (These frescoes were rediscovered in 1934 after being covered over with more 'fashionable' paintings in the mid 19th century.) In the **Room of the Oil Lamp**, the lamp hangs from the hand of a *putto* (cherub) painted onto the ceiling. Just along from here, the end room has a portrait of the artist in hunting garb, next to a lolloping hound. The **Bacchus Room** is dedicated to winemaking: Bacchus is depicted showing farmhands how to make wine, while the wealth of natural resources within the estate is celebrated in an elaborate chimneypiece carved with the figure of Abundance. Finally the **Room of the Tribunal of Love** celebrates union through celestial images of a bride and groom.

Before you leave, don't miss taking a closer look at the nymphaeum and fish pond round the back, which gushes water from the source that supplies the villa. Vittorio lined the arc of the pool with Olympian divinities, while the four splendid giants are the work of Marcantonio Barbaro himself, who fancied himself as a sculptor.

The villa has a small snack bar and a rather fabulous shop selling wine (including a gutsy little Merlot), honey and oil from Azienda Agricola Villa di Maser.

Cortina d'Ampezzo is Italy's chicest ski resort where the great and the good come to ski, be seen and to revel in the off-piste action. The big peaks of *Le Dolomiti* (the Dolomites mountain range) start here: Cortina lies at 1224 m beneath Tre Cime di Laveredo (2999 m) and Cinque Torri (2366 m), with Marmolada (3343 m), Sasso Lungo (3179 m) and Torri del Vaiolet (2243 m) to the west. The Dolomites stretch further west into the Trentino-Alto Adige region.

Cortina has been on the society ski map since the mid 19th century but it was hosting the 1956 Winter Olympics that turned the town into a goldmine. The ice rink and bobsleigh track are still in use and, despite being 50 years old, have a futuristic magic to them. In summer, winter sports' enthusiasts give way to hikers, Nordic walkers, rock climbers and cyclists, all keen to soak up the glorious scenery.

The town itself consists of one long main street, corsa Italia, that has everything you could ever need, plus a lot that you don't need but may covet. Yes, Cortina has the flashiest high-altitude high street in Italy and prices to match.

### Chiesa di Santi Filippo e Giacomo

*Corso Italia.*
Mon-Sat 0800-1200.

Cortina's grand church was built in 1775 by an architect called Promperg-Costa. Its white campanile (1858) looks beautiful against the surrounding peaks. Highlights of the interior include the rose marble altar, the fabulously decorative cupola and a wooden tabernacle by Andrea Brustolon.

## Tip...

If you are in Cortina on a Sunday morning, it's worth attending Mass to hear the singing of the Schola Cantorum, founded in 1882.

Sella mountain range in the Dolomites, west of Cortina.

**Tip...**

While wandering around the town, you may notice the locals speaking a Germanic dialect, known as *Ladin*, which is common to the Dolomiti Trento-Adige region.

## Essentials

⊖ **Bus station** Lungosile Mattei, T0436-867921 (Cortina Express), T0437-217111 (Dolimiti Bus), dolomitibus.it.

🕒 **Train station** It used to be possible to reach Cortina by train but the Austrian-built railway was closed in the 1960s, when skiers and holidaymakers started to drive to the resort. Today, the nearest train station is at Calalzo di Cadore, T848-888088, trenitalia.it, 30 km or 20 mins south of Cortina by bus.

Ⓢ **ATMs** corso Italia.

⊕ **Hospital** Istituto Codivilla Putti di Cortina d'Ampezzo, via Codivilla 1, T0436-883111.

✛ **Pharmacy** Farmacia San Giorgio, corso Italia 25, T0436-862449, Mon-Sat 0900-1300 and 1530-1930.

↷ **Post office** largo delle Poste, T0436-862411, Mon-Sat 0830-1830.

❶ **Tourist information offices** APT, piazzetta San Francesco 8, T0426-3231, cortina.dolomiti.org, daily 0930-1230.

### Museo Ciasa de ra Regoles

*Corso Italia, T0436-2206, musei.regole.it.*
Tue-Sun 1000-1230 and 1600-2000, €5.

This municipal building houses a number of small museums that will provide welcome distraction for any non-skiers in your party. The **Museo** Paleontologico Rinaldo Zardini has an intriguing display of fossilized sponges, gasteropods, cephalopods and corals that reveal the Dolomites' origins under a tropical sea. The **Museo Etnografico** is a nod to the social history of the area with some churns, riddles, tools and traditional costumes. Finally, the **Museo d'Arte Moderna Mario Rimoldi** has a surprisingly large collection of 20th-century figurative art, including works by De Chirico, Guidi, Guttuso and Tomea.

### Stadio Olimpico del Ghiaccio

*Via dello Stadio 1, T0436-881811.*
Daily 1030-1230 and 1530-1830,
€9 per hr including skate hire.

The 30 m by 60 m open-air rink was built for the seventh Winter Olympics in 1956. It was later covered and can now be used in both winter and summer. As well as ice-skating, the stadium has a bar, solarium and a children's playground. 'New wave' curling lessons are available (curlingcortina.it) and an adults-only Ice Disco Dance is held once a week.

# Mountain highs

## Skiing & snowboarding

Cortina has 140 km of pistes spread throughout eight ski areas. These form three main groups, all connected by ski buses, lifts and/or cable cars: Lagazuoi Col Gallina and the Cinque Torri; Tofana, Pocol and Cristallo; and Faloria and Mietres. The buses are often packed and chaotic in high season but, once you are on the piste and see the beauty of the mountains, transport disorder is the last thing on your mind.

The Cortina Valley ski pass is available from **Skipass Cortina** (via Marconi 15, T0436-862171). Prices depend on the time of year: pre season (early-mid Dec) for one/three/six days €32/92/162; season (mid-late Jan, mid Mar-late Apr) €35/101/178; high season (late Dec-early Jan, early Feb-mid Mar) €40/115/177.

Ski and snowboard lessons are available from **Scuola Sci e Snowboard Dolomiti** (via Roma 83, T0436 862264, dolomitiscuolasci.com, €53 per hour in high season). For something different, try **Cortina Cross Country Ski School** (c/o Fiames Sport Nordic Center – GIS, T0436-4903, scuolafondoskicortina@dolomiti.org, from €50 per hour in high season).

A comprehensive list of cross-country, snow-shoeing and snowboarding trails is available from the tourist office. Freestylers, meanwhile, will find hours of fun at **Snowpark Faloria** with its half-pipe, rails and jumps. Located at the bottom of Canalone Franchetti, it can be reached by the Vitelli chairlift.

# Sloping off: what pistes might suit you

There are 66 ski runs in total: 32 of these are blue (easy), 22 are red (medium difficulty) and 12 are black (difficult).

**Novice skiers**  Pocol-Socrepes area (and the lower lifts on Cristallo), as well as several at Faloria.

**Intermediate skiers**  Tofana, Faloria and Cinque Torri.

**Advanced skiers**  Lagazuoi, Cristallo and Tofana.

**Snowboarders**  Pocol-Socrepes for novices; Faloria and Cinque Torri will thrill experienced snowboarders.

## Cable car trips

Even if you don't ski, you can still reach the mountain tops by riding one of Cortina's dramatic cable cars. All operate daily from mid December to March and from mid June to September between 0900 and 1700.

**Freccia nel Cielo** (T0436-2517, €22 return) The 'arrow in the sky' departs from the town (close to the Stadio Olimpico) and stops at Col Druscie (1770 m) and Ra Valles (2550 m), finishing at Tofana di Mezzo (3191 m) surrounded by glaciers and jutting peaks aplenty. There are restaurants at each of the stops.

**Funivia Faloria** (T0436-2517, €14 return) departs from a chalet next to the bus station. Not quite as utterly vertiginous as the Freccia nel Cielo, this cable car ascent still offers some thrills above the treetops and a steep climb over the jagged, sparkling cliffs of Monte Faloria (2126 m). There are 30 pistes to choose from for your descent, or you can snuggle down with a *cioccolato caldo* at the restaurant, feast on the vistas of Cortina and take the cable car back down again.

**Falzarego–Lagazuoi** (T0436-867301, €13 return, catch the frequent Dolomitibus from the bus station to Passo Falzarego). This cable car takes you 2752 m up the cliffside of Lagazuoi. At the top you'll find **Rifugio Lagazuoi** (T0436-867303, mid Jun-Sep and mid Dec-Mar) which has 360 degrees of mind-blowing views, a bar, restaurant and 18 beds (ranging from bunks to double rooms with private facilities). Also here is the **Museo all'aperto del Lagazuoi**, one of a number of open-air museums that tell the story of the fighting that took place in the Dolomites during the First World War; a guide to the tunnels and trenches you can visit is available at the *rifugio*. Make sure you're properly kitted out for walking before you go. In winter, skiers can head back down via the Valle Nascosto trail into Armentarola and the Sella Ronda, passing a beautiful frozen turquoise waterfall on the way. In summer, you can take your bike on this cable car and cycle back down the designated track.

# Tip...

Gradients can be very tough so make sure you know your capabilities. If you intend to cycle on the roads, watch out for huge tour buses and speedy, open-topped cars, especially on bends.

## Cycling

Although the twisting roads are popular with serious cyclists slicing by at high speeds, it's mountain biking that is the real draw in this area. The local tourist office has a whole sheaf of maps showing bike routes to suit all strengths of thigh and its website (dolomiti.org) details 15 mountain bike tracks ranging from the easy Route 2 – a 90-minute leisurely pedal that follows the old railway line to Passo Cimabanche – to the much tougher Route 12 to Forcella Ambrizola, which takes you through woods and pastures to Rifugio Palmieri and the mirror-like Federa or da Lago and up Forcella Ambrizola, where the views will make your knees tremble even if the ride hasn't.

Another great bike ride with a bit of culture thrown in is the 36-km Cortina to Pieve di Cadore section of La Lunga Via delle Dolomiti. This takes you through the Valle di Cadore along the old railway track to the birthplace of Tiziano Vicello (Titian). You can visit his humble little house (via Arsenale 4, Pieve di Cadore, T0435-32262, mid Jun-mid Sep Mon-Sat 0930-1230 and 1530-1830, €2) and see a statue of him outside the Palazzo della Comunità Cadorina.

Bikes can be hired from **Cicli Cortina** (via Majon 148a, T0436-867215, ciclicortina@libero.it) from €20 a day.

## Hiking & climbing

During the summer months the Dolomites are a magnet for walkers, Nordic walkers and climbers. However, the vast network of trails mean there will be many occasions when you'll only have a marmot, chamois or eagle for company. There are 42 earmarked routes for walkers around the Cortina area from low-lying lakeside rambles to high-altitude super-hikes; contact the tourist office for details.

As always, a good map, a compass, suitable clothing and boots that will cope with a change in the weather (which happens frequently in this area) are necessary. If you are inexperienced or would like a guide to show you the way, contact the **Gruppo Guide Alpine Cortina** (corso Italia 69a, T0463-868505, guidecortina.com, daily 0800-1200 and 1600-1900). Prices vary hugely, depending on distance and group size.

Rock climbers are also spoiled for choice with bouldering, sports climbs and classic routes. Cinque Torrei has something to suit all climbers, while the Crepe de Oucera Alti (1800 m) near Passo Giau is considered one of the best crags in the eastern Dolomites. There are also a number of *vie ferrate* (iron paths) in the area, which have cables, bridges and ladders to help you along. The website planetmountain.com is a useful place to check out climbs in the area.

# Sleeping

### Hotel Ca' del Galletto €€
*Via S Bona Vecchia 30, T0422-432550, hotelcadelgalletto.com.*
This box of a hotel doesn't seem very appealing from the outside but it has the comfort, space and mod-cons that make all the difference: sound-proofed rooms (always a boon in Vespa-mad Italy), efficient air-conditioning and a swimming pool. The restaurant staff and the porters are engaging and full of tips on Treviso. Situated to the north of the *centro storico*, it's 10 minutes by bus 51 from the train station or five minutes by taxi.

### Hotel Scala €€
*Viale Felissent, T0422-307600, hotelscala.com.*
This elegant villa lies just outside the city walls, next to the gardens of Villa Manfrin. It has 20 plain rooms that have recently been done up. The bathrooms are fresh and the furnishings are sturdy. The tiled and beamed breakfast room has a buffet table that heaves with brioche, *formaggio* and cakes: a generous spread, indeed, served by pleasant staff.

### Hotel Al Sole €€
*Via Collegio 33, T0423-951332, albergoasole.com.*
It has a great location near the town centre but wearers of high heels will have to be careful tottering up and down the cobbled road to this hotel. The rooms are large and well looked after, and the bathrooms are lovely: some have jacuzzi showers. The staff are obliging and will take time to give you the low-down on the area. Breakfast on the sunny terrace with its amazing views must be the hotel's USP. There's also a garage round the back where you can park.

### Self-catering
### Al Morer
*Via Risorgimento 12, T0423-55060, almorer.it.*
**€60 per night for a double room with cooking facilities.**
Just 10 minutes from the centre of Asolo, this self-catering agriturismo sits amongst vineyards, mulberry bushes and cypresses. It's pretty basic but nice and clean and has everything you need, including a terrace for breakfast or evening drinks.

### Hotel Ancora €€
*Corso Italia 62, T0436-3261, hotelancoracortina.it.*
Right on the main piazza, this hotel offers affordable comfort right in the middle of all the action. The bedrooms have hand-made bedsteads, polished wooden floors and some fabulous views (even in the cheaper rooms). Breakfast and lunch are served in a vaulted dining room and the welcoming reception area has an intricately carved wooden ceiling and a ceramic stove with seats around it. There's also the café, which serves great pastries, and an art gallery that hosts regular exhibitions and events.

### Meuble Montana €€
*Corso Italia 94, T0436-860498, cortina-hotel.com.*
Closed Nov and Jun.
The Meuble's good-natured staff stay busy keeping the 31 rooms spotless. The beds are so comfortable and the bedding so plentiful, you'll be as warm as pie. Just be prepared to be woken by the bells of nearby Chiesa di Santi Filippo e Giacomo at 0700. Breakfast is hale and hearty, which is exactly what you need in the mountains. In the warmer months, you can rent out bikes from reception. If you're coming in winter, look at the weekly half-board deals: you'll get a much better price.

# Eating & drinking

Treviso

## Torre del Spin €€
*Via Inferiore 7, T0422-543829.*
Mon 1800-2200, Tue-Sat
1200-1430 and 1800-2200.
Favoured by the locals, this eatery
serves superb Trevigiani home
cooking. The menu is chalked up
on a board and, if you're lucky, will
include fabulous *zuppa de mare*
and *risotto al radicchio*. It can be
busy at lunchtime, so get in quick.

### Cafés & bars

### Beltrame
*Piazza dei Signori 27,*
*T04225-40789.*
Fri-Wed 0800-0100.
Great coffee and nice Trevigiani
snacks are served on the piazza.
It's open very late and becomes
a pleasant little drinking den
from about 1800.

## Tip...

**Radicchio in piazza** is a little
festival that takes place in
Treviso before Christmas and
celebrates dishes with radicchio
in them, accompanied by
plenty of drinking and general
merrymaking. The tourist office
website has exact dates.

### Biffi
*Piazza dei Signori 28,*
*T0424-540784.*
Tue-Sun 0700-0100.
Come here for beer, wine and
snacks, including the traditional
Trevigiani *panino alla porchetta*
(roast suckling pig sandwich).
This is where all the action is.

Asolo

## Ca' Derton €€€
*Piazza d'Annunzio 11,*
*T0423-529648.*
Tue-Sat 1230-1400 and
1930-2200, Sun 1230-1400.
Just a few steps from the main
piazza, this restaurant offers
fragrant and adventurous
interpretations of the dishes of
the Veneto. Its *tagliatelle e*
*intingolo di pernice* (pasta with
partridge sauce) is intensely rich
in flavour and the *branzino di*
*mare e verdure, al vapore di timo*
(sea bass and vegetables with a
thyme perfume) will have
grabbed you by the nostrils
before you taste a morsel.

**Vineyards around Guia, near Valdobbiadene.**

# Treviso tastes

*casatella* – local creamy cow's
cheese.

*chiocciole* – little snails (also
called scios)

*formaggio imbriago* – a sharp
cow's cheese aged amongst
grapes to give it a sweet, dark-
red rind. It first came about when
the locals hid their cheese from
the Austrians.

*panino porchetta* – roast suckling
pig sandwich.

*prosecco* – a white, usually
sparkling, wine which is produced
just north of the city between
Conegliano and Valdobbiadene.

*radicchio rosso di Treviso* – red
chicory; bitter but very tasty.
This vegetable is so loved and
celebrated it even has its own
website (radicchioditreviso.it)
with some great recipes.

*sopa coada* – pigeon broth.

*Tiramisu* – 'pick me up'. The
Trevigiani say this creamy,
spongy, coffee concoction was
invented here.

### Ristorante Due Mori €€
*Piazza D'Annunzio 5,*
*T0423-952256.*
Tue-Sun 1200-1400 and
1900-2200
This relaxed but sizeable
restaurant has some marvellous
views and the capable staff,
winding back and forth with
plates and charm, make it a happy
holiday find. *Flan di carciofi*
(artichoke flan) will excite the
most jaded palate, and the aroma
of the *coniglio brasato con polenta*
(rabbit stew) will leave meat-
eaters salivating. There's also a
small wine bar a few doors down.

### Antica Osteria Al Bacaro €€
*Via Robert Browning 165,*
*T0423-55150.*
Thu-Tue 1000-2400.
This traditional hostelry has been
in the Cavaliere family since 1892.

The heart-warming home
cooking hits all the right spots:
choose from huge plates of
asparagus risotto, *pasta con
funghi del bosco* (woodland
mushrooms), platters of grilled
vegetables and cheese. More
than that, with local characters
constantly popping in and out,
it's got a buzz that makes it a
great place to see, hear and
experience small town life.

#### Cafés & bars
### Alle Ore
*Via Robert Browning 185,*
*T0423-952070.*
Tue-Sun 0800-2100.
On the main thoroughfare, this is
a rather swish spot for a coffee,
an *ombre* (little glass of beer or
wine) or a softy.

### Caffè Centrale
*Via Roma 72, T0423-952141.*
Wed-Mon 0800-2400.
Robert Browning, Ernest
Hemingway and Eleanora Duse
have sampled the espresso and
cappuccino here.

#### Cortina d'Ampezzo

### Ristorante Tivoli €€€€
*Via Lacedel 34, T0436-866400,*
*ristorantetivoli.it.*
Jun-Sep and Dec-Easter
Tue-Sun 1230-1400 and
1930-2200.
This is considered the best
restaurant in town. Sit by the
large windows or on the terrace
to enjoy the jaw-dropping
beauty of the twinkling lights
in the Cortina basin or the sun
setting the mountainsides
aflame. It's a Michelin-

starred establishment so high expectations will be met: even the simple, casually chic construction of *pappardelle con finferli* (tiny mountain mushrooms) is a knee trembler.

### Al Camin €€€
*Via Alverà 99, T0436-862010.*
Tue-Sun 1200-1500 and 1900-2230.

If you follow the river Bigontina for 10 minutes to the outskirts of town, you will find this rustic little restaurant. Wood panelled and with a big fireplace, it serves large helpings of local dishes such as *canederli al fegato* (potato dumplings stuffed with liver) and *casunziei rossi* (pasta stuffed with beetroot).

### El Toula €€€
*Località Ronco 123, T0436-3339.*
Late Jul-early Sep and Dec-Mar Tue-Sun 1200-1430 and 1900-2200.

On the way to Passo Falzarego, just 3 km from Cortina, this converted hay barn (*toula*) serves first-rate local dishes using mountainous ingredients, such as juniper berries and *capretto* (kid meat), plus a scintillating smattering of international dishes. The wood-panelled walls are lined with wine bottles from all over Italy and upstairs the picture frame windows have captivating views.

### Ristorante Pizzeria Vienna €€
*Via Roma 66-68, T0436-866944.*
Tue-Sun 1730-2300.

Don't be put off by the exterior, this pizzeria is the best deal in town with the friendliest people, too. The specialities are oversized *canederli* and *casunziei*, both stuffed with a multitude of meat or vegetable fillings and served with a variety of sauces. Takeaway pizzas are also available.

## Cafés & bars

### Enoteca
*Via del Mercato 5, T0436-862040.*
Tue-Sun 1000-2300.

Normally packed with lovers of fine wine, this Enoteca sells wine by the bottle together with cold cuts and cheese. The narrow original bar is a beauty.

### La Terrazza Viennese
*Hotel Ancora, Corso Italia 62, T0436-3261.*
Daily 0800-2200.

If the slopes aren't your thing, you can still get a mountain buzz from the pastries they serve in this genteel Austro-Hungarian style salon.

### LP26
*Largo delle Poste 26, T0436-862284.*
Tue-Sun 0800-0200.

Café and *pasticceria* purveying custardy, marmaladey, chocolatey pleasures.

# Entertainment

### Cortina d'Ampezzo

## Cinema
### Eden
*Corso Italia, T0436-2967.*

With only 280 seats, this cosy little cinema shows the usual blockbusters plus occasional independent films with subtitles.

## Clubs
### Bilbò Club
*Largo delle Poste 7, T0436-5599, bilbocortina.com.*
Fri-Sun 2100-0300.

One of the most happening clubs in Cortina, it hosts house, euro-pop and alternative nights during the ski season. Check out the website for details.

## Music
Founded in 1861, the **Corpo Musicale di Cortina d'Ampezzo** (Corso Italia 83, T0436-2673) does a bit of oom-pa-pa matched with a rousing repertoire of folkloric and classical tunes. Visit the office to see when and where they are playing. The **Schola Cantorum** is a 40-strong polyphonic choir specializing in holy music. It accompanies Mass and all the most important religious festivals at Cortina's church.

# Shopping

## Treviso

### Art & antiques
Treviso's antiques market is held around Borgo Cavour on the fourth Sunday of every month.

### Clothing
**Benetton**
*Piazza Indipendenza 5, T0422-559911.*
Mon-Sat 0900-1300 and 1500-1930, Sun 1000-1300 and 1500-1930.
Treviso is the home of Benetton. This megastore is huge and has things you may not see elsewhere.

### Food & drink
Even if you don't want to buy anything, Treviso's morning fish market (Mon-Sat) is in the loveliest of locations on an island in the canal.

**Abbiati Vini e Spiriti**
*Via Municipio 43, Treviso, T0422-582635.*
Mon-Sat 0900-1230 and 1530-1900.
Come here for a bottle of *radicchio rosso*-flavoured grappa and other local beverages.

### Outdoor equipment
**North Face**
*Via Padova 21, Cornuda, nr Treviso, T042-383 9133.*
Mon 1430-1930, Tue-Sat 1000-1300 and 1430-1930.
North Face outdoor gear is made near Treviso. For super bargains head to this factory outlet.

## Asolo

### Art & antiques
Asolo's antiques market takes place every second Saturday afternoon and all day Sunday, except in July and August.

**Galleria Asolana Preziosi Ed Antichità di Vettorato Gianna**
*Via Robert Browning163, T0423-55320.*
Mon 1530-1930, Tue-Sat 1000-1230 and 1530-1930.
Twentieth-century and antique bits and bobs in a treasure trove of a shop.

**Tessoria Asolana**
*Shop: via Canova 317, T0423-952062, tessoriaasolana. com. Workshop: via Schiavonesca Marosticana 15 (down the hill), T0423-950877.*
Shop: Mon-Sat 1000-1200 and 1630-1830. Workshop: by appointment Mon-Fri 0800-1200 and 1430-1630.
The silks available from this workshop have been handwoven on wooden looms since 1848. You can buy beautiful scarves and fabric for upholstery or clothing.

### Food & drink
**Cantina Cirotto**
*Via Bassanese 51, T0436-952396.*
Mon-Fri 0930-1300 and 1600-1900.
At the bottom of the hill leaving Asolo, this cantina sells prosecco Rubino d'Asolo and Perla d'Asolo to quaff or carry home.

**Gastronomia Sgarbossa Ennio**
*Via Robert Browning 151, T0423-529109.*
Mon-Sat 0900-1230 and 1530-1930, Sun 1530-1930.
Had Robert Browning (who once lived upstairs) been alive today, he would never have been out of this shop, which sells every kind of bean, wine, vinegar, cheese, oil and *salume* – indeed, all things artisan and scrumptious.

## Cortina d'Ampezzo

### Clothing
Cortina d'Ampezzo's main street, corso Italia, is chock-a-block with luxury boutiques. The sales in January and July have a few bargains but, in general, this is one pricey town.

## Activities & tours

### Department stores

**La Cooperativa**
*Corso Italia 40, T0436-861245.*
Daily 0900-1230 and 1530-1930.
Fabulous department store that
sells everything from clothing to
souvenirs to books.

### Food & drink

**La Piazzetta**
*Corso Italia 53, T0436-3436.*
Tue-Sat 0830-1300 and
1600-1930, Sun-Mon
1600-1930.
Lovely cheese and bread from
this salumeria.

### Outdoor equipment

**North Face**
*Corso Italia 124, T0436-3467.*
Mon 1530-1930, Tue-Sun
0900-1230 and 1530-1930.
Outdoor gear from the
Treviso-based firm.

**Peak Performance**
*Via XXIX Maggio, T0436-866958.*
Mon 1500-1930, Tue-Sun
0900-1230 and 1500-1930.
Look swish on the slopes with
some of the colourful names and
top brands found here.

**Slalom**
*Via Franchetti 6, T0436-890666.*
Mon 1500-1930, Tue-Sun
0900-1230 and 1500-1930.
Splash out on new salopettes at
this reasonably priced (for Cortina)
ski shop. You can also hire skis here.

### Cultural

**Veneto Tours**
*T349-1016700,*
*theothersideofvenice.com.*
**From €200 per couple per day.**
There's not much Veneto Tours
don't know about the Veneto.
They offer flexible walking or
chauffeur-driven tours, packed
with information and spirited
attempts to fit as much in as
possible.

### Food & wine

**Lezioni di Cucina**
*Via Collegio 33, Asolo,*
*T0423-951332, albergoasole.com.*
The chef of Albergo al Sole in
Asolo offers cooking lessons at
La Terrazza restaurant on the
themes of *pesce*, *pane e dolci* and
pasta. They cost €100 per person,
with special deals for guests of
the hotel.

### Treviso

Airport (20 mins by bus).
Hourly train services to Venice
(30 mins) and Feltre (40 mins)
from piazzale Duca d'Aosta.
Frequent buses to Venice (30 mins).

### Asolo

Bus to Cornuda (20 mins) for
rail connections to Treviso
(30 mins direct or 50 mins via
Montebelluno). Bus to Treviso
(55 mins) and to Bassano del
Grappa (25 mins).

### Cortina d'Ampezzo

Bus to Venice (4 hrs 20 mins)
and Milan (6 hrs 30 mins).
Also to Calalzo di Cadore for
rail connections to Venice (2 hrs
20 mins; allow 4 hrs including bus
from Cortina) and Padua (3 hrs).

Above and right: Lezioni di Cucina.

# Contents

Ponte degli Alpini at Bassano del Grappa.

Vicenza & around

# Introduction

Vicenza is one of Italy's most beautiful cities but it is not one of its best known. The Romans snatched it from the Gauls in AD 49 but after the fall of the empire it changed hands many times and was always a poor relation to Verona and Padua until the Venetians took charge in 1404. The 1500s saw the emergence of this remarkable city, thanks to the extraordinary talent and commitment of Andrea Palladio. The Renaissance's rediscovery of classicism, the liberal arts and the humanities created a fertile ground for the ideas of the architect who, reintroduced the columns, domes and porticos of classical architecture to transform the city and architecture itself. Not *everything* in Vicenza was designed or built by Palladio but there can be few other cities where the work of a single architect can be seen round every corner.

With its famous gold fairs (in January, May, September), Vicenza today is the third most productive city in Italy; not bad for a place that has only 120,000 inhabitants. So, it's well off, friendly and stunning, particularly first thing in the morning. Is it the perfect city? Not quite. The US army base, located outside the city and about to expand, is a noticeable presence: take an early morning stroll around Vicenza and you'll see the streets become a training ground for huffing, sweating troops.

To the south of Vicenza lie the Berici hills, while, to the north, in the foothills of the Sette Comuni, are the splendid medieval towns of Thiene, Marostica and Bassano del Grappa.

## What to see in...

### ...one day

Start with a walk along **corso Palladio** before heading into **piazza dei Signori** to see the basilica, loggia and piazzas. Then head to the **Teatro Olimpico** and the **Museo Civico**. After lunch, stroll to **Villa Valmarana ai Nani** and **La Rotonda**. The views from nearby **Santuario di Monte Berico** and the walk back to the city will give you an appetite for a plate of *baccalà alla Vicentina* (fish stew).

### ...a weekend or more

Spend a good hour or two at the **International Andrea Palladio Architecture Centre** and the **Palladian Museum** to grasp the scientific and philosophical thinking behind Palladio's buildings. Head to the foothills of the Sette Comuni where the medieval towns of **Thiene** and **Marostica** still retain their fortified grandeur. Then visit **Bassano del Grappa**: never more beautiful than in the late afternoon sun, and never more lively than during the *passeggiata*.

## Piazza dei Signori

Piazza dei Signori is situated on what is believed to have been the original Roman Forum and is linked to piazza delle Biade to the east, piazza delle Erbe to the south and piazzetta Palladio to the west. The border with piazza delle Biade is marked by two columns which were constructed to remind the Vicentini who were in charge: the Venetian lion of St Mark (1464) spreads its wings atop one, while Christ (1649) looks down from the other.

Dominating the piazza is the **Basilica Palladiana** (or Palazzo della Ragione). Palladio liked to bring sacred design into secular use, so, although it's called a Basilica, this is a judicial rather than religious building. The Gothic hall with its large ship's keel roof was built in the mid 15th century by Domenico da Venezia. Palladio won the commission to refurbish it in 1549, while he was still relatively inexperienced. His idea was to sheathe the building in a two-storey loggia, with Doric columns on the ground floor and Ionic columns on the upper. Entablatures topped both rows of columns and were crowned with a balustrade populated by 23 deeply flattering statues of the Albanese family. Palladio had been dead for 34 years before the final Ionic row was finished in 1614.

# Essentials

❶ **Getting around** Local buses are provided by AIM: useful routes include bus 13, which stops near La Rotonda and Villa Valmarana ai Nani, and bus 18, which goes up to Santuario di Monte Berico. **FTV** buses serve regional destinations, including Vicenza to Thiene to Vicenza (bus 15); Thiene to Marostica to Bassano del Grappa to Thiene (bus 44); Vicenza to Marostica to Bassano del Grappa to Vicenza (no.5). Taxis are available from piazza la Stazione 1 (T0444-324396) and via Lago di Levico 11 (T0444-920600).

❷ **Bus station** AIM (T0444-394911, aimvicenza.it) and FTV (T0444-223111, ftv.vi.it) are both based next to the train station at viale Milano 78.

❸ **Train station** Vicenza Stazione FS, piazzale della Stazione, campo Marzio, T0444-325046, trenitalia.it.

❹ **ATM** There are a number of ATMs on corso A Palladio.

❺ **Hospital** Ospedale di Vicenza, viale Ferdinando Rodolfi 1, T0444-753111.

❻ **Pharmacy** Farmacia Al Redentor, piazza delle Erbe 21, T0444-321951, Mon-Sat 0930-1230 and 1330-1930; **Farmacia Centrale Valeri**, corso A Palladio 136, T0444-544804, Mon-Sat 0900-1300 and 1600-1700.

❼ **Post office** piazza Garibaldi Giuseppe 1, T0444-322554, Mon-Sat 0830-1830.

❽ **Tourist information** piazza Matteotti 12, T0444-944770, vicenzae.org, daily 0900-1300 and 1400-1800; piazza dei Signori 8, T0444-544122, daily 1000-1400 and 1430-1830; at the train station, Apr-Sep Mon-Sat 0900-1400, Sun 1300-1800.

# Tip...

Vicenza's **Card Musei e Palazzi** costs €8, €5 under 15s, students under 26 and over 65s, lasts three days and allows admission to the Teatro Olympia, Museo Civico and the Museo Naturalistico Archeologico. It is available from those sites and from the tourist information offices.

Basilica Palladiana and Torre di piazza in Piazza dei Signori.

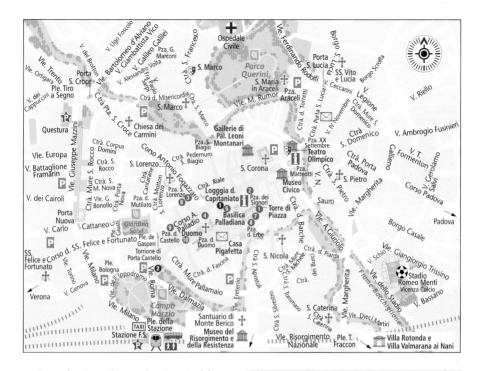

Across the piazza, the grandiose **Loggia del Capitaniato** (also known as Loggia Bernarda) was the former headquarters of the city's Venetian rulers and is now home to the city council. Palladio was commissioned to design it in 1571 to mark the Republic's victory in the Battle of Lepanto and he sought to match the Basilica in size and majesty. However, the project ran out of steam, leaving the loggia with three bays rather than the intended seven and making it look slightly misshapen. Nevertheless, it is far more imposing than most town halls.

The **Torre di Piazza** (or Torre di Bissari) was begun in the 12th century and added to once in 1311, then, again, in the 15th century until it reached its full height of 82 m. It's a slender thing, with a base that is just 7 m wide. Next to it is the **Palazzo del Podestà**. Built in the 12th century by the Bissari family, it was bought by the authorities in the 13th century and given numerous makeovers.

# Listings

**❶ Sleeping**

1 Albergo Due Mori  *contrà di Rode 26*
2 Campo Marzio  *viale Roma 21*

**❶ Eating & drinking**

1 Amici Miei Restaurant and Drinks  *piazza Biade 6*
2 Antica Casa della Malvasia  *contrà delle Morette 5*
3 Art Café  *corso Fogazzaro 52*
4 Caffé Natura  *via Battisti 17*
5 Dai Nodari  *contrà Do Rode, 20*
6 Gran Caffé Garibaldi  *via Cavour 7*
7 Hisyou  *piazza delle Erbe 9*
8 Il Grottino  *piazza dell'Erbe 2*
9 Pasticceria Sorarù  *piazzetta Palladio 17*
10 Righetti  *piazza Duomo 3*

# A stroll through Palladio's legacy

Inside the city walls (built by the Veronese della Scala family who ran things until the Venetians showed up in 1404), corso Andrea Palladio is the main thoroughfare and, running east to west, is the original central axis of the town's Roman *decumanus maximus*. A walk along the corso is a good way to discover the architectural wealth bequeathed by Palladio and continued by his protégé Vincenzo Scamozzi.

Begin at the west end in **Giardini Salvi**, a peaceful public park where the hexastyle doric **Loggia Valmarana** sits astride the Seriola stream. The *centro storico* begins at porta Castello. As you enter the piazza, far to the right is the rather faded **Palazzo Porto Breganze**, built by Scamozzi soon after his master's death in 1580. It represents just a slice of the building designed by Palladio, which had seven bays rather than the two Scamozzi completed.

On the right-hand side as you start along corso Palladio is the stately **Palazzo Thiene Bonin Longare** (corso A Palladio 12, May-Sep Wed-Fri 0900-1200 and 1500-1800, Sat 0900-1200, Oct-Apr Tue-Wed 0900-1200 and 1500-1800), which is made of brick not stone (Palladio was experimenting). It was started by Palladio in 1562 and completed by Scamozzi in 1593. The building now houses the Banca Popolare Vicentina but is open on certain days to allow visitors to see the frescoes by Paolo Guidolini and Giacomo Chiesa. Further along, **Palazzo Capra-Clementi** (corso A Palladio 45),

Above: The ponderous statue of Palladio beside the Basilica.
Opposite page: Another Palladio masterpiece.

built in 1540, would have been a good example of the young Palladio's work if the various owners had not tampered with the façade.

If you turn right down contra Battisti, you'll come to the Duomo (see page 221); instead, turn left along corso Fogazzaro to reach **Palazzo Valmarana Braga Rosa** (corso Antonio Fogazzaro 16, T392-656868, palazzovalmaranabraga.it, Wed 1000-1200 and 1500-1800), completed by Palladio in 1565. Tightly packed into a street of houses that were once all owned by the Valmarana family, its huge arched doorway and imposing cornice make it stand out from the others. It was bombed during World War Two but the interior has been restored and there's some nice stucco work and frescoes inside, if you have a free half hour on a Wednesday.

Back on corso Palladio, if you head right down corso Cavour, it will take you to piazza dei Signori for the Basilica Palladiana and Loggia del Capitaniato (see page 217) or you can turn left onto contrà Porti to find **Palazzo Barbarano Porto** at No 11. Built by Palladio in 1571 for the nobleman Montano Barbarano, it is the only city palazzo that Palladio completed. Palladio's desire for symmetry was severely tested on this difficult site but he succeeded in creating a unified building. It now houses the **International Andrea Palladio Architecture Centre** and the **Palladian Museum** (T0444-323014, Easter-Sep Tue-Sun 1000-1800, Oct-Easter Tue-Thu 1000-1500, Fri-Sun 1000-1800, €5, €3 concessions). Many of Palladio's original drawings were bought by Lord Burlington (the 'Apollo of the Arts') and taken to London but there are still some to see here. Also on contrà Porti, at No. 15, is the house where Luigi da Porto, considered to be the author of the original version of *Romeo and Juliet*, lived and died in 1529 (he is buried in Chiesa di Santa Corona). **Palazzo Iseppo da Porto** (contrà Porti 21) was built in 1552 and is one of Palladio's first palazzi.

Return to corso Palladio and then turn left onto contrà San Gaetano Thiene. The historical seat of Banca Popolare Vicentina is **Palazzo Thiene** (contrà San Gaetano Thiene 11, T0444-542131, palazzothiene.it, May-Jun and Sep Wed and Fri 0900-1200 and 1500-1800, Sat 0900-1200, Oct-Apr

Tue-Wed 0900-1200 and 1500-1800.) Although the designs for this palazzo appear in Palladio's *Quattri Libri dell'Architettura*, the building doesn't look like one of Palladio's creations. It is believed that Palladio merely supervised the architect Giulio Romano on this project.

Take the next left off corso Palladio to reach Chiesa di Santa Corona (see page 221), which houses the **Valmarana crypt**, designed by Palladio as an elegant and fitting tribute to his loyal patron. Further up contrà Santa Corona is **Palazzo Leoni Montanari** (see page 221).

Back on corso Palladio you'll see the lovely little balconies and loggias of **Palazzo dal Toso Franceschini da Schio** at No 147. The building is referred to as Ca' d'Oro because of its similarity to the famous Venetian palazzo. Finally, the walk ends with a look at Palladio's modest former home at No 163, although you could carry on a little further to the **Teatro Olimpico** (see page 220), one of Palladio's masterpieces.

## Around the region

Piazza delle Erbe, behind the Basilica, also has a tower known as the **Torre del Tormento**. This former prison and torture chamber was a place of dread in medieval times. The piazza also hosts the town's market and has a few interesting bars and restaurants.

### Teatro Olimpico

*Piazza Matteotti 11, T0444-222800.*
Jul-Aug Tue-Sun 0900-1900, Sep-Jun 0900-1700, €7 includes admission to Museo Civico and Museo Naturalistico Archeologico, valid for 3 days.

In 1555 Palladio founded the Accademia Olympica, a culturally enriching club for the great and the good of Vicenza, and used this to build enthusiasm for the creation of an indoor theatre in the Roman style.

Scamozzi's stage set inside Paladio's Teatro Olimpico.

There's not much to see on the outside except for an iron gate, some architectural remnants and lush ivy caressing the courtyard walls, but Palladio's and Scamozzi's genius was unleashed on the interior.

Palladio's trademark obsessions – proportion, perspective and symmetry – all come together in a remarkably innovative way, creating the illusion that the stage recedes further than it does. The stage forms a rectangle, while the auditorium is a semi-circle with wooden bench seating on a fairly steep rake. A second tier is created by a wooden colonnade with plaster corniceing and detailed figures. The ceiling was later painted to resemble a celestial sky with flitting clouds.

After Palladio's death in 1580, his son Silla oversaw the completion of the auditorium, while Scamozzi got to work on the stage. The permanent stage set looks like stone but is in fact finely carved in wood. It is angled, with a mid-stage opening that, by clever use of foreshortening, depicts the streets of Thebes. Goethe called it "indescribably beautiful" during his 1786 Grand Tour.

The Teatro Olimpico is both the first and last of its kind: the first modern theatre and the only surviving Renaissance theatre. Its first performance was *Oedipus Rex* in 1585. In the late 16th century, the killjoys of the counter-Reformation closed the theatre but, after the Second World War the Academy regrouped and reopened Vicenza's theatrical treasure trove. It now hosts regular summer seasons of music and drama (see page 231).

### Museo Civico

*Palazzo Chiericati, piazza Matteotti, T0444-321348.*
Sep-Jun Tue-Sun 0900-1300, Jul-Aug Tue-Sun 1000-1300.

Palazzo Chiericati was designed by the city architect in 1550-57. With its unusual layout, open loggias on both the ground floor and *piano nobile,* and elevated, stand-alone position, it is an intriguing building. It makes more sense, however, when you consider that this was once the port area (formerly known as piazza dell'Isola) and the palazzo was designed to sit on the edge of the water.

On the ground floor, the Neri Pozza bequest has three rooms of 19th- and 20th-century Italian artists, while on the second floor, the Pinacoteca is a series of eight understated rooms that are home to Vicenza's huge and impressive civic art collection. Arranged chronologically, you can see the developing techniques, styles and themes used during the Renaissance and Baroque periods. Worth looking out for are Hans Memling's *Calvary* (c1470), Tintoretto's soaring *St Augustine Healing the Lame* (1550), Anthony Van Dyck's *The Three Ages of Man* (1625) and Giovanni Battista Piazzetta's *Ecstasy of St Francis* (1732).

## Chiesa di Santa Corona

*Contrà Santa Corona 2.*
Daily 0830-1200 and 1430-1800.

Built to house a fragment of Jesus' crown of thorns, this Romanesque church has an unfathomable construction which makes it difficult to get your bearings once you are inside. At the fifth altar is Giovanni Bellini's *Baptism of Christ* (c1505), and Veronese's beautiful but fanciful *Adoration of the Magi* (c1570). The artist has transported the nativity scene out of a cattle shed and into some magnificent Roman ruins, with some rather coquettish camels and a comical dog looking on. The church also holds the tomb of Luigi da Porto and the Valmarana crypt by Palladio.

In the cloisters next door, the **Museo Naturalistico Archeologico** (contrà Santa Corona 4, T0444-320440, Tue-Sun 0900-1700, €8) houses a rather disappointing collection of Paleolithic and Roman artefacts dug up from the Berici hills, as well as some stuffed insects.

## Gallerie di Palazzo Leoni Montanari

*Contrà Santa Corona 25, T0444-578875, palazzomontanari.net.*
Tue-Sun 1000-1800.

This gallery exhibits a fairly comprehensive array of Russian icons and some 18th-century Venetian paintings, including those by the Guardi brothers and Pietro Longhi.

## Duomo

*Piazza Duomo, T0444-320996.*
Mon-Fri 1000-1200 and 1530-1730,
Sat 1030-1200, Sun 1000-1200.

Stones in the Duomo's crypt suggest that the old Roman building sited here may have been an early *domus ecclesia* or house of prayer. In the fifth century it became a Christian basilica, which was remodelled in the 11th century, then rebuilt by Lorenzo da Bologna in 1482. Palladio added a drum apse and entablature in 1557, but attaching the Pantheon-esque cupola proved rather complicated and was only completed in 1564, after he'd perfected the technique at the cathedral in Brescia. Lorenzo Veneziano's 14th-century golden altarpiece, *Dormitio Virginis* has a certain one-dimensional charm.

## Palazzo Vescovile

*Piazza Duomo 11, T0444-226300, vicenza.chiesacattolica.it.*
Mon-Fri 0900-1200.

Across the road from the cathedral is the neoclassical Palazzo Vescovile (Bishop's Palace). It has a beautiful Renaissance courtyard with big round arches called the Zeno Loggia, which was built by Bernardino da Milano in 1494.

## Casa Pigafetta

*Contrà Pigafetta.*

This ornate Gothic palazzo was built in the mid 15th century by Stefano da Ravenna and became home to Antonio Pigafetta (1480-1534), Vicenza's famous explorer. He made his name as one of only 18 survivors (out of 237 men) who returned from Magellan's expedition of 1519-22 which circumnavigated the globe. The climates, seas, amazing flowers, weird animals and strange languages they encountered are wonderfully described in Pigafetta's *La Relazione del primo viaggio intorno al mondo* (Report on the First Voyage around the World), one of the first and most authoritative texts on the geographical discoveries of the 16th century. There is no public access to this building but still much to admire from the outside, including the old French motto above the door: *"Il n'est rose sans espine"* ('there is no rose without thorns').

## Santuario di Monte Berico

*Viale X Giugno 87, T0444-320998, monteberico.it.*
Oct-Mar 0600-1230 and 1430-1800,
Apr-Sep 0600-1230 and 1430-1900.
Bus: 8 Viale Roma.

Don't miss the short and beautiful hike up Monte Berico to visit this church. Setting off from the eastern corner of campo Marzio and onto viale X Giugno, cross the bridge and follow the signs up the hill. You'll walk along a cypress-lined path and pass a number of shrines. The Santuario was built in honour of the Madonna who appeared in 1426 then again in 1428 to advise that if the locals built a church here, Vicenza would be saved from the plague. They took her advice and the city was spared, so on 8 September every year, the locals process up this path to thank the Madonna for her good counsel.

# A bicycle tour of Vicenza's villas

This 7-km route is mainly on asphalt and paths that wind past the loveliest villas and lush, fragrant trees. It should take a leisurely three hours if you stop at all the sights; longer if Villa Valmarana ai Nani is open.

You begin at Palladio's **Arco delle Scalette** on porta Monte Palladio, a revival of the Roman triumphal arch. Follow the Riviera Berica, a signposted track that runs parallel to the road of the same name. After about 200 m, turn right into via Giambattista Tiepolo. After a gentle incline you'll reach **Villa Valmarana ai Nani** (see page 223). Walk your bike across the garden paths and down the steps to stradella Valmarana. Follow this path and you'll soon reach Villa Almerico Capra Valmarana, better known as **La Rotonda** (see page 224). This is considered Palladio's magnum opus but, in fact, there are many other Palladian buildings that are just as wonderful. Follow the route back to the edge of the gardens at Villa Valmarana, then turn off left into via San Bastiano. This will take you on to viale X Giugno, which leads to **Santuario di Monte Berico** (see left). Be sure to take in the fabulous views from the city from piazzale della Vittoria before cycling back down viale X Giugno or the little procession path to the left.

Villa Valmarana ai Nani.

On reaching the church, soak up the views from piazza della Vittoria before venturing inside. The domed Baroque basilica we see now was built by Carlo Borrello in 1688 and contains two artworks that are worth closer inspection: Bartolomeo Montagna's *Pietà* (1505), which despite its rudimentary style emotively conveys Mary's grief, and Veronese's *The Great Supper of St Gregory the Great* (1572). The composition of this painting echoes the artist's *Feast in the House of Levi*, which hangs in the Accademia in Venice (see page 121) but, in this picture, the Pope takes centre stage and Jesus, dressed as a pilgrim, is placed on his right-hand side. During the occupation of the Veneto in 1848, Austrian troops slashed the canvas in a frenzied attack, tearing it to shreds, but it has since been totally reconstructed and restored. In the sacristy there are three intricate wood-inlaid closets by Pier Antonio dell'Abate da Modena: the one showing a bird in a cage is particularly delightful.

### Villa Valmarana ai Nani

*Via dei Nani 28, T0444-321803, villavalmarana.com.* Mar-Oct Sat-Sun 1000-1200 and 1400-1600, €8. Bus: 8 Viale Roma or €8-10 in a taxi from the centro storico.

Believe it or not, this villa is not by Palladio! It was commissioned by Giovanni Bertoli, who bequeathed it to his daughter, a nun in Padua, meaning it became the property of her convent. Giustino Valmarana bought the villa in 1715 and the architect Francesco Muttoni developed it further. There are actually three buildings within the large gardens: the *palazzina* (main villa), completed in 1669, and the *foresteria* (guest house) and *scuderia* (stables), both of which were built around 1720.

The *'ai nani'* in the villa's name refers to the 17 dwarves with attitude that line the boundary wall. They were carved by Francesco Uliaco, who allegedly worked from some drawings by Tiepolo. It was a Baroque conceit to incorporate dwarves into the decoration of buildings and these are some of the most spirited you will find. There is a popular belief that the Valmarana family had a daughter of

## Tip...

**Concerti in Villas** is a series of classical concerts that take place in the grounds of La Rotonda and other villas during June and July. Contact the tourist office for more details.

restricted height and hoped that the presence of these statues and a number of staff who also had physical abnormalities might ensure she felt normal.

The reason this villa is so celebrated is because of the magnificence and inventiveness of its frescoes by the Venetian painter Giambattista Tiepolo (1724-1804) and his son Giandomenico. They were commissioned by Giustino Valmarana in 1757 and have a dreamlike palette and use of perspective that pulls you in. You can tell by the colour and ingenuity of the frescoes, inspired by classical love stories and literature, that Tiepolo's imagination was given a free rein here. In the entrance hall of the *palazzina* is a remarkable portrayal of Iphigenia in Aulis (from the Greek play by Euripides), framed by architectural features. The four rooms off the hall host scenes from Homer's *Iliad*, Virgil's *Aeneid*, *Orlando Furioso* by Ludovico Ariosto and *Gerusalemme Liberata* by Torquato Tasso, an epic poem based on the first crusade.

Tiepolo gave each of the five rooms in the *foresteria* a different theme: peasants working the land throughout the seasons; China; carnival cherubs; Olympus; and 'the room of the loggia' (which was decorated by Girolamo Mengozzi and Antonio Visentini). These frescoes very nearly ended up in Paris but it wasn't Napoleon who sought to plunder them, it was Mussolini, who wanted them for the embassy there. Thankfully, Giustino Valmarana, who was a Christian Democrat Senator at the time and Giuseppe Bottai, one of Il Duce's right-hand men, managed to persuade him to leave them here. The Valmarana family still own the villa and *foresteria* today.

### La Rotonda (Villa Almerico Capra Valmarana)

*Via Rotonda 29, T0444-321793.*
Garden: mid-Mar-Oct Tue-Sun 1000-1200 and
1500-1800, Feb-mid-Mar Tue-Sun 1000-1200 and
1430-1700, closed Nov-Mar; €5.
Villa: mid-Mar-Oct Wed 1000-1200 and
1500-1800, closed Nov-Mar; €10.
Bus: 8 Viale Roma (infrequent); €8-10 in a taxi
from the *centro storico*.

Connected to the Villa Valmarana ai Nani by way of a
pleasant shady path, La Rotonda was commissioned
in 1566 by the wealthy Vicentine cleric, Paolo
Almerico, as a summer pavilion. The design is a
simple square, with a dome and four identical
porticos of the Ionic order on each side, which
overlook the countryside. Inside, the symmetry
continues with the central dome and four corridors
leading to each of the porticos. Palladio took great
pride in the way the landscape, materials, location,
symmetrical forms and mathematical precision
came together in such beauteous harmony.

> **"**
> The place is nicely situated and one of the loveliest
> and most charming that one could hope to find; for it
> lies on the slopes of a hill, which is very easy to reach.
> The loveliest hills are arranged around it, which
> afford a view into an immense theatre…because one
> takes pleasure in the beautiful view on all four sides,
> loggias were built on all four façades.
> **"**
>
> *Quattri Libri dell'Architettura* (Andrea Palladio)
> describing La Rotonda.

He died before it was finished but, once more,
Scamozzi completed the work, flattening the
original design of the dome. The frescoes inside are
by Alessandro Maganza and Louis Dorigny, with
stuccoes by Agostino Rubini and Domenico
Fontana. La Rotunda has been copied numerous
times; there are versions of it as far away as Delhi and
Washington. It was also used as the film set for
Joseph Losey's *Don Giovanni* in 1979.

## Villa Porto-Colleoni-Thiene

*Via Garibaldi 2, Thiene,*
*T0445-380879, castellodithiene.com.*
Tours: Mid Mar-mid Sep Sun 1500, 1600 and
1700, €8, €5 under 13s. 20 km north of Vicenza
on the S349.

Often called the Castello, this villa was never
actually a castle but certainly resembles one. It is
believed to be the work of Domenico da Venezia
who worked with Palladio on the Duomo and the
Palazzo della Ragione between 1448 and 1453.
Entered by a loggia with five huge arches, the
solid rectangular structure contains a vast atrium.
Francesco Porto inherited the villa in 1507 and
raised the roof, adding two symmetrical white
marble staircases at either side of the loggia.
He also developed the gardens which to this
day are kept in the Renaissance style.

The villa is celebrated for its frescoes by
Veronese's top pupils Battista Zelotti (1526-1578)
and Giovanni Antonio Fasolo (1530-1572). They did
their master proud with their depictions of classical
mythology on the walls of the hall. At either side of
the fireplace crouch Vulcan and Venus with Cupid
in her arms. Bands of cherubs, bundles of fruit and
sheep skulls line the cornices of the four walls, which
show scenes from Roman history: the meeting of
Massinissa and Sofonisba after the Roman victory
over Carthage; Muzio Scevola standing defiant in
front of the Etruscan King Porsenna; a blonde
Cleopatra turning against Augustus; and the
freeing of a lady from Carthage at Scipione.

Also worth a look are the stables downstairs.
These were designed by Francesco Muttoni
(1668-1747) and have mosaic cobbled floors and red
marble columns with carved *putti* (cherubs) on top.

## Marostica

*14 km east of Thiene on the S248.*

This compact medieval town was formerly
celebrated for its cherries but now it's famous for
a human chess game, which is held on the second
weekend of September in even years. After World
War Two, Vucetich Mirko wrote a play in which two
suitors, Renaldo and Vieri, fell in love with Lionora,
the beautiful daughter of the local lord. To win her
hand they challenged each other to a duel but the
lord of Marostica didn't want to lose either of them,
so instead he ordered the love rivals to play a chess
game in the town square: whoever won would
marry Lionora while the loser would marry her
younger sister, Oldrada. So, the joy of chess is
celebrated, avoiding bloodshed and hurt
feelings and providing the opportunity for
some pomp, dancing and fireworks. Some visitors
feel a bit cheated when they realise there is no
historical basis to the story and it is just fictional

## Tip...

Marostica's legendary cherries are still grown in
this area and harvested in June. You can buy huge
quantities very cheaply on the roadside or in local
shops and markets. They are utterly delicious but
watch out for the juice: it can stain terribly!

**Above: Marostica is famous for its cherries. Opposite page: La Rotonda.**

## Around the region

Everyday chess in Marostica.

medievalism, but it has done wonders for tourism in the town and gives the locals a chance to dress up in 14th-century costume.

If you can't make it to the chess game itself, visit the **Museo dei Costumi e delle Armi della Partita a Scacchi** (Castello Inferiore, piazza Castello, T0424-72127, daily 1430-1830, €1), which displays the lavish costumes and weaponry that are worn by the chess pieces, Lionora, the king, the knights, the foot soldiers and so on: heavy doublet, hose and leg-of-mutton sleeves for the fellows and brightly coloured *bliauds* (tunics) with wimples for the ladies. The museum is housed in the town's lower castle on the main piazza, which is linked to another castle on the hill (Castello Superiore) by means of crenellated walls that fully enclose the town.

### Bassano del Grappa

The green and fruitful area at the foot of Monte Grappa, where the river Brenta opens out onto the plains, has been inhabited by settlers since the Bronze Age. More recently it was the site of wartime heroics, when the Italians routed the Austrians in 1917-18, thanks to the Alpini, elite mountain soldiers who fought an unrelenting battle in the most difficult and dangerous conditions up in the Grappa. Their bravery is referenced throughout Bassano del Grappa with the tricolore and their motif cap with a feather. Three of the five Alpini brigades were disbanded

after the Cold War ended but even those who are no longer in the army still consider themselves Alpini *"in congedo"* or 'on leave'. Every year, in late spring, members of the Associazione Nazionale Alpini gather together for a veci (reunion) in one of the towns in the area (the Bassano reunion is always the most trumpeted) to commemorate lost friends, drink and sing. You might not understand a word of *La Montanara* but hearing the men's voices and watching their chests puff with pride is a moving experience.

Bassano is best known for its grappa, the intense liquor made from the leftovers of wine production. The town is also famous for its majolica ceramics and for white asparagus (see page 233).

### Ponte Vecchio

Bassano town sits on either side of the river Brenta, linked by this sturdy, covered wooden bridge (also known as the ponte degli Alpini). Originally designed by Palladio in 1569, it has been destroyed a number of times by combat and flash floods but, apart from some tweaking by engineers to increase its strength, it remains true to the architect's vision. You can see still see evidence of the battles that have been fought here: bullet holes riddle the walls of buildings at either end of the bridge.

### Museo Civico

*Piazza Garibaldi, T0424-522235.*
Tue-Sat 0900-1830, Sun 1530-1830,
€4.50, €3 under 14s and students, includes admission to Museo della Ceramica.

In the cloisters of the 14th-century church of San Francesco are some Roman artefacts and some paintings by the Da Ponte or Bassano family, Jacopo and Francesco. There is also a room devoted to Canova and one to Tito Gobbi, a local baritone made good.

## Museo della Ceramica

*Palazzo Sturm, via Schiavonetti, T0424-524933.*
Tue-Sat 0900-1230 and 1530-1830, Sun 1530-
1830, €4.50, €3 concessions, includes admission
to Museo Civico.

The majolica of Bassano has been famous in ceramic
circles since the 16th century, so, if you delight in
decorative dishes, this is a good place to spend an
hour or so. For those less interested in ceramics, the
palazzo itself has some charming frescoes, rococo
rooms and lovely views over the river.

## Museo degli Alpini

*Taverna Bar Alpini, via Angarano 2, ponte Vecchio,
T0424-503662.*
Tue-Sun 0830-2000.

A room of the pub is dedicated to the feathered
*fratelli* and shows some heart-rending photographs
and relics of their icy heroics.

## Museo della Grappa

*Distillerie Poli, via Gamba 6, T0424-524426.*
Daily 0900-1930.

The almost-gripping story of grappa is told in a
super-smooth way in this commercial museum.
Invariably, you wait for a taste of the good stuff,
which is not always forthcoming.

## Grotte di Oliero

*Via Oliero di Sotto 85, Valstagna, T0424-558250.*
Park and caves: daily 0900-1900. Boat trips:
Mon-Sat 0930-1200 and 1400-1700,
Sun 0900-1700, €7, €5 under 15s.
14 km from Bassano on the SS47 turn left to
Campolongo bridge and follow the signs to
'Grotte di Oliero'.

The subterranean waters of the Oliero springs were
discovered in 1822 by Alberto Parolini. A winding
track takes you down a hill and under Rock
Rampion to paths that surround the underground
lake. The ground can be slippery and it can feel

Bassano del Grappa.

rather chilly, so make sure you are properly shod
and clothed. Tools, discovered in the *Covolo degli
Assassini* (Cave of the Murderers) show that it was
once inhabited; there are also signs that a
two-storey house was once tucked into the
crevices. There are three other caves: the Sisters'
Cave, Lord's Cave and Parolini Cave; each more
difficult to reach than the last. A boat takes you to
the Parolini Cave, which is an other-worldly 14-m
high chamber of alabastrine stalactites. It is also
home to the olm, an amphibian troglobiont or
cave salamander that is native to Croatia. Parolini
introduced them as an experiment and they live
here quite happily.

The park above offers some lush meanderings
amongst flora and fauna indigenous to the region.
Also here is the **Museo di Speleologia e Carsismo,**
which lovers of geology and speleology might
enjoy. It has a nice little café and benches for picnics.

# Sleeping

## Campo Marzio €€

*Viale Roma 21, T0444-545700,*
*hotelcampomarzio.com.*

You'll either love the '70s vibe of the brown reception area at this business hotel or it will make you wince. Either way, if you have booked a superior room, not to worry: they are much fresher, lighter and altogether more delightful. There are 35 rooms in total and the location is very convenient: right between the station and the historical centre and close to the buses that run to the outlying villas and hills.

## Albergo Due Mori €

*Contrà di Rode 26, T0444-321886,*
*hotelduemori.com.*

Bang in the centre of things, just a short shuffle from piazza dei Signori, this beautifully refurbished palazzo has 30 spacious rooms (27 are en suite) which are decorated in neutral tones and furnished in an art nouveau style. Breakfast is €5 extra but is well worth it. There is also a lift for those who don't want to heave their bags up the stairs.

## Bob and Jenny's Bed and Breakfast €

*Borgo Berga 140, T0444-320884,*
*bed-breakfast-italy.com.*

This B&B is located in a lovely little neighbourhood in the Berici Hills, just a gentle amble away from the Santuario di Monte Berico and a stroll from some great bars and restaurants. The family that run it are hugely engaging and offer a whole host of information on what to do, how to get there and where to eat and drink. They will also do pick-ups from the station. There are two bedrooms and a two-night minimum stay.

### Self-catering

## Villa Pasini €€

*Via Roma 4, Arcugnano, nr*
*Vicenza, T0444-270054,*
*villapasini.com.*

Tucked away in the hills between olive groves and vineyards, this spectacular villa is run by a Californian woman, Cynthia. The chic bedrooms are accessed through a courtyard and are actually suites with small kitchenettes so you can make your own supper. Breakfast, which is included, is served outside in summer or in your room during cooler months. The rural location suits those with a car; a taxi from the city centre will set you back €12.

## Al Castello €€

*Piazza Terraglio 19,*
*T0424-228665.*

Not far from the ponte Alpini, this small hotel has 11 variously sized rooms, all with simple but good quality wooden furnishings and spotless bathrooms. It's run by a mother and son who delight in making everything *'buona'*. The breakfast room may be small but it caters for big appetites (good value for an extra €6) and there is a bar downstairs with seats outside for aperitivi hour.

Below: Bassano del Grappa.

# Eating & drinking

## Amici Miei Restaurant & Drinks €€€

*Piazza Biade 6, T0444-321061, amicimiei.vi.it.*
Mon 1830-2400, Tue-Sat 1130-1500 and 1830-2400.

This upmarket bar is adorned with photos of the Vicentini glitterati. An aperitivo from the huge wine and drinks list (including bizarre-coloured cocktails) helps you settle into the chic, modish surroundings. Simple knock-out dishes include *penne con salsa di asparagi* (pasta with asparagus) and *gelato alla zenzero* (ginger ice cream). And, what could be better than stumbling full-bellied and merry out of here into the majesty of piazza dei Signori?

## Hisyou €€€

*Piazza delle Erbe 9, T0444-321044.*
Mon 1930-2400, Tue-Sun 1200-1500 and 1930-2400.

Opening a sushi restaurant in the shadow of the basilica in the heart of Vicenza must have been a huge gamble but it has paid off: the locals can't get enough of the sashimi and tappanyakis. The minimalist utility decor and gentle lighting create an unassuming atmosphere. Sapporo beer and saki make a nice change from Valpolicella, too.

## Dai Nodari €€

*Contrà do Rode 20, T0444-544085.*
Tue-Sun 1200-2200.

Tucked away on a little back street not far from the basilica, this huge bar/restaurant with outdoor seating has a laid-back vibe and cheerful staff and attracts a good cross-section of Vicentini diners. Tasty versions of pasta dishes, all the regional classics, as well as a good range of simple food, such as baked *branzino* (sea bass) and grilled vegetables, mean it caters for everyone.

## Antica Casa della Malvasia €

*Contrà delle Morette 5, T0444-543704.*
Tue-Sun 1130-1500 and 1830-2300

Palladio might have designed Vicenza but in this, the city's oldest restaurant, you can eat the food that built the Vicentini. Big fat *bigoli con l'anatra* (pasta with duck sauce) and the fabulously stewy *baccalà alla Vicentina*. It's superb value for money and well suited to those who want to get stuck in to the local wines, as it has over 80 different bottles to choose from.

## Righetti €

*Piazza Duomo 3, T0444-543135.*
Mon-Fri 1200-1430 and 1900-2200.

This place might be self-service but the food goes way beyond cafeteria fare. With lashings of pasta, a good selection of grilled meat and vegetables, and risotto on Tuesday and Friday evenings, there is much to keep even the biggest fusspot happy. The mix of locals, including finely clad ladies, proves that this is one of the most popular eateries in Vicenza. You can sit inside or out.

## Picnic spots

**Campo Marzo** (via Roma) It's next to the train station but the expanse of green means the background bustle isn't a problem.

**Giardino Salvi** (corso Santi Felice e Fortunato) There's some lovely shady areas next to the canal if you want to escape the sun.

**Parco Querini** (contrà Chiara V Aracelli) This well tended park with a creamy white pavilion and statues is a romantic spot that's popular with canoodlers.

Loggia Valmarana at Giardino Salvi.

## Cafés & bars

### Art Café
*Corso Fogazzaro 52,*
*T0444-321047.*
Tue-Sun 0800-2300.
The location on piazza San Lorenzo ensures a constant stream of locals and visitors come to drink here.

### Caffè Natura
*Via Battisti 17, T0444-234372.*
Tue-Sun 0800-2000
If you've had your fill of coffee, this place sells beautiful smoothies and fruit-studded cakes that are so fresh tasting you could fool yourself into thinking they were good for you.

### Caffè Vicenza
*Corso A Palladio 73b,*
*T0444-321368.*
Daily 0800-2200.
This place is right on the main drag, surrounded by swanky shops, so you'll get an eyeful of the local talent and they'll also get an eyeful of you.

### Gran Caffè Garibaldi
*Via Cavour 7, T0444-544147.*
Wed-Mon 0900-2400.
Sitting outside on the piazza drinking cappuccino in this notable café is an unmissable Vicenza experience. And you won't have to move either as they serve lunch and dinner too. Upstairs is posh and rather expensive but worth a peek.

### Il Grottino
*Piazza della Erbe 2.*
Tue-Sun 1700-0200.
Right behind the basilica, this bar is open every night for apertivi, snacks and music.

### Osteria Ca' d'Oro
*Contrà San Gaetano da Thiene 8,*
*T0444-323713.*
Daily 1200-1430 and 1900-2230.
Close to the palazzo that resembles Venice's Ca' d'Oro, this bar is popular with a young crowd and with those who think they are young.

### Pasticceria Sorarù
*Piazzetta Palladio 17,*
*T0444-320915.*
Thu-Tue 0830-1300 and 1530-2000.
Whether you're inside amongst the columns, marble and mirrors

## Vicenza dishes

*baccalà alla Vicentina* cod cooked very slowly with onions and parmesan cheese, served with soft polenta.

*bigoli con l'anatra* homemade egg pasta served with bolognese made from Thiene duck.

*capretto sullo spiedo* roasted kid, best served with roasted *zucca* (pumpkin).

*castrato con risi e bisi* rice and peas from Lumignano; it's more of a broth than a risotto.

*polenta brustola* toasted polenta.

*sorpressa* a kind of salame from the Pasubio and Recoaro valleys, generally eaten with a slice of grilled polenta.

*torresani* pigeons from Breganze, served with fried polenta.

Grappa.

# Entertainment

or outside watching the stylish Vicentini stride by, you'll find the coffee and artisan pastries are as good as the surroundings.

## Osteria Terraglio €€
*Piazza Terraglio 28,*
*T0424-521064.*
Tue-Sun 0830-1500 and 1700-0200.
This rustic restaurant packs them in and is one of the most spirited places in town. The menu runs the whole gamut: juicy salads, cured meats, roasted vegetables (including the local white asparagus), grilled fish and pasta with robust sauces. There are lots of wines to choose from, too, but you don't have to flash your cash as the house white is most enjoyable. Tuesday is jazz night.

### Cafés & bars
**Bar Paninoteca al Porton**
*Via Gamba 3, T0424-524079.*
Mon 0800-1430, Wed-Sun 0800-2400.
The chunky wooden benches outside and the flowers in the window boxes give this a jolly, Alpine, beer-drinking atmosphere. Great coffee and fulsomely filled panini.

## Vicenza

### Cinema
**Cinema Odeon**
*Corso A Palladio 186,*
*T0444-543492.*
Tue-Sun 2000.
Come here for the usual Hollywood fare dubbed into Italian. Independent and arthouse films also occasionally feature on the bill.

**Cinema Teatro Araceli**
*Borgo Scrofa 20, T0444-514253.*
Cinema buffs will love the traditional cinema experience and the singular line-up of classic movies.

### Clubs
**Totem Club**
*Via Vecchia Ferriera 166,*
*T0444-291176.*
Thu-Fri 2200-0400,
Sat 2300-0500.
To the west of the city, this club holds avant-garde, house and Gothic industrial nights and entertains a mainly studenty, alternative crowd.

**Villa Bonin**
*Viale del Commercio 8,*
*T0444-348168.*
Wed, Fri-Sat 2300-0400.
Near the Fiera on the other side of the train line, this mammoth bar, club and restaurant is a rather slick operation and full of the most gorgeous people you'll have ever seen: *'Megabella!'*

### Theatre
**Teatro Olimpico**
*Piazza Matteotti 11,*
*T0444-222800.*
For information on performances and ticketing, contact the tourist information office in piazza Matteotti. Tickets €10-30.
Can there be a more amazing venue to experience a live performance? There's a jazz festival in May, orchestral works in June and drama (tending on the classical side) in September and October.

# Shopping

**Vicenza**

### Art & antiques

An antiques market is held in piazza dei Signori on the second Sunday of every month. The items are all quite randomly displayed but there are some joys to behold: a glove stretcher in the shape of a bird's beak, for instance.

### Books

**Librerià Athena**
*Contrà San Gaetano Thiene 2a, T0444-326103.*
Mon-Sat 0930-1300 and 1600-1900.
Some fascinating discoveries can be made in this small but satisfying little bookshop.

Above: Get yer lamps 'ere!
Right: Beans at Il Melario, Bassano del Grappa.

### Clothing & accessories

The whole of corso Palladio is lined with high-street clothes shops, including Zara, H&M, Bata, Conbipel, Golden Point (socks and tights), Sephora (make up and perfume), Intimissini (undies), Max & Co, and others.

### Department stores

**Coin**
*Piazza Castello 190, T0444-546044.*
Mon 1530-1930, Tue-Fri and Sun 1000-1930 and 1530-1930, Sat 1000-1300 and 1530-2000.
Good old trusty Coin: always there when you need new flip flops, pants, make-up, shorts, etc.

### Food & drink

**Dolci Tentazioni**
*Corso A Palladio 23, T0444-321068.*
Mon-Sat 0900-1300 and 1500-1930.
Fabulous chocolates, honey and different flavoured salts and peppers.

**Il Ceppo Gastronomia**
*Corso A Palladio 196, T0444-544414, gastronomiailceppo.com.*
Mon-Sat 0900-1300 and 1500-1900.
The best quality and most comprehensive selection of carry-out cold dishes, bread, cheese and salami you will find in Vicenza: perfect for picnics. You can also take goodies home with you in vacuum packs, such as a slice of Bastardo del Grappa (a much-loved local cheese).

**Piaceri e Peccati**
*Corso A Palladio 150, T0444-327417, piaceriepeccati.it.*
Mon-Sat 0930-1300 and 1500-1930.
Purveyors of fine sweeties, herbs, oils, jams: indeed, all things tasty.

### Gifts

**Cartoleria Zamperetti**
*Corso A Palladio 66, T0444-321265.*
Mon-Sat 0930-1300 and 1500-1900.
Pretty coloured paper, envelopes and leather-bound books.

# Activities & tours

### Food & drink

Bassano del Grappa is famous for its *asparago bianco* (white asparagus), which has been cultivated underground in this area since the 15th century. It can be found in abundance in fruit and vegetable markets all over Veneto from the last week in April until 13th June. There is considerable pride amongst the growers of these spears and the last harvest is always announced, so that customers know that anything they buy thereafter must have been refrigerated and will therefore have an impaired flavour.

Thursday is market day in Bassano and a great opportunity to buy some dried mushrooms and beans to take home.

**Il Melario**
*Via Angaro 13, T0424-502168.*
Daily 0900-1300 and 1500-1900.
There is an amazing array of dried mushrooms and beans for sale here, as well as grappa galore.

### Cultural tours

**Veneto Tours** (T349-1016700, theothersideofvenice.com) offer a great day-long Palladian tour of Vicenza, either on foot or chauffeur-driven, from €200 for two people. Their passion for Palladio make their tours of his palazzi and villas particularly insightful: perfect if you only have a day in the area and want to pack as much in as possible. A shorter half-day walking tour of the city and surrounding villas with enthusiastic guides is offered by **Avventure Bellicose** (T041-970499, tours-italy.com) from €37; prices vary depending on type of tour, length and number of people in the group.

### Cycling

**Dolcevita Bike Tours** (T070-920 9885, dolcevitabiketours.com) run a great seven-day self-guided tour of the Veneto starting from Vicenza. The route heads past a number of the most famous villas (including the splendid Villa Barbaro) to Marostica, Asolo, Bassano del Grappa, Treviso, Venice, Chioggia and Padua, before returning to Vicenza. It's a comprehensive and not too hilly route. The price (around €750) includes an orientation session before you go, accommodation, meals, baggage transfer, all road maps and, of course, a bike!

Hourly train services to Milan (2 hrs 30 mins) Venice (50 mins), Padua (20 mins) and Verona (30-45 mins). Also buses from viale Milano to Venice (1 hr) Padua (50 mins) and Verona (1 hr 40 mins); and to Thiene (20 mins), Marostica (30 mins) and Bassano del Grappa (1 hr).

**Wheely great views around Vicenza.**

# Contents

Verona

Looking across the Adige to Sant'Anastasia.

# Introduction

A lthough it's famous for a love story that never happened, Verona is anything but a fake. The Romans, who arrived in 300 BC, had big ambitions for Verona. Their monumental amphitheatre – still in operation today – and Teatro Romano show just how grand their plans were. The Roman Empire may have crumbled but centuries of power struggles, including those involving the Scaligeri family and the Venetian Republic, have left behind a legacy of fine Gothic churches and Romanesque palazzi. These create a beautiful backdrop for a city that enjoys the good life: wine is produced in the surrounding hills and Verona's performing and visual arts scenes draw thousands of visitors each year.

With a population of 260,000, Verona is quite a small city but its wealth and history imbue it with the confidence of a much larger urban centre, and its 20,000 students add youthfulness and an air of excitement. However, it is also politically conservative: the influx of new immigrants and other threats to its way of life are much debated in the city's bars and cafés. Italy is changing fast and Verona isn't happy.

The city is on the main routes to Milan and Venice and has excellent transport links; Lake Garda is only an hour away. The river Adige, rushing down from the Dolomites, swirls round Verona and has created a promontory where the very best of the city is located. This compact centre is easy to explore on foot. There is much to see in Verona but this is also a city for socialising, drinking aperitivi, eating well and shopping better.

The Arena at night during the opera season.

## What to see in…

…one day

A walk through the **piazzas** and a visit to the **Scaligeri tombs**, **Arena**, **Casa di Giulietta** and the **Teatro Romano** can all be done in a day, leaving plenty of time for cappuccino and aperitivo breaks, meals and shopping.

…**a weekend or more**
Invest in a Verona Card and you will be able to see all the sights. Go to **Castelvecchio** early on the second day, then take in the **churches** or the modern art or photographic **galleries** before heading to **Giardini Giusti**. The **Museo della Radio Epoca** (near to Tomba di Giulietta) and the **Museo Civico di Storia Naturale** are worth a look if you've still got time on your hands. If you're here for longer, a trip to the **Torri del Benaco** will blow away the excesses of la dolce vita in the city.

# Essentials

**➊ Getting around** The centre of Verona is compact enough to explore happily on foot. There are orange AMT buses for travel around the city and blue APTV buses for transport to outlying destinations. The **Verona Card** (€8 for one day; €12 for three days) admits you to a number of Verona's sights and allows free travel on AMT buses. It can be bought in shops, museums, monuments and tobacconists (look for the T sign). Tourists can hire bikes for free from the tourist information office at Porta Nuova train station by leaving an identity card or passport. **Radio Taxi**, T045-532666.

**➋ Bus station** Autostazione di Verona Porta Nuova, piazzale XXV Aprile, T045-887 1111 (AMT), T045-805 7811 (APTV), amt.it, apt.vr.it.

**➌ Train station** Porta Nuova FS, piazzale XXV Aprile, T045-800 0861, trenitalia.it.

**➍ ATMs** at the train station; via Mazzini; piazza Erbe.

**➎ Hospital** Ospedale Civile Maggiore Borgo Trento, piazzale Stefani 1, T045-812 1111.

**➏ Pharmacy** call T1100 for the three nearest open pharmacies.

**➐ Post office** piazza Viviani 7, T045-805 1111, Mon-Sat 0830-1830.

**➑ Tourist information offices** IAT, via degli Alpini 9, T045-806 8680, tourism.verona.it, Mon-Sat 0900-1900, Sun 0900-1500; IAT, Porta Nuova FS, T045-800 0861, Mon-Sat 0900-1800, Sun 0900-1500.

## Arena

*Piazza Bra, T045-800 3204, arena.it.*
Jun-Aug (opera season) Tue-Sat 0900-1530,
Sep-May Mon 1330-1930, Tue-Sat 0830-1930,
€4, €1 children, €3 students and over 65s.
For details of opera performances and tickets,
see page 255.

Verona's Roman amphitheatre, the third largest Roman structure in Italy (behind Rome's Colosseum and Capua's amphitheatre) was built around AD 30. Although a major earthquake in 1117 destroyed most of the *ala* (outer ring) and many of its stones have been 'borrowed' over the years to prop up other building projects in the city, it is still in amazingly good nick. The elliptical structure is 139 m long and 110 m wide with 44 tiers of stone seats. For the best view, climb the steps to the top, where only some of the *ala* remains, giving you excellent views of piazza Bra and across the Adige.

The Romans used the Arena for *ludi* (games and shows) that honoured the gods. These could be theatrical performances (*ludi scaenici*), chariot races (*ludi circenses*) or the grisly execution of felons and prisoners of war. (There is no evidence to suggest Christians were slain here.) Up to 30,000 spectators (the entire population of Roman Verona) could watch these events and the clever design allowed this mass of people to flow freely, using the 64 *vomitorio* (entrances) and the *ambulatori* (corridors). Nowadays, due to health and safety regulations, audiences are restricted to 15,000.

In the 16th century a body of learned friends with political backing formed the Arena Conservators, who sought to protect the building and make it safe for use but it wasn't until 1913 that it staged its first opera: Giuseppe's Verdi's *Aida*. Aida remains, perhaps, the most popular opera to be performed here and seems entirely appropriate in such an ancient setting. Other favourites include Puccini's *Tosca*, Bizet's *Carmen* and Rossini's *The Barber of Seville*, all of which suit the scale and extravagance of the Arena and benefit from its amazing acoustics.

During opera season there is always a buzz around the piazza, where the sets for forthcoming

Above: The *ala* of the Arena. Opposite page: The Arena.

productions are stored and gladiators pose for camera-toting tourists for a Euro or two. You can visit during the day as a sightseer but the best way to see and experience the Arena is to attend an opera. These shows are spectacular, with exaggerated colours, lights, costumes and drama. The crowd is pretty eye-popping too: the local glitterati sit on plush red chairs at the front and totter off in their Gucci heels for a prosecco during the interval, while up at the back, families with children spread out on the marble seats (or steps, rather) and tuck into picnics. You can hire cushions and buy drinks from cheeky-chappy coke sellers with an eye for the ladies. When you enter the Arena you will be given a candle or *mocoleto* with a card to catch the hot wax. Come the moment of darkness, everyone lights their candle and the whole arena twinkles: *che spettacolo*! What a show!

## A cheap night at the opera

Who needs the posh seats when you can sit with the proles and get carried away with the crowd?

- Book your tickets online at arena.it as soon as you know you're coming to Verona. This saves disappointment and means you'll only have to queue for a short time to pick them up.

- For a few Euros you can rent a cushion. This isn't a good time to penny-pinch; you'll regret it, if you don't.

- Go to the toilet before you arrive. Getting up and down the huge steps is awkward and the queues during the interval are colossal.

- Take some snacks and drinks that are easy to consume by hand. There's no room for tablecloths, glasses and cutlery.

- Bring some binoculars so you can see exactly what's happening on stage and observe the rest of the Veronese audience at play.

# Piazzas
# of power
A walk through central Verona

**B**egin at **piazza Bra**, where you can admire the Roman Arena while sipping a coffee in one of the many bars that make up the Listone. The balcony at No. 18 is famous as the venue for Garibaldi's 'Rome or death' speech in 1867. To the hard right is a double-arched gate, the portoni Bra, which leads to Porta Nuova train station and the city walls.

Walk along the arcaded 17th-century Gran Guardia, which was built by Domenico Curtoni (c1610), and part of an interior city wall. These fortifications were

the work of the della Scala or Scaligeri family, who ruled Verona in the 13th century and needed to keep their numerous enemies out of the city (see page 243). Walking round the piazza, on your right you'll see the flashy neoclassical Palazzo Barbieri (1848), which is now the city hall, while across from the Arena are pleasant cedar- and pine-filled gardens. Walk through these to see a statue of Victor Emanuel II, first king of the united Italy.

To your left is the Arena and, ahead, the Louis Vuitton shop which marks the start of via Mazzini. This glamorous thoroughfare leads towards **piazza**

**Erbe**, which was built on the site of the former Roman forum. A market is still held here (Mon-Sat 0800-1900) but it has dwindled in size and quality: if you're looking for a Romeo and Juliet snowstorm to take home, here's where to find it. Standing at the **Fontana Madonna Verona** (1368), which was constructed out of a font from Sant'Anastasia, you'll see the column of San Marco that denotes the presence of the Venetians, who added Verona to their territory in 1405. Napoleon's men pulled it down when Venice fell in 1797 but it was re-erected in 1886. Behind the column is the huge baroque **Palazzo Maffei**, which stands on the site of the old Roman Capitol. It is crowned with statues of Hercules, Jupiter, Venus, Mercury, Apollo and Minerva. If you dine in the wonderful Maffei (see page 253), be charming to the waiter and he may just take you downstairs to see the ruins. To the left of Palazzo Maffei is **Torre del Gardelo**, built in 1370. Its bell is now at Castelvecchio. Shops line the western side of the piazza with a small *piazzetta* housing the Romanesque **Domus Mercatorum** (1301) or Merchants' House. Near the Fontana you will also see the **Berlina**, a canopied construction from the 12th century where ceremonies involving the *podestà* or mayor were held.

Now walk along via della Costa and through the **Arco della Costa** (arch of the rib) – so called because a whale bone dangles inexplicably from it – to the grander **piazza dei Signori**. Immediately to the right, at 83 m high, is the **Torre dei Lamberti** (T045-803 2726, Mon 1330-1930, Tue-Sun 0930-1930, €4. €3 concessions, €1 children) which affords the best views of Verona. It was built in the 12th century, although the belfry wasn't added until 1464. Further on and into piazza dei Signori there are three arches to your right. The first small arch leads to cortile Mercato Vecchio, a pink and white brick courtyard where **Palazzo del Comune** (also called Palazzo della Ragione, the Palace of Reason, built in 1193) sits at the top of a magnificent Renaissance staircase, the **Scala della Ragione**.

The second larger arch leads to via Dante where there are some exposed Roman excavations. The third and final arch leads to cortile del Tribune and the **Scavi Scaligeri** (the Roman excavations which you can see in the cortile under glass) and the **Centro Internazionale di Fotografia** in Palazzo Viviani (see page 244).

Looking across the piazza and straight at the statue of Dante, the building to your left (near the entrance to Piazza Erbe) is the 17th-century Venetian-style **Domus Nova** and the Renaissance **Loggia del Consiglio** (1492), the meeting room for government. The building is crowned with five statues: Vitruvius, local Roman poet Catallus, Pliny the Elder, Emilio Marco and Cornelius Nepos. Straight ahead is the Renaissance loggia by Fra' Giocondo (1493) which was home to the Council during Venetian rule.

The statue of Dante recognizes Verona's love of the great medieval humanist who visited his chums, the Scaligeris, in 1306, and then again in 1314. He may have loved Verona enough to have returned but the city's beauty did not still his raging heart. The poet, having fallen foul of the Florentine ruling elite, had been exiled from his beloved Florence, stripped of his property and left impoverished and destitute. Sorely aggrieved at the time, he developed deep grudges against those who crossed him and took his revenge by trapping them for eternity (at least literary eternity) in the rings of hell in his *Inferno*. Pause for a coffee or a Spritz close to his statue by Ugo Zannoni (1865) and be grateful you never fell foul of the man.

Above: Piazza dei Signori, as seen from the Torre dei Lamberti.
Opposite page: Piazza Erbe.

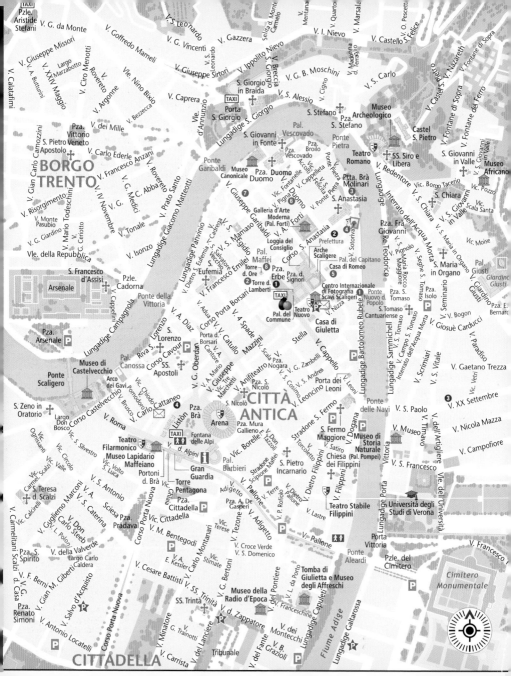

# Listings

## Arche Scaligeri

*Via Arche Scaligeri, T045-803 2726.*

The 14th-century Gothic iron fence and the raised temples covered with overbearing *baldachini* (canopies) do not provide the most soothing setting for the tombs of Verona's infamous ruling family. But, then again, the Scaligeris were soldiers, murderers and tyrants, so, perhaps, there really is no rest for the wicked. The biggest tomb, a pyramidal affair with a convoluted Gothic pinnacle topped by a horse and rider, is that of Cangrande II. The *baldachino* for Mastino II competes with an even more over-the-top one for Cansignorio, while Mastino I's more humble tomb sits against the wall of the church of **Santa Maria Antica**. Rather overshadowed by its surroundings, this modest Romanesque church dates back to the seventh century and was the favoured place of worship for the Scaligeri family. The copy of Cangrande I's equestrian statue (the original is in Castelvecchio) surmounting the doorway suggests it became as much a monument to Scaligeri power as a house of God.

## The Scaligeri

The Scaligeri (or the della Scala family) are the most famous in Veronese history and held the office of *podestà* (mayor) for many generations. Mastino I (the 'mastiff') was the first Scaligeri elected to the position in 1259 and, liking it so much, he passed a law making him *podestà* until his death. He was assassinated by aggrieved *signori* in 1277 and the election of his son, Alberto, to the role instigated 30 years of fighting with the rival San Bonifacio and Este families. Alberto's son, Cangrande I ('big dog' – real name Bartolemeo), inherited the title in 1311 and despite his brutality, left a legacy of grand buildings and artistic treasures. A fierce soldier, autocrat and patron of the arts, he bankrolled Giotto, Dante and Petrarca, as well as significantly expanding Veronese territory. His nephew, Mastino II, took over when he died in 1351 and gained more territory for Verona, before losing much of it to a consortium of families opposed to Scaligeri rule. His son, Cangrande II, took the reins but was deeply disliked – even by his own family – and was eventually murdered by his brother, Cansignorio ('noble dog'), who also dispatched his other brother, Paolo Alboino. Cansignorio left a beautiful legacy of public buildings and statues but his murderous ways turned the Veronese against him and he was forced to flee Verona in 1387. His nephew, Guglielmo, Cangrande II's son, sought to regain the family's reputation but died following a bloody battle to rout the Milanese in 1404, thus ending 145 years of Scaligeri dominance in the city.

The Scaligeri's fondness for canine-related names is unexplained.

## Galleria d'Arte Moderna

*Vicolo Volto Due Mori 4, corso Sant'Anastasia,
T045-800 1902, palazzoforti.it.*
Tue-Fri 0900-1900, Sat-Sun 0900-2000,
€6, €5 under 14s and students.
Temporary exhibitions upstairs.

The 13th-century Palazzo Forti is situated on a former Roman site and has undergone various transformations over the years. Napoleon famously stayed here as a guest of Francesco Emilei, whom he swiftly condemned to death for insurrection. The gallery eschews the 'white cube' aesthetic and instead makes the most of its historic surroundings. As you enter through a beautiful courtyard, you'll notice some nicely lit glass-covered Roman excavations underfoot. The gallery has made some impressive acquisitions over the last few years, including photography by Cindy Sherman, video installations by Bill Viola and sculpture by Louise Bourgeois.

Via Arche Scaligeri.

### Tip...

What about Romeo? No. 4 via Arche Scaligeri is the house of the Montecchi (or Montague) family. Casa di Romeo is a private residence but you can eat in the Osteria al Duca below (see page 253).

## Centro Internazionale di Fotografia

*Cortile del Tribunale, piazza Viviani 5,
T045-800 7490.*
Tue-Sun 1000-1900.

Located amongst the excavated ruins of long-abandoned Roman sewers, this gallery provides a great setting for some prestigious exhibitions by mainly Italian photographers.

## Casa di Giulietta

*Via Cappello 23, T045-803 4303.*
Mon 1330-1930, Tue-Sun 0830-1930,
courtyard free, house €4.

Originally built in the 13th century for the Cappello family, this courtyard palazzo was converted into a museum to Shakespeare's tragic heroine in the mid 1990s, although there is nothing to connect the Cappellos with the fictional Capulets. As you walk along via Cappello you will become aware that there is a bit of a bottleneck ahead: young Veronese hang around smoking, shouting and flirting while groups of elderly tourists stand with puzzled, scrunched-up faces that say, "Is this it?". Well as far as a fictional setting for a fictional character goes, it is. The passageway is covered with graffiti: declarations of love in marker pen and Tippex, layered on so thick that the names and sentiments are barely legible and become one multi-coloured blur. There are clusters of colourful padlocks bearing the names of besotted lovers and, at the other side of the dark alley, the scrawls continue despite dramatic threats of hefty fines by the authorities. For those too scared to face a fine, Post-it notes have been employed and create a fluttering relief.

Visitors expecting a pristine dream scene can barely hide their disappointment at the untidy graphic displays of love and the gangs of raucous young people but there is something truly magical about Juliet's house and balcony. After all, *Romeo and Juliet* is a story of young, all-consuming, destructive love that didn't care about the old folks and their expectations. So, while the tourist attraction itself is a manufactured stage set, the youth of Verona have stuck two fingers up to the authorities and claimed Juliet and her balcony as their own.

Inside the courtyard, all eyes focus on the balcony, although hands veer towards the statue of Juliet cast in bronze at the back wall: rubbing her

Below: Casa di Giulietta.
Right: Tokens and scrawls of affection, outside Casa di Giulietta.

"There is no world without Verona walles
But purgatorie, Torture, hell itself:
Hence banished, is banisht from the world,
And world's exile is death." (Romeo)

*William Shakespeare, 'Romeo and Juliet', 1597*

## Romeo & Juliet, fact & fiction

A love-struck heroine who fakes her own death in order to escape her circumstances and be with her true love is a theme that appears in several classical and Renaissance texts: Ovid's *Metamorphosis*, Masuccio Salernitano's *Il Novelino* (1476) and Luigi da Porto's *Historia novellamente ritrovata di due Nobili Amanti* (1530). Shakespeare was undoubtedly aware of previous treatments of the story before he put quill to paper. However, it was the Bard who popularized it, developed the theme of love within conflict and gave the relationship between the young, infatuated lovers its emotional intensity. What's more, there are a few grains of truth in the tale. There was certainly a deep-seated conflict between the Guelphs (represented by the Montagues or Montecchi, who did exist) and the Ghibellines (represented by the Capulets or Capuletti, who maybe didn't) from the 12th to the 14th centuries. It is also true that young men seeking to prove themselves can sometimes turn to brutality – recent proof of this is the garlanded shrine on via Cappello to Nicolà Tommasoli (29), murdered by a gang of men in their 20s who were celebrating Berlusconi's re-election in May 2008. As for the poison you can drink that renders you dead for a few hours; in the Middle Ages, *morion* or death wine made from the mandragora root was secretly administered to those who were to be tortured so that they could appear dead.

breast apparently brings luck in love. You can enter the Renaissance-style palazzo to see the bed and some costumes from the 1968 Franco Zefferelli film and an original fresco by Veronese.

## Tomba di Giulietta & the Musei degli Affreschi

*Via del Pontiere 35, T045-800 0361.*
Mon 1345-1930, Tue-Sun 0830-1930, €3.

It's not just the tourist industry that milks Juliet for all she is worth. The Capuchin monastery of San Francesco al Corso is in on the act too, claiming to house Juliet's final resting place. This could so easily have been a cheesy pastiche but in this vaulted room deep in the crypt, with a Gothic window imbuing a golden hue to the crumbling bricks, there is an atmosphere that is quite moving. And, when you realize the sarcophagus is empty, it makes your hair stand on end. If you are too embarrassed to admit to visiting the tomb of a non-existent woman, there is the thin excuse of the fresco museum upstairs.

## Castelvecchio & Museo Civico d'Arte

*Corso Castelvecchio 2, T045-806 2611.*
Mon 1330-1930, Tue-Sun 0830-1930,
€8, €3 under 14s.

Built by Cangrande II in 1357 as a discreet little pied-à-terre, the castle consists of two huge blocks that sit on either side of the ponte Scaligero: one served as a military base and stores; the other as the ruler's residence. Following the fall of the Scaligeri, the castle was occupied in turn by the ruling Visconti family, officials from the Venetian Republic and then Napoleon's men.

The castle now holds the civic art museum. Downstairs a collection of carvings and statues from the Middle Ages is displayed in a serene exhibition space by Carlo Scarpa (1906-1978), the Venetian architect whose modernist vision was informed

Below: Castelvecchio at night. Opposite page: The crenellated Ponte Scaligero at Castelvecchio .

and resourced by materials popular in the past. Light flows in through the windows caressing the somewhat clumsy sculptures of Jesus and the Saints and casting a hazy light that assists the spiritual context. Upstairs there are paintings and decorative arts by Tintoretto, Tiepolo, Veronese, Bellini and Pisanello. It is also worth strolling around Scarpa's gardens in the courtyard, which mix greenery with old (the statue of Cangrande) and new (a tufa waterpool) features. It has a few welcome places to sit down for some sensory respite.

The red-brick crenellated **ponte Scaligero** links the castle with the Arsenale across the Adige. It was bombed by the Americans during World War II but rebuilt soon after using the remains that they dug out of the river. There are walkways along the battlements and a number of observation points which provide great photo opportunities.

### Basilica San Zeno Maggiore

*Piazza San Zeno, T045-592813.*
Mar-Oct daily 0830-1800, Nov-Feb Tue-Sat 1000-1600, Sun 1300-1700, €2.50. Visitors discouraged during Mass.

This 12th-century basilica is dedicated to Verona's patron saint, San Zeno (died AD 380), who was the city's eighth bishop and also the patron saint of fishermen. Made of local rose brick and creamy toned tufa, it glows in the late afternoon sun. The 62-m campanile and the nave with its ship's keel ceiling and Gothic adornment were added in the late 1300s. Two marble lions support the columns of the porch which is intricately carved with scenes from Genesis by Nicolò, dating from 1135. Within the bronze panels of the wooden doors and the bas relief above there are simple, almost comic, images from the life of San Zeno. Inside, Lorenzo Veneziano's *Crucifixion* (1360) hangs on the west wall. You won't be the only one to admire Andrea Mantegna's altarpiece *Madonna and Child Enthroned with Saints* (1457-59): Napoleon pilfered it for his collection in Paris. The Romanesque cloister with Gothic arches may be a mish-mash of styles but it is undoubtedly tranquil.

### Museo della Radio Epoca

*ITIS Galileo Ferraris, via del Pontiere 40, T045-505855, museodellaradio.com.*
Mon-Fri 0900-1800, €4.

Not far from the Tomba di Giulietta is this wonderful collection of radios, from art deco to swingable handheld sets. This museum documents their development with nerdy but sincere enthusiasm. (For those who are wondering, Galileo Ferraris was the physicist who discovered alternating currents.)

## Around the region

### Duomo

*Piazza Duomo, T045-592 813.*
Mon-Sat 0930-1800, Sun 1300-1800, €2.50.
Strictly no bare legs or shoulders.

As grand as some of the Venetian churches, Verona's cathedral took 500 years to complete and is full of splendid craftsmanship. The architect Sansovino designed the choir and the Cappella Nichesola, which houses Titian's vibrant *Assumption* (1540). Through an old door in the far wall you can access **San Giovanni in Fonte**.

> ## Tip...
>
> The Chiese Verona card (chieseverona.it) admits you to Verona's five main churches for €5.

**View towards the Duomo.**

This carefully renovated Romanesque church would seem austere were it not for the rich tones of its marble. Its huge baptismal font (1200) is made from a single block, carved with scenes from the Gospel (some of them gruesome). Next to it is the church of **Sant'Elena**, built in the ninth century. Excavations under glass show the mosaics and stones of an even earlier Christian church, dating from AD 362.

From the piazza in front of the Duomo you can visit the cloisters, a beautiful arched courtyard now home to private residents. Also on piazza Duomo is the **Biblioteca Capitulare**, which houses artworks and hundreds of rare liturgical and jurisprudential texts, and the **Museo Canonicale** (Fri 1000-1230, Sat 1000-1300 and 1430-1800, Sun 1430-1800, €2.50), a much celebrated collection of paintings and statues of the saints and the Madonna dating from the 12th to the 18th centuries.

### Sant'Anastasia

*Piazza Sant'Anastasia, T045-592813.*
Mon-Sat 0930-1800, Sun 1300-1800, €2.50.

This big Gothic bruiser of a church is softened by an enchanting fresco by Antonio di Pisanello and by the two marble hunchbacks – one stooped, one sitting – that support the water fonts. These were carved by Paolo Veronese's father in 1495.

### San Fermo Maggiore

*Stradone San Fermo, T045-800 7287.*
Mon-Sat 0930-1800, Sun 1300-1800, €2.50.

The layers of Verona's history are laid bare in the structure of this fascinating church. The original fifth-century church housed the relics of the saints Fermo and Rustico. A few walls remain but it was largely replaced in the 11th century by a Romanesque church (now accessed from the cloisters). In the 13th century, a Gothic church was built on top; this is the big gingerbread edifice you see today.

## Santa Maria in Organo

*Via Santa Maria in Organo.*
Mon-Sat 0930-1800, Sun 1300-1800, €2.50.

You'll find this little church next to the Giardino Giusti. It has a wooden choir lovingly carved by Giovanni da Verona (1457-1525), a monk whose talent for intarsia and marquetry is without parallel.

## Teatro Romano & Museo Archeologico

*Rigaste Redentore 2, T045-800 0360.*
Mon 1330-1930, Tue-Sun 0830-1930 (ticket office closes at 1845), €3. For information about performances and the Shakespeare festival in July: T045-807 7201, estateteatraleveronese.it.

Climb all the steps to the top of the hill and you'll realise how perfectly located this Roman theatre is. But it's not until you see Palladio's model of it in the archaeological museum that you can appreciate just how breathtakingly beautiful it must have been.

Like the Arena, the Teatro Romano suffered the effects of an earthquake and has lost some of its stones to other buildings in the city but there is still enough here to stage an awesome performance. What remains are the *scena* (stage) and the semicircular *cavea* (auditorium) as well as some deep steps which still serve as seating. The back wall of the stage (*scaenae frons*) has been rebuilt. Roman plays tended to copy the Greek style but were certainly bawdier with more rough and tumble.

Head up the steps to the archaeological museum, housed in the former convent of San Girolamo. There are some small rooms showing Estruscan and Roman figurines, ceramics and tools from digs around the city. However, it is the views out of the tiny windows that will catch your eye. The larger rooms have Roman busts without noses, headless sculptures, some interesting mosaics as well as Palladio's model of the theatre. The high point is the walk through the former residential wing into the gardens, where tombstones, capitals, columns and even an old chariot are displayed. Sitting amongst these ruins, looking out over the remarkable panorama is a generous reward for the toil up the hill.

View across the Adige from the Museo Archeologico.

## Giardino Giusti

*Via Giardino Giusti 2, T045-803 4029.*
Apr-Sep 0900-2000, Oct-Mar 0900-1900, €4.50.

The Palazzo Giusti is located in a residential area, just along from the Teatro Romano, and gives no hint of the treat that lies behind its walls. Beyond the courtyard is a Renaissance garden whose timeless beauty has inspired poets, including Goethe on a visit in 1786. You can read his musings on one of the first trees you see as you enter. Laid out in 1580 by Agostino Giusti, the gardens follow a simple symmetry, structured by cypresses, box hedges and gravel paths that lead up to a stone-terraced wood. The palazzo blocks any views of the city but the sense of enclosure is welcome in such a dreamy setting.

## Museo Civico di Storia Naturale

*Lungadige Porta Vittoria 9, T045-807 9400, museostorianaturaleverona.it.*
Mon-Thu and Sat 0900-1900, Sun 1400-1900, €3.

If it's raining, this museum of botanic, zoological and geological objects will help while away a couple of hours. It is an archetypal civic museum and has a dusty, dated feel but don't let first impressions put you off. There are some huge fossils of weird prehistoric fish, the bones of a species of brown bear that once roamed the wilds of the northern Veneto, an abundance of taxidermy and a display of limestone and marble which may inspire you to do up the bathroom when you get home.

# Escape to the lake

**W**ide and surrounded by plains at its southern end, progressively narrower and enclosed by mountains to the north, Lake Garda is an exceptionally beautiful place that is just about big enough to be able to cope with the hordes of package holidaymakers that descend on it each summer. The beaches and lakeside towns have plenty of facilities for watersports and boat trips and there's solitude to be found if you head away from the coastline and up into the hills. Veneto borders the eastern shores and on summer weekends, the exodus towards the lake is something to behold – although, traffic-wise, not something you want to get stuck in.

At the southern end of the lake, **Peschiera** is served by the main Verona–Milan train line as well as by frequent buses from Verona. It has little to warrant a visit in itself but offers the best onward travel options to the eastern shore of the lake. Nearby, on a narrow peninsula jutting out in the southern part of the lake, is **Sirmione**. It's over-touristed but does boast sulphurous springs, a Scaligieri castle and remains which may once have been a Roman spa or, alternatively, Catullus's villa. Heading up the eastern side of the lake, **Garda**, **Torri del Benaco** (see below) and **Malcesine** are more traditional towns in attractive settings. Malcesine has a cable car that takes passengers up to the high slopes of **Monte Baldo**, while, at the northern end of the lake, **Torbole** has a thriving windsurfing industry and some surf culture to go with it.

Just one hour from Verona is the pretty, cobbled and laid-back harbour town of Torri del Benaco. It might not have much in the way of culture but it is less overrun with tourists than some of its

Torri del Benaco.

neighbours and has bucketloads of charm. Behind Hotel Gardesena, corso d'Alighieri is a shop-lined street with some good cafés and pizzerias. The small, pretty harbour is filled with colourful boats and there's a narrow, shingly beach towards the northern end of town, although this can be busy in the height of summer. The **Lido** (viale Marconi 4, T045-629 0405) to the south charges sunbathers for the use of umbrellas and loungers and, in the evening, becomes a cool place to hang out, with drum-and-bass and hip-hop DJs eyeballing the ladies. Otherwise, one of the lake's best swimming spots, **Baia delle Sirene** on the Punta San Vigilio, is only a five-minute bus journey south of Torri (€1.60 single). There's a pay beach here (€9 a day), with shingle and grassy terraces, and a rockier free beach a short (250 m) walk along the coast road and then through a steep olive grove (handy for changing). A boat sells ice-creams, drinks and sandwiches to both beaches. Those who fancy a bit more activity on the lake could arrange a windsurf or sailing course with **Fraglia Vela** (via Gardesana 205, Frazione Navene, T045-657 0439, fragliavela.org) a well-run sailing centre, located north of Torri del Benaco near Malcesine.

If a day trip is not enough, stay at the **Hotel Gardesana** (€€, piazza Calderini 20, Torri del Benaco, T045-722 5411, hotel-gardesana.com). This 15th-century former harbourmaster's house is located right on the harbour looking out over the lake. Its 34 rooms are nice enough but it's the terrace that is a winner: you'll want to sit there all day long. It also has a decent restaurant.

**How to get to Torri**: Leave Verona from the west and head for the northbound A22 motorway (for Brennaro). Turn off at Affi and head to Garda. Continue on the SS249 north to Torri del Benaco.

# Sleeping

### Due Torri Hotel Baglioni €€€
*Piazza Sant'Anastasia 4,*
*T045-595044, baglionihotels.com.*
If you want to luxe it up in
Verona, this is where to do it.
It's just around the corner from
some of the best bars in the city
and right next to the church, so
both sins and redemption are
well catered for. The bedrooms
are plush and the sparkling
marble bathrooms are perfect
places to pamper yourself.
Lounge around in the lavish
public rooms, if you're not put off
by the staff's air of cool hauteur.

### Albergo Aurora €€
*Piazza Erbe, T045-594717,*
*hotelaurora.biz.*
In a great location right on piazza
Erbe, this hotel has a typical
Italian reception area, with
efficient female staff doing all
the work while the men seem
to just sit around reading
newspapers. Its 19 rooms are
plain but have everything you
need (including air-conditioning
units). However it's the fabulous
roof terrace overlooking the
piazza that is the selling point.
This is where breakfast is served.

### Ca' dell'Orto €€
*Via Francesco da Levanto,*
*T045- 830 3554, cadellorto.it.*
Bus 61/62.
Only 2 km (a 25-min walk or a €15
taxi ride) from the city centre,
following the bend of the river
Adige, this 'aparthotel' has nicely
furnished and fully equipped

Piazza Erbe.

rooms (those on the top floor
have huge skylights) and
well-kept grounds with a pool.
Breakfasts are bountiful.

### Hotel Torcolo €€
*Vicolo Listone 3, T045-800 7512,*
*hoteltorcolo.it.*
Closed Feb.
Just off piazza Bra, this hotel
is run with old-fashioned
hospitality by two thoroughly
modern ladies. Popular with
opera goers, it appeals to those
who appreciate a bit of care and
attention. The rooms are nothing
fancy but still good quality and
the bathrooms are spick and
span. Breakfasts are extra (€8-13)
and are served in the courtyard
but, if you're ravenous, you will
get more for €13 from one of the
cafés nearby.

### B&B In The Sun €
*Via San Vincenzo 3A,*
*T045-551786, bbinthesun.com.*
Bus 51.
Located 6 km north of the city
centre on the vineyard-swathed
Torricelle hills, this large
farmhouse has been converted
with style and enthusiasm.
The rooms are simple and
contemporary with firm beds
and down-filled pillows, and the
rural location ensures a good
night's rest, uninterrupted by the
Vespas that punctuate sleep in
the city. Breakfast is all organic
and if you want to cook your
own dinner you can use the
kitchen. There are even laundry
facilities. A taxi to here costs
€15-20.

*Self-catering*
### L'ospite di Federica de Rossi
*Via XX Settembre 3,*
*T045-803 6994, lospite.com.*
€70-130 for two per night.
We're not surprised that Ms de
Rossi is proud to put her name
to this establishment. Its six
simply furnished apartments
are of varying sizes so can
accommodate singles, couples
and even small families. All are
spotless and kitted out with
everything you need. This is an
excellent base for a holiday in the
Veneto. Federica or Flavio are
always on hand to offer advice
and will go the extra mile to
make sure you have everything
you might need.

# Eating & drinking

### Ristorante Maffei €€€
*Piazza Erbe 38, T045-801 0015, ristorantemaffei.it.*
Daily 1200-1400 and 1900-2200.
This is where the locals go for a special night out. The Maffei kitchen experiments with new colours and textures to add something extra to classic dishes. Their risotto with melon puree or bigoli cooked in Amarone are so good, you'll find yourself writing about them on postcards home. There's seating both inside and in the courtyard recessed from the piazza and some beautifully lit Roman ruins downstairs.

### Carro Armato €€
*Vicolo Gatto 2a, T045-803 0175.*
Mon, Tue amd Thu-Sat 1000-0200, Sun 1000-2400.
This is an excellent spot for some informal dining with, perhaps, a greater emphasis on drinking. The heavy wooden benches and sturdy tables make you feel as though you could easily take on

Above: Osteria Sottoriva.
Below: Osteria al Duca.

the wine list and menu but beware: portions are generous. Everything has a made-by-mamma feel about it. Simple dishes, such as *gnocchi di patate* served with a sweet tomato sauce and a dollop of ricotta, earn cries of *'buonissimi!'*

### Enoteca Segreta €€€
*Vicolo Samaritana 10, T045-801 5824, enotecasegreta.com.*
Mon-Sat 1900-0200.
As well as being an excellent restaurant, this enoteca is a great place for wine tasting and aperitivi. The owner is a sommelier and for the tasting he serves wines combined with a different cheese or salume from Verona. He tells you the history of the wine and the vineyard it comes from.

### Osteria al Duca €€
*Via Arche Scaligeri 2, T045-594474.*
May-Oct Mon-Fri 1200-1430 and 1800-2230, Nov-Apr Mon and Wed-Sat 1200-1430 and 1830-2230.
Book in advance as this place is popular with returning American tourists who are chummy with the

owners, the Montecchi family. You will eat a fine meal here from the meat- and fish-orientated menu: *bigoli con le sarde* (bigoli pasta with sardines) or *agnello arrosto* (roast lamb) with fragrant fried potatoes are typical. An ample two-course lunch costs just €13: a bargain considering the quality. Puddings are also good, especially the *biscotti* dipped in *vin santo*.

### Osteria Trattoria al Duomo €€
*Via Duomo 7a, T045-800 4505.*
Mon-Sat 1100-1430 and 1800-2230.
This wonderful tavern feels and sounds like it's the spiritual home for rock children of the 1960s and '70s. The wine list is long (and cheap) and the food is splendid: nothing particularly fancy, just substantial, wholesome dishes like *bigoli con ragu d'asino* (bigoli pasta with donkey sauce) and cherry tomato-tossed spaghetti with the perkiest rocket. The tiramisu is great, but copious use of confectioner's squirty cream renders many puddings a let-down.

### Pane e Vino €
*Via Garibaldi 16a, T045-800 8261.*
Wed-Mon 1100-1500 and 1800-2300.
Just down the road from the Scaligeri tombs, this popular trattoria offers a €10 lunch that includes starter, main course and half a carafe of wine and water. The food is so good and the

service is so forthcoming that you keep thinking, "what's the catch?" There isn't one. It's all hearty stuff: risotto, beef cooked in Amarone and *bollito con la peará* (boiled meat served with bread sauce). Doesn't sound much, but it's delicious.

### Cafés & bars

**Bar al Ponte**
*Via Ponte Pietra 26, T045-56 9608.*
Tue-Sun 1200-2400.
Walking down from ponte Pietra, if you blink you might miss this bar because it is below street level. It has a little terrace on the river offering a breathtaking view and a gentle breeze. It's particularly lovely by candlelight.

**Caffè Coloniale**
*Piazzetta Viviani 14c, T045-801 2647.*
Tue-Sat 0745-2400,
Sun 0945-2400.
Located between piazza Erbe and Casa di Giulietta, this is run by real coffee enthusiasts. You can opt for a fancy, cream-laden Viennese version or a heady Moroccan blend. There are seats inside and out.

**Caffè Monte Baldo**
*Via Rosa 12, T045-803 0579.*
Mon-Sat 1000-1500 and 1700-2100.
This is one of the oldest osterie in Verona. It offers *tartine* (canapés) and wine, oysters on Friday and Saturday, and it's open for lunch during the week.

Piazza Erbe.

# What the locals say

Verona is famous for its excellent cuisine and wines. It's traditional for us Veronesi to meet friends and to go out for an aperitivo before dinner. So, you can choose among *osterie*, *cantine* and bars where you can have a simple Spritz (aperol, white wine and soda) or a glass of good wine. Piazza Erbe is packed with bars where you can sit outside, but if you want to try something different, I recommend **Bar al Ponte**, **Caffè Monte Baldo**, **Cantina Il Bugiardo**, **Enoteca Segreta**, **L'Aquila Nera Caffè** and **M27**.

*Federica de Rossi*

**Caffè Turbino**
*Corso di Porta Borsari 15d, T045-803 1313.*
Mon-Sat 0715-2100.
A very small café with a very large chandelier and an even larger reputation. It's been packing them in for years. If you like the coffee, you can buy some to take home.

**Cantina Il Bugiardo**
*Corso Portoni Borsari 17, T045-591869.*
Tue-Sun 1100-2200.
This cantina is very popular for its *bocconcini* (bread topped with all

kind of delicacies) and other snacks to eat with a good glass of wine.

**Cappa Café**
*Piazzetta Bra Molinari 1, T045-800 4549.*
Daily 0730-0200.
This rather boho spot does a lovely cappuccino and has a terrace round the back that looks out over the Adige towards San Pietro.

# Entertainment

## L'Aquila Nera Caffè
*Via Pelicciai 2, T045-801 0172, aquilaneraverona.com.*
Daily 1700-2300.
A very elegant café where you can sit down in a comfortable armchair and relax. Great choice of wine, champagne, plus a rich buffet.

## M27
*Via G Mazzini 27/a, T045-803 4242.*
Tue-Sun 0800-0200.
A place to discover. Great list of snacks, aperitivi and drinks, plus the best freshly prepared sandwiches in town. Open late.

## Osteria Sottoriva
*Via Sottoriva 9a, T045-801 4323.*
Thu-Tue 1100-2230.
Want to know what the best wines of the Veneto are? Try them here, in this convivial bar.

## Ponte Pietra
*Via Ponte Pietra 23.*
Mon 1530-2000, Tue-Sun 1100-2200.
The local's favourite gelateria: home-made flavours sold on a little street behind the Duomo.

## Savoia
*Via Roma 1b, piazza Bra, T045-800 2211.*
Tue-Sun 1100-2200.
A top-quality range of artisan ice creams are on offer here. Try a slider (ice cream sandwiched between wafers) or the Gianduiotto, served in a cup: it's a chocolate-lover's dream.

Cinema
## Teatro Stimate
*Piazza Cittadella, via Montarino 1, T045-800 0878.*
Shows art house and independent films with, joy of joys, subtitles rather than dodgy dubbing. English-language films on Tuesdays.

Clubs
## Alter Ego Club
*Via Torricelle 9, T045-915130, alteregoclub.it.*
Jun-Sep Fri-Sat 2230-0300 (sometimes 0600).
House, prog and euro pop are served up to a molto-trendy crowd at this bizarre club in the hills. A taxi will cost around €18 from the centre of Verona. Check the website for details.

Gay & lesbian
## Caffè Bukowski
*Via Amanti 6.*
Wed-Mon 1900-0200.
This rather avant-garde disco has happy hours in the early evening but doesn't really get going until 2200. The music is a mix of everything from Hi-NRG to Elvis to, er, Dido.

## Romeos Club
*Via Giolfino 12, Zona Porta Vescovo, T045-840 3215, romeosclubverona.blogspot.com.*
Tue-Sat 2300-0530.
There are thumping euro beats at this shirts-off gay club. It also hosts occasional film nights.

Music & theatre
Tickets for the Verona Jazz Festival (June), the Shakespeare Festival (June to August) and the Dance Festival (August), as well as tickets for visiting artists and shows, are available from **Assessorato alla Cultura di Verona** (Palazzo Barbieri, angolo Via Leoncino 61, T045-806 6485, estateteatrale veronese.it, box office Mon-Sat 1030-1300 and 1600-1900 and on day of performance). As well as the venues listed here, festival events are held in the Teatro Romano, Corte Mercato Vecchio and Giardino Giusti.

## Arena
*Piazza Bra, T045-800 3204, arena.it.*
This is the ultimate venue for opera in the summer, plus

# Tip...
The most fitting way to enjoy the Shakespeare Festival is to track down the **Sognando Shakespeare Company** who perform on the streets of Verona. The tourist information office can give you the programme of where to find them.

# Shopping

occasional gigs by big international rock and pop acts visiting Verona. The opera season starts in June and runs until August with four or five different operas on different nights. Tickets start at €25 for the marble stairs at the back and go up to €160 for the plush red seats at the front. Performances start at 2100 and can last until midnight.

### Interzona
*Via Scuderlando 4, T045-505 0054, izona.it.*
This edgy venue hosts a diverse programme of rock, punk, folk, jazz and video art performances in a disused industrial unit in the south of the city. Check the website for details. You'll need a taxi to get there and back.

### Teatro Filarmonico
*Via dei Mutilati 4, T045-805 1891, arena.it. Box office: Via Roma 3, T045-800 5151.*
Daily 1000-1200 and 1630-1930 or until 2100 on the day of performance.
Bombed by the Americans during the war, this grand venue has finally been restored to its former glory and hosts classical concerts, ballets and opera during the winter season.

Most shops are open from 0930 to 1300, when they close for a long lunch and siesta, before opening again from 1600 to 1900. Most are closed on a Sunday and some are also closed on a Monday morning. There are sales in Verona in January and February and from late July to early August.

## Art & antiques
There is an outdoor antiques market along via Sottoriva on the second Sunday of every month. In addition to the ones listed here, you'll find a number of antique shops on and around corso Sant' Anastasia.

### Antichità Smeraldo
*Vicolo Due Stelle 5. T045-800 7055.*
Antique demi-johns, chandeliers and porcelain are just some of the things you'll find in this cornucopia.

### Cavaliere
*Stradone Port Palio 41, T329-897 7848.*
You can find some timeless old luggage here that wouldn't have looked out of place on the Orient Express in the 1920s.

## Books
### Bazzani Stampe Antiche – Libreria Antiquaria
*Via Stella 20, T045-597621, libreriabazzani stampeantiche.com.*
Behind a 16th-century arch,

this roomy shop sells beautiful old books and maps.

### FNAC
*Via Cappello 34, T045-806 3811.*
This French-owned megastore sells music and electronics, as well as books, and has a café with internet access.

### Ghelfi & Barbato
*Via Mazzini 21, T045-597732.*
On the main drag, this is the place to find a large selection of maps and travel guides in English, as well as cookbooks.

### Liberia Novecento
*Via Santa Maria in Chiavica 3, T045-4231586.*
A mix of early 20th century English and Italian travel guides, art books, prints, political manifestos and some curious tomes that defy categorization.

## Clothing
There's some excellent clothes shopping to be done in Verona. The main streets to explore are via Mazzini (for Gucci, Diesel, Furla, Mandarina Duck, Armani), via Cappello (for more designer names) and corso Porta Borsari (for shoes) but the web of little streets that run off these thoroughfares have some great little independent boutiques too.

### Cecile
*Via Salvatore, corte Reggia 9.*
Vintage and second-hand shops are not exactly ten-a-penny in

Italy but this is a treasure trove with Prada and even some Pucci calling your name.

## Love Therapy
*Via Mazzini 4.*
Three floors of funky and fabulous fashions curated by Elio Fiorucci, as well as homewares, make-up, perfumes, sunglasses and bijou gifts.

## Mimma
*Corso porta Borsari 57a, T045-801 0380.*
Colourful clothing and shoes for kids that you'll not see anywhere else.

## Opticus
*Via Roma 5, T045-594804, opticusverona.it.*
Eccentric and customized spectacles and sunglasses in every colour.

Department stores
## Coin
*Via Cappello 30, T045-803 4321.*
Great underwear, homewares and accessories at reasonable prices.

## Upim
*Via Mazzini 6, T045-596701.*
Lots of run-of-the-mill items but the kitchen section is particularly good.

Food & drink
## Calimala Chocolat
*Vicolo Crocini 4a, T045-800 5478.*
Hand-made chocolates and sweet treats.

## L'Enoteca
*Via Sottoriva 7, T045-590366 enotecaverona.com.*
A monumental selection of wines housed in Roman cellars. Moreover, the jovial staff know their stuff. Check out the website for wine-tasting events.

## PAM
*Via dei Mulati 3, T045-803 2822.*
Great for picnics, this supermarket is full of fresh local produce and every basic ingredient, as well as coffee, pasta and alcohol at knock-down prices.

## Salumeria Albertini
*Corso Sant' Anastasia, T045-803 1074.*
Whether you are taking home a **panettone** or a piece of **baccalà** (dried cod) for gran or just fancy a few slices of **sopressa** (sausage) and some bread, Albertini's is pricey but good.

Souvenirs
The market in piazza Erbe (Mon-Sat 0800-1900) does a nice line in cheesy Romeo and Juliet snowstorms and Arena di Verona ashtrays.

Via Cappello.

# Activities & tours

### Cultural

If you want to learn the language, Verona is one of the best cities to take an Italian course.

### Lingua IT

*Via Francesco Emilei 24, T045-597975, linguait.it.*
€610 for a 4-week, 80-hour course and €390 for a 2-week, 40-hour course.

Just off Piazza Erbe, this young, on-the-ball language school delivers well-structured intensive courses that provide great value for money and a fighting chance of understanding and being understood in Italian.

### Football

Verona has two teams that share the **Stadio Marc'Antonio Bentegodi** at piazzale Olimpia. **AC Chievo Verona** (Via Galvani 3, T045-575779, chievoverona.it) are known as the '*mussi volanti*' or flying donkeys and are in Serie A. **Hellas Verona FC** (Verona Point, via Cristoforo 30, T045-575005, hellasverona.it), nicknamed the 'Mastiffs', have an old-school following that has stuck with them despite a fall in fortunes: they now play in the Lega Pro Prima Divisione, equivalent to the English First Division. Check out their websites for dates of home games or the daily *Corriere dello Sport* or L'Arena newspapers.

### Food & wine

The Provincia di Verona tourist information website (tourism. verona.it) has information about local *cantine* that welcome visitors and a route map in the 'Enjoying our Land' section. The Verona area is particularly famous for its Valpolicella and Soave. Italy's most important wine trade fair, **Vinitaly** (vinitaly.com) is held in Verona over five days in April. Although this is primarily for wine trade professionals, there are

Bottega del Vino restaurant and cellar.

events around town, such as 'Vinitaly for you' in Gran Guardia, that are aimed at those who simply enjoy wine.

### Creo Events

*Via delle Argonne 1,*
*T045-803 6485, creoevents.it.*
Creo's wine tastings are not only fun but hugely informative: you visit a wine cellar in a cantina and hear all about the soil, weather and wine-making methods while rolling an Amarone over your tongue (€50 per person). They also offer cookery courses with Gabriele Ferron, the 'Ambassador of Rice in the World', who will

show you how to make a perfect risotto (€50 per person).

### Wellbeing
### Villa dei Cedri

*Piazza di Sopra 4, Colà di Lazise,*
*T045-759 0988, villadeicedri.com.*
Mon-Thu 0900-2100, Fri-Sat 0900-0200, Sun and public hols 0900-2300, €16-21.
Just 25 km from Verona, this spa beside a lake with hot thermal waters is open all year round. It's lit up at night creating a magical, steaming environment for pure relaxation.

Hourly train services to Milan (2 hrs), Venice (1½ hrs), Vicenza (30 mins) and Padua (45 mins). Frequent buses to Venice (2 hrs), Vicenza (45 mins) and Padua (1 hr).

Sottoriva.

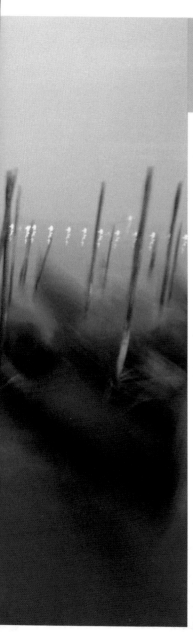

# Contents

**Practicalities**

Gondolas on the Bacino di San Marco.

# Getting there

 **Air**

## From UK and Ireland

Direct flights to Venice Marco Polo leave from London Heathrow (**bmi**, **British Airways**); Belfast, Bristol and East Midlands (**easyJet**) and London Gatwick (**easyJet**, **British Airways**). During the summer months there are also daily flights from Edinburgh and Leeds (**Jet2**). **Ryanair** have twice daily flights to Treviso from Dublin, Liverpool and London Stansted. **British Airways** have daily flights to Verona Valerio Catullo from Gatwick.

# Going green

Venice is much more convenient for rail travel from the UK than cities further down the Italian peninsula. It won't do for a weekend away but if you have the luxury of time, it's worth considering as a way to limit your carbon footprint, avoid the increasingly strict hand luggage rules and frequent delays at airports and for the chance of a short stay in Paris or Milan. If you start your journey by Eurostar, you have to get off at Paris Nord and traverse the city to board again at Paris Bercy. This can be bothersome if you hit the Paris rush hour and/or have a lot of luggage. If you travel by day, you'll also have to change trains at Milan but at least you'll be treated to some amazing scenery en route – French vineyards, Alpine villages and the Italian lakes – which you'll miss if you take the direct overnight sleeper.

## From North America

Alitalia, British Airways and **Iberia** are some of the airlines that fly directly from New York to Venice Marco Polo (transit time around 12 hours). **Air France**, **Air Canada**, **Alitalia**, **British Airways**, **Delta** and **KLM** fly direct from Canada to Venice Marco Polo.

## From rest of Europe

There are direct flights to Venice Marco Polo from many European cities including Berlin, Amsterdam, Paris and Stockholm. Carriers include **Air France**, **Alitalia**, **Austrian**, **easyJet**, **Lufthansa** and **Swiss**. **Ryanair** connect a number of European cities with Treviso and **Transavia** fly daily from Amsterdam to Treviso and Verona.

**Airport information**

Venice Marco Polo (T041-260 9260, www.veniceairport.it) lies on the mainland due north of Venice. The Arrivals hall has an **APT di Venezia** tourist office (T041-541 5887, daily 0900-1800) and a number of car hire companies, including **Avis** (T041-541 5030, avis.co.uk, **Europcar** (T041-541 5654, europcar.co.uk) and **Hertz** (T041-541 6075, hertz.com); all are open daily 0800-2400. The airport is 19 km by road and 8 km by sea from the city centre. A waterbus service runs roughly every half hour from the airport to destinations in the city (around €12 per person); buy tickets at the **Alilaguna** (alilaguna.it) stand in Arrivals. Water taxis are convenient but are much more expensive (up to €100). Bus services go to piazzale Roma every 30 minutes (€1.10).

Treviso (T042-231 5131, trevisoairport.it) is a **Ryanair** hub, located 6 km from Treviso city centre and 34 km from Venice. The Arrivals hall has a small **Treviso IAT** tourist office (T0422-263282, Mon and Fri 0830-1400 and 1630-1700, Tue and Thu 1430-1700, Wed 0800-1030 and 1330-1900, Sat 1430-1900 and 2000-2230) and a number of car hire companies, including **Avis** (T0422-433351, avis.co.

uk) and **Hertz** (T0422-297027, hertz.com). **ATVO** (atvo.it) runs a bus service from the airport to piazzale Roma in Venice (€6 single, €10 return with 7-day validity, 1 hr). Alternatively, take bus no.6 to Treviso Centrale train station (€1 at airport, €2 on board, 15-20 mins) from where there are frequent rail connections to Venice Santa Lucia FS.

**Verona Valerio Cattullo** (T045-809 5666, aeroportoverona.it) is 12 km south of Verona. The Arrivals hall has a **Verona APT** tourist office (T045-861 9163, Apr-Nov Mon-Sat 0900-1800, Sun 0900-1500, Dec-Mar Mon-Sat 0900-1600, Sun 0900-1500). Car hire is available from **Avis** (T045-987571, avis.co.uk) and **Hertz** (T045-861 9042, hertz.com). **APTV** (aptv.it) run the Aerobus service to and from the train and bus station at porta Nuova every 20 minutes (€4.50, 15 mins). Taxis are available just outside the Arrivals hall and cost around €13 into the *centro storico*.

## Rail

There are direct rail links to Venice, Padua, Vicenza and Verona from European cities, including Paris, Munich, Vienna and Geneva. It is also eminently possible to travel by rail from the UK by taking the **Eurostar** (eurostar.com) service from London St Pancras to Paris Gare du Nord (from £59 return, 2 hrs 25 mins) and then crossing Paris to the Gare de Bercy

to catch a direct overnight sleeper (from £60 return) to Venice Santa Lucia. The train stops at Brescia, Verona, Vicenza and Padua en route. Daytime travel is also possible but you'll have to spend a night in either Paris, Milan or Geneva. Buy tickets through **Rail Europe** (T0870-584 8848, raileurope.co.uk, raileurope.com) or **SNCF** (voyages-sncf.com).

For luxury, there's the **Venice Simplon-Orient Express** (orient-express.com), which runs from London Victoria to Venice Santa Lucia, via Paris, Innsbruck and Verona, between March and November, with departures on Thursday and Sunday mornings; it arrives in Venice the following evening. Prices start at £1550 for a one-way trip or £2325 for a return. The Hotel Cipriani is owned by the same company and offers special deals for Orient Express travellers.

For comprehensive information on rail travel throughout Europe, consult seat61.com.

## Road

### Car

If you're up for the 1500 km journey and can afford the petrol, you could drive from the UK to Venice. The journey will take a leisurely 24 hours (if you're lucky). The most popular route is down through France, entering Italy through the Mont Blanc tunnel just north of Turin, then on to Milan, where you join the A4 across northern Italy to Venice.

Having a car is a bonus if you want to explore rural Veneto but is utterly useless in Venice itself. Avoid paying €22-26 per day at Venice's Tronchetto car parks by parking your car at Mestre on the mainland (Parking Serenissima, viale Stazione 11, T041-938021) for €6 per day, before entering the city by train (€1, journey time 8 mins).

### Bus/coach

Eurolines (T041-538 2118, eurolines.com) run long-distance coaches from all over Europe to piazzale Roma in Venice and to the bus stations in Treviso, Padua, Vicenza and Verona. From London to Venice or Verona takes just over 30 hours and costs from £50 for a one-way ticket booked 30 days in advance.

## Sea

Ferries between Greece and Venice (hellasferries.gr) set sail four times per week, with prices starting at €54 (27-hour passage).

# Getting around

## Rail

Italy's hugely extensive, efficient and affordable rail network is the best way to get around the country on a city-based trip. It is served by air-conditioned and splendid Eurostar Italia trains (ES); direct and convenient InterCity trains (IC), and the slightly less regular and slower Regional trains (REG). All can be booked at trenitalia.com; booking is advised for Eurostar Italia and InterCity services.

Ticket prices are sure to be a pleasant surprise: a single from Venice to Verona, for example, costs €12; from Vicenza to Venice costs €7. As well as standard fares there are also cheaper Amica fares, available in advance, and first class tickets, which are not that much more expensive. Booking and buying tickets at the counter in a station usually involves a long wait so look for the ticket-dispensing machines. These take cash and/or credit or debit cards, have a number of language functions and offer all the options, prices and timings. Remember, you must validate train tickets at the yellow stamping machines before boarding, although on many Italian trains it is possible to travel 'ticketless' by quoting a booking reference to the conductor instead. In general, it's cheaper and more convenient to book individual journeys online or to buy the ticket at the station than it is to buy a pass for multiple journeys; Eurostar Italia and InterCity services often have a surcharge which makes rail passes less cost-effective.

Venice Santa Lucia is the city's central train station, supplemented by Venice Mestre on the mainland. The main rail route through Veneto runs from Venice Santa Lucia to Milan via Mestre, Padua Centrale (40 mins), Vicenza Centrale (1 hr) and Verona Porta Nuova (1½ hrs). This is well served by Eurostar and InterCity trains with one every hour or so. Slower, regional trains also operate on this route and are occasionally the most suitable option, especially on Sundays or at night. The route north from Venice to Treviso Centrale (30 mins) is a regional service that continues towards Belluno and Calalzo di Cadore for the Dolomites and Cortina

d'Ampezzo. (The infrequent direct train to Calalzo di Cadore takes 2 hrs 45 mins but you are more likely to have to change at Treviso or Ponte nelle Alpi.) Train travel around the interior is a bit trickier. There are regional lines linking Treviso with Cornuda via Montebelluna (for Asolo, 1 hr) and Padua with Bassano del Grappa (1 hr). Visitors to the Colli Euganei can use the route from Padua to Montegrotto Terme (15 mins) and Monselice (25 mins). **Trenitalia** (T89-20-21, trenitalia.it) has details of all routes.

## Road

### Car
Having your own vehicle is more of a burden than a bonus in Venice, requiring you to pay parking fees to keep your car at Tronchetto or Mestre for the duration of your stay in the car-free city. However, if you plan to tour the region, having your own transport will allow you to visit more rural destinations that are difficult to reach by bus or train.

## Tip...

Unleaded petrol is *benzina*; diesel is *gasolio*. Expect to pay €1.25 for a litre of petrol and €1.30 for a litre of diesel.

EU nationals taking their own car into Italy need to have an International Insurance Certificate (also known as a *Carta Verde*) and a valid national or EU licence. Those holding a non-EU licence need to take an International Driving Permit with them.

Speed limits are 130 km per hour on *autostrade* (motorways), 110 km per hour on dual carriageways and 50 km per hour in towns. (Limits are 20 km per hour lower on motorways and dual carriageways when the road is wet.) *Autostrade* are toll roads, so keep cash in the car as a back-up even though you can use credit cards on the blue 'viacard' gates. **Autostrade** (T055-420 3200, autostrade.it) provides information on motorways in Italy and **Automobile Club d'Italia** (T06-49981, aci.it) provides general driving information. It also offers roadside assistance with English-speaking operators on T116.

Key routes in the region include the **A4**, which runs across southern Veneto, linking Milan with Verona, Vicenza, Padua and Mestre (for Venice), before continuing east as the **A1** to Trieste, and the **A27**, which leads north from Mestre, becoming the **SS51** near Belluno and continuing to Cortina d'Ampezzo. If you intend to drive in the Dolomites, take extra care, certainly in winter due to the icy conditions but also in summer when there are a lot of cyclists on the road. If you're driving in winter, also watch out for frozen fog and treacherous conditions on the A4, especially around Padua, and be prepared to abandon your journey if necessary.

Be aware that there are restrictions on driving in historic city centres, indicated by signs with black letters ZTL (*zona a traffico limitato*) on a yellow background. If you ignore these signs, you are liable for a fine. Parking is usually available outside the *centro storico* for €2-5 an hour depending on the location. City hotels will either provide parking for guests or will be able to direct you to the nearest car park.

Since July 2007 on-the-spot fines for minor traffic offences have been in operation; typically they range from €150 to €250 (always get a receipt). Note the following legal requirements: the use of mobile telephones while driving is not permitted; front and rear seatbelts must be worn, if fitted; children under 1.5 m may only travel in the back of the car. Italy has very strict laws on drink driving: the legal limit is 0.5g per litre of blood compared to the UK's 0.8g. If your car breaks down on the carriageway, you must display an emergency triangle and wear a reflective jacket in poor visibility. Car hire companies should provide both of these, but check the boot when you pick up your car.

## Car hire

Car hire is available at all three international airports in the region. You are advised to book your hire car before you arrive in the country, especially at busy times of year. Car hire comparison websites and agents are a good place to start a search for the best deals: try avis.com, europcar.co.uk and hertz.co.uk. Check what each hire company requires from you: some companies will ask for an International Driving Licence alongside your normal driving licence; others are content with an EU licence. You will also need a credit card, so, if you book ahead, make sure that the named credit card holder is the same as the person renting and driving the car. Most companies have a lower age limit of 21 years, with a young driver surcharge for those under 25, and require that you've held your licence for at least a year. Confirm the company's insurance and damage waiver policies and keep all your documents with you when you drive.

Even if you are planning a driving tour around Veneto, it goes without saying that there is no point hiring a car at the airport just for it to sit at the Tronchetto car park while you enjoy the sights of Venice. Save money by catching the bus or vaporetto from the airport to the city and arranging to pick up your hire car from Tronchetto when you are ready to move on.

## Bicycle

If your thighs are up to it and you are confident on roads populated with fast and crazy drivers, cycling around the rural areas of Veneto can be

memorable. Arm yourself with a good map: the Edizioni Multigraphic's *Carta Turistica Stradale* (1:50,000) has enough detail for most cyclists, while the 1:25,000 version is useful for those who like to go off road. Bikes are allowed on many train services: check out trenitalia.it for more information. The **European Cycling Federation** (ecf.com) promotes cycling in Europe and has some good advice as well as links to companies that provide biking tours in the region.

## Bus/coach

With trains so fast, cheap and efficient, it is only in the more rural areas that buses provide a useful service. Check with the local tourist information office to confirm times and pick-up points, as well as to find out where to buy tickets (it's often a nearby newsagent or tobacconists). Padua, Treviso, Vicenza and Verona all have city bus services. Again, you can buy tickets from newsagents, tobacconists (look for a big T sign) and even some cafés: if you intend to make a number of journeys, buy a stash of tickets at once. Always remember to validate your ticket when you board by stamping it in the machine located at the front and sometimes also at the back of the bus.

# Directory

## Customs & immigration

UK and EU citizens do not need a visa but will need a valid passport to enter Italy. A standard tourist visa for those from outside the EU is valid for up to 90 days.

## Disabled travellers

Northern Italy is beginning to adapt to the needs of disabled travellers but access can still be very difficult due to the age of many historic buildings or the lack of careful planning. For more details and advice, contact a specialist agency before departure, such as **Accessible Italy** (accessibleitaly.com) or **Society for Accessible Travel and Hospitality** (sath.org). Despite its 420 or so bridges, Venice is endeavouring to be as accessible as possible. **Informahandicap Venezia** provide information on accessible routes, sights, hotels and will advise how to get hold of the keys that operate the chair lifts on many of its bridges (T041-274 8144, comune.venezia.it).

## Emergencies

Ambulance T118; **Fire service** T115; **Police** T112 (with English-speaking operators), T113 (*carabinieri*); **Roadside assistance** T116.

## Etiquette

*Bella figura* – projecting a good image – is important to Italians. Take note of public notices about conduct: sitting on steps or eating and drinking in certain historic areas is not allowed. In Venice strict rules are enforced, especially around piazza San Marco, where you can be fined €50 on the spot for lying down or eating a picnic. Elsewhere in the city, 'hosts' and 'hostesses' have the power to fine you for littering, swimming in the canals, riding bicycles or walking about the city shirtless or in swimwear.

Covering arms and legs is necessary for admission into some churches – in rare cases even shorts are not permitted. Punctuality, like queuing, is an alien concept in Italy, so be prepared to wait on occasion but not necessarily in line or order.

## Families

The family is highly regarded in Italy and children are well treated (not to say indulged), particularly in restaurants (although more expensive restaurants may not admit children). Note that lone parents or adults accompanying children of a different surname may sometimes need proof of guardianship before taking children in and out of Italy; contact your Italian embassy for current details (Italian embassy in London, T020-7312 2200).

## Health

Comprehensive medical insurance is strongly recommended for all travellers to Italy. EU citizens should also apply for a free European Health Insurance Card (ehic.org), which replaced the E111 form and offers reduced-cost medical treatment. Late-night pharmacies are identified by a large green cross outside. To obtain the details of the three nearest open pharmacies dial T1100; out-of-hours pharmacies are also advertised in most local newspapers. The accident and emergency department of a hospital is the *pronto soccorso*.

## Insurance

Comprehensive travel and medical insurance is strongly recommended for all travellers to Italy.

You should check any exclusions, excess and that your policy covers you for all the activities you want to undertake. Keep details of your insurance documents separately. Scanning them, then emailing yourself a copy is a good way to keep the information safe and accessible. Ensure you are fully insured if hiring a car, or, if you're taking your own vehicle, contact your current insurer to check whether you require an international insurance certificate.

## Money

The Italian currency is the Euro (€). To change cash or travellers' cheques, look for a *cambio* (exchange office); these tend to give better rates than banks. Bank are open Monday to Friday 0830 to 1300 with some opening again from 1500 to 1600. ATMs that accept major credit and debit cards can be found in every city and town (look around the main piazzas). Many restaurants, shops, museums and art galleries will take major credit cards but paying directly with debit cards such as Cirrus is less common than in the UK, so having a ready supply of cash may be the most convenient option. You should also keep some cash handy for toll roads, if you're driving.

## Police

There are five different police forces in Italy. The *carabinieri* are a branch of the army and wear military-style uniforms with a red stripe on their trousers and white sashes. They handle general crime, drug-related crime and public order offences. The *polizia statale* are the national police force and are dressed in blue with a thin purple stripe on their trousers. They are responsible for security on the railways and at airports. The *polizia stradale* handle crime and traffic offences on the motorways and drive blue cars with a white stripe. The *vigili urbani* are local police who wear dark blue (in summer) or black (in winter) uniforms with white hats and direct traffic and issue parking fines in the cities. The *guardia di finanza* wear grey uniforms with grey flat hats or green berets (depending on rank). They are charged with combating counterfeiting, tax evasion and fraud.

In the case of an emergency requiring police attention, dial 113, approach any member of the police or visit a police station (below). If it's a non-emergency, dial 112 for assistance.

**Cortina d'Ampezzo**: corso Italia 33, T0436-866200.
**Padua**: Piazzetta Palatucci 5, T049-833111.
**Treviso**: via Cornarotta 24, T0422-411806.
**Venice**: fondamenta di San Lorenzo, Castello 5053, T041-270 5511.
**Verona**: via del Pontiere 32, T045-807 7458.
**Vicenza**: viale Giuseppe Mazzini 213, T0444-357511.

## Post

The Italian post service (poste.it) has a not entirely undeserved reputation for unreliablility, particularly when it comes to handling postcards. You can buy *francobolli* (stamps) at post offices and *tabacchi* (look for T signs). A postcard stamp costs from €0.60 for both EU and transatlantic destinations; for letters over 20g and parcels, there is a maze of prices and options.

## Safety

Statistically, the crime rate in Veneto is lower than in Italy as a whole. However, it is always advisable

## Telephone

The dialling codes for the main cities in Veneto are:

Venice 041; Padua 049; Treviso 0422; Cortina d'Ampezzo 0436; Vicenza 0444; Verona 045.

You need to use these local codes, even when dialling from within the city or region. The prefix for Italy is +39. You no longer need to drop the initial '0' from the area codes when calling from abroad. For directory enquiries call T12.

## Time difference

Italy uses Central European Time, GMT+1.

## Tipping

It is increasingly common for service to be included in your bill on top of the cover charge. Where this isn't the case (and, sometimes, even when service is included in the bill), tipping is expected but don't tip unless you are genuinely happy with the service: you do your fellow travellers a disservice if you do. There is no need to tip when buying coffees or drinks but a token of appreciation for good, smiling, grudge-free service, is always appreciated. Having said that, always check your bill before paying it. It's amazing how often extra orders and random prices can appear on your bill in Italy. This goes for shops too.

to take general care at night or when travelling, especially around train stations: don't flaunt your valuables; take only the money you need and don't carry it all in one wallet or pocket. Pick-pockets and bag-cutters operate on public transport, so try not to make it obvious which stop you're getting off at, as it gives potential thieves a timeframe in which to work. Car break-ins are common, so always remove valuables and secure other luggage in the boot. Beware of scams, con artists and sellers of fake goods: you can be fined a considerable amount of money for buying fake designer goods. In general, don't take risks you wouldn't at home.

## Voltage

Italy functions on a 220V mains supply. Plugs are the standard European two-pin variety.

# Language

In hotels and bigger restaurants, you'll usually find English is spoken. The further you go from the tourist centre, however, the more trouble you may have, unless you have at least a smattering of Italian. Around the shores of Lake Garda English, German and Italian are spoken almost equally.

You will also find that the heavy Veronese dialect is spoken, especially as you go out of the city into the surrounding countryside. A slight variant on the Veneto dialect, once the official language of Venice, the dialect spoken today in and around Verona has changed little in centuries and exhibits Germanic influences. Characteristic sounds are short, clipped and nasal, or come from the back of the mouth.

Stress in spoken Italian usually falls on the penultimate syllable.

Italian has standard sounds: unlike English you can work out how it sounds from how it's written and vice versa.

## Vowels

**a** like 'a' in cat

**e** like 'e' in vet, or slightly more open, like the 'ai' in air (except after c or g, see consonants below)

**i** like 'i' in sip (except after c or g, see below)

**o** like 'o' in fox

**u** like 'ou' in soup

## Consonants

Generally consonants sound the same as in English, though 'e' and 'i' after 'c' or 'g' make them soft (a 'ch' or a 'j' sound) and are silent themselves, whereas 'h' makes them hard (a 'k' or 'g' sound), the opposite to English. So ciao is pronounced 'chaow', but chiesa (church) is pronounced 'kee-ay-sa'.

The combination 'gli' is pronounced like the 'lli' in million, and 'gn' like 'ny' in Tanya.

## Basics

thank you   *grazie*
hi/goodbye   *ciao* (informal)
good day (until after lunch/ mid-afternoon)   *buongiorno*
good evening (after lunch)   *buonasera*
goodnight   *buonanotte*
goodbye   *arrivederci*
please   *per favore*
I'm sorry   *mi dispiace*
excuse me   *permesso*
yes   *si*
no   *no*

## Numbers

| | | | |
|---|---|---|---|
| one | *uno* | 17 | *diciassette* |
| two | *due* | 18 | *diciotto* |
| three | *tre* | 19 | *diciannove* |
| four | *quattro* | 20 | *venti* |
| five | *cinque* | 21 | *ventuno* |
| six | *sei* | 22 | *ventidue* |
| seven | *sette* | 30 | *trenta* |
| eight | *otto* | 40 | *quaranta* |
| nine | *nove* | 50 | *cinquanta* |
| 10 | *dieci* | 60 | *sessanta* |
| 11 | *undici* | 70 | *settanta* |
| 12 | *dodici* | 80 | *ottanta* |
| 13 | *tredici* | 90 | *novanta* |
| 14 | *quattordici* | 100 | *cento* |
| 15 | *quindici* | 200 | *due cento* |
| 16 | *sedici* | 1000 | *mille* |

## Gestures

Italians are famously theatrical and animated in dialogue and use a variety of gestures.

*Side of left palm on side of right wrist as right wrist is flicked up* Go away

*Hunched shoulders and arms lifted with palms of hands outwards* What am I supposed to do?

*Thumb, index and middle finger of hand together, wrist upturned and shaking* What are you doing/what's going on?

*Both palms together and moved up and down in front of stomach* Same as above

*All fingers of hand squeezed together* To signify a place is packed full of people

*Front or side of hand to chin* 'Nothing', as in 'I don't understand' or 'I've had enough'

*Flicking back of right ear* To signify someone is gay

*Index finger in cheek* To signify good food

Bona gente i Veneti massa bona!

## Questions

ow? *come?*

ow much? *quanto?*

vhen? *quando?*

vhere? *dove?*

vhy? *perché?*

vhat? *che cosa?*

## Problems

I don't understand *non capisco*

I don't know *non lo so*

I don't speak Italian *non parlo italiano*

How do you say ... (in Italian)?
*come si dice ... (in italiano)?*

Is there anyone who speaks English?
*c'è qualcuno che parla inglese?*

## Shopping

this one/that one   *questo/quello*
less   *meno*
more   *di più*
how much is it/are they?
   *quanto costa/costano?*
can I have ...?   *posso avere ...?*

## Travelling

one ticket for...   *un biglietto per...*
single   *solo andata*
return   *andata a ritorno*
does this go to Verona?
   *questo va a Verona?*
airport   *aeroporto*
bus stop   *fermata*
train   *treno*
car   *macchina*
taxi   *tassi*

## Hotels

a double/single room
*una camera doppia/singola*
a double bed   *un letto matrimoniale*
bathroom   *bagno*
Is there a view?   *c'è un bel panorama?*
can I see the room?   *posso vedere la camera?*
when is breakfast?   *a che ora è la colazione?*
can I have the key?   *posso avere la chiave?*

## Time

morning   *mattina*
afternoon   *pomeriggio*
evening   *sera*
night   *notte*
soon   *presto/fra poco*
later   *più tardi*
what time is it?   *che ore sono?*
today/tomorrow/yesterday   *oggi/domani/ieri*

## Days

Monday   *lunedi*
Tuesday   *martedi*
Wednesday   *mercoledi*
Thursday   *giovedi*
Friday   *venerdi*
Saturday   *sabato*
Sunday   *domenica*

## Conversation

alright   *va bene*
right then   *allora*
who knows!   *bo! / chi sa*
good luck!   *in bocca al lupo!* (literally, 'in the mouth of the wolf')
one moment   *un attimo*
hello (when answering a phone)   *pronto* (literally, 'ready')
let's go!   *andiamo!*
enough/stop   *basta!*
give up!   *dai!*
I like ...   *mi piace ...*
how's it going?   (well, thanks) *come va?* (bene, grazie)
how are you?   *come sta/stai?* (polite/informal)

# Menu reader

## General

*affumicato* smoked
*al sangue* rare
*alla griglia* grilled
*antipasto* starter/appetizer
*aperto/chiuso* open/closed
*arrosto* roasted
*ben cotto* well done
*bollito* boiled
*caldo* hot
*cameriere/cameriera* waiter/waitress
*conto* the bill
*contorni* side dishes
*coperto* cover charge
*coppa/cono* cone/cup
*cotto* cooked
*cottura media* medium
*crudo* raw
*degustazione* tasting menu of several dishes
*dolce* dessert
*fatto in casa* homemade
*forno a legna* wood-fired oven
*freddo* cold
*fresco* fresh, uncooked
*fritto* fried
*menu turistico* tourist menu
*piccante* spicy
*prenotazione* reservation
*primo* first course
*ripieno* a stuffing or something that is stuffed
*secondo* second course

## Drinks (bevande)

*acqua naturale/gassata/frizzante* still/sparkling water
*aperitivo* drinks taken before dinner, often served
  with free snacks
*bicchiere* glass
*birra* beer
*birra alla spina* draught beer
*bottiglia* bottle
*caffè* coffee (ie espresso)
*caffè macchiato/ristretto* espresso with a dash of
  foamed milk/strong
*spremuta* freshly squeezed fruit juice
*succo* juice
*vino bianco/rosato/rosso* white/rosé/red wine

## Fruit (frutti) & vegetables (legumi)

*agrumi* citrus fruits
*amarena* sour cherry
*arancia* orange
*carciofo* globe artichoke
*castagne* chestnuts
*cipolle* onions
*cocomero* water melon
*contorno* side dish, usually grilled vegetables or
  oven baked potatoes
*fichi* figs
*finocchio* fennel
*fragole* strawberries
*frutta fresca* fresh fruit
*funghi* mushroom
*lamponi* raspberries
*melagrana* pomegranate
*melanzana* eggplant/aubergine
*melone* light coloured melon
*mele* apples
*noci/nocciole* walnuts/hazelnuts
*patate* potatoes, which can be *arroste* (roast),
  *fritte* (fried), *novelle* (new), *pure'di* (mashed)
*patatine fritte* chips
*peperoncino* chilli pepper
*peperone* peppers
*pesche* peaches
*piselli* peas
*pomodoro* tomato
*rucola* rocket
*spinaci* spinach
*verdure* vegetables
*zucca* pumpkin

## Meat (carne)

*affettati misti* mixed cured meat
*agnello* lamb
*bistecca* beef steak
*braciola* chop, steak or slice of meat
*carpaccio* finely sliced raw meat (usually beef)
*cinghiale* boar
*coda alla vaccinara* oxtail
*coniglio* rabbit
*manzo* beef
*pollo* chicken
*polpette* meatballs
*polpettone* meat loaf
*porchetta* roasted whole suckling pig
*prosciutto* ham – *cotto* cooked, *crudo* cured

*salsicce* pork sausage
*salumi* cured meats, usually served mixed (*salumi misto*)
  on a wooden platter
*speck* a type of cured, smoked ham
*spiedini* meat pieces grilled on a skewer
*stufato* meat stew
*trippa* tripe
*vitello* veal

### Fish (*pesce*) & seafood (*frutti di mare*)
*acciughe* anchovies
*aragosta* lobster
*baccalà* salt cod
*bottarga* mullet-roe
*branzino* sea bass
*calamari* squid
*cozze* mussels
*frittura di mare* small fish, squid and
  shellfish lightly covered with flour and fried
*frutti di mare* seafood
*gamberi* shrimp/prawn
*grigliata mista di pesce* mixed grilled fish
*orata* gilt-head/sea bream
*ostriche* oysters
*pesce spada* swordfish
*polpo* octopus
*sarde, sardine* sardines
*seppia* cuttlefish
*sogliola* sole
*spigola* bass
*stoccafisso* stockfish
*tonno* tuna
*triglia* red mullet
*trota* trout
*vongole* clams

### Dessert (*dolce*)
*cornetto* sweet croissant
*crema* custard
*dolce* dessert
*gelato* ice cream
*panettone* type of fruit bread eaten at Christmas
*semifreddo* a partially frozen dessert
*sorbetto* sorbet
*tiramisù* rich 'pick-me-up' dessert
*torta* cake
*zabaglione* whipped egg yolks flavoured with
  Marsala wine
*zuppa inglese* English-style trifle

**Useful phrases**
can I have the bill please? *posso avere il conto per favore?*
is there a menu? *c'è un menù?*
what do you recommend? *che cosa mi consegna?*
what's this? *cos'è questo?*
where's the toilet? *dov'è il bagno?*

### Other
*aceto balsamico* balsamic vinegar, usually from Modena
*arborio* type of rice used to make risotto
*burro* butter
*calzone* pizza dough rolled with the chef's choice of
  filling and then baked
*casatiello* lard bread
*fagioli* white beans
*formaggi misti* mixed cheese plate
*formaggio* cheese
*frittata* omelette
*insalata* salad
*latte* milk
*lenticchie* lentils
*mandorla* almond
*miele* honey
*olio* oil
*polenta* cornmeal
*pane* bread
*pane-integrale* brown bread
*pinoli* pine nuts
*provola* cheese, sometimes with a smoky flavour
*ragù* a meaty sauce or ragout
*riso* rice
*salsa* sauce
*sugo* sauce or gravy
*zuppa* soup

# Index

# Index

# Index

# Index

# Index

# Footprint credits

**Text editor**: Sophie Blacksell
**Assistant editor**: Alice Jell
**Picture editor**: Kassia Gawronski
**Layout & production**: Angus Dawson
**Maps**: Compass Maps Ltd

**Managing Director**: Andy Riddle
**Commercial Director**: Patrick Dawson
**Publisher**: Alan Murphy
**Editorial**: Sara Chare, Ria Gane,
Jenny Haddington, Felicity Laughton,
Nicola Gibbs
**Design**: Mytton Williams
**Cartography**: Sarah Sorenson, Rob Lunn,
Kevin Feeney, Emma Bryers
**Sales & marketing**: Liz Harper,
Hannah Bonnell
**Advertising**: Renu Sibal
**Business Development**: Zoë Jackson
**Finance & Administration**: Elizabeth Taylor

## Print

Manufactured in Italy by EuroGrafica
Pulp from sustainable forests

## Footprint Feedback

We try as hard as we can to make each
Footprint guide as up to date as possible
but, of course, things always change.
If you want to let us know about your
experiences – good, bad or ugly – then
don't delay, go to footprintbooks.com
and send in your comments.

Every effort has been made to ensure
that the facts in this guidebook are
accurate. However, travellers should still
obtain advice from consulates, airlines etc
about travel and visa requirements before
travelling. The authors and publishers
cannot accept responsibility for any loss,
injury or inconvenience however caused.

# Publishing information

FootprintItalia Venice & Veneto
1st edition
© Footprint Handbooks Ltd
April 2009

ISBN 978-1-906098-56-8
CIP DATA: A catalogue record for this
book is available from the British Library

® Footprint Handbooks and the Footprint
mark are a registered trademark of
Footprint Handbooks Ltd

**Published by Footprint**
6 Riverside Court
Lower Bristol Road
Bath BA2 3DZ, UK
T +44 (0)1225 469141
F +44 (0)1225 469461
www.footprintbooks.com

**Distributed in North America by**
Globe Pequot Press

# Another slice of Italy

## **Footprint** Lifestyle guides

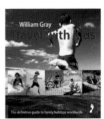

Books to inspire and plan some of the world's most compelling travel experiences.
Written by experts and presented to appeal to popular travel themes and pursuits.

*A great book to have on your shelves when planning your next European escapade*
**Sunday Telegraph**

## **Footprint** Activity guides

These acclaimed guides have broken new ground, bringing together adventure
sports and activities with relevant travel content, stunningly presented to help
enthusiasts get the most from their pastimes.

*This awesome guide has been hailed as 'the new surfer's bible'*
**Extreme Sports Channel**